D1649043

STEPCHILDREN OF PROGRESS

SUNY Series in the Anthropology of Work
June Nash, Editor

STEPCHILDREN OF PROGRESS

The Political Economy of Development
in an Indonesian Mining Town

Kathryn May Robinson

State University of New York Press

Published by
State University of New York Press, Albany
©1986 State University of New York

For information, address State University of New York
Press, State University Plaza, Albany, N.Y., 12246

Library of Congress Cataloging in Publication Data

Robinson, Kathryn M   1949–
    Stepchildren of progress.

    (SUNY series in the anthropology of work)
    Originally presented as the author's thesis (Ph.D.—
Australian National University, 1983).
    Bibliography: p.
    Includes index.
    1. Nickel industry—Indonesia—Saroako. 2. Economic
anthropology—Indonesia—Saroako. 3. Saroako
(Indonesia)—Economic conditions. 4. Saroako
(Indonesia)—Social conditions. I. Title. II. Series.
HD9539.N52I547 1986   307.7'66'095984   86-5847
ISBN 0-88706-119-2
ISBN 0-88706-120-6 (pbk.)

10 9 8 7 6 5 4 3 2 1

Contents

Illustrations

Tables

Preface

This book is principally based on data collected during twenty-three months of field work in Soroako, Sulawesi Selatan, Indonesia, between July 1977 and March 1979, and from December 1980 to January 1981.

Soroako, a village on the Island of Sulawesi (also known as Celebes), has undergone dramatic changes in the last decade as a consequence of the establishment there of a foreign-owned nickel mining and processing venture. This book focuses on the consequences of the new development, mainly for the 1,000 indigenous Soroakans, whose former agricultural land is now the site of the mining town. It presents an analysis of developing capitalist relations of production in the mining town, investigating changes not only in the sphere of production—manifested in daily life as new forms of work—but also in culture and ideology. New ideological forms have arisen in the context of the evolving class structure.

The metaphor in the book's title derives from the evaluation the Soroakans make of the new order: they call themselves the 'stepchildren' of the progress occuring around them.

I have glossed the indigenous language of Soroako as *Bahasa Soroako* to avoid ambiguity, since I use *Soroakan* to refer to the indigenous population, rather than the language. When the Indonesian language appears in the text it is unmarked, but *Bahasa Soroako, Bugis,* and *Toraja* are marked with S., B., and T., respectively.

All money values in rupiah have been converted to U.S. dollars, using the rate that applied during most of the initial field-work period: Rp.414 = US$1.

Some of the references posed problems for the citation in the text. Consequently, a number of unpublished historical documents have been listed separately at the end of the bibliography, and their assigned numbers are cited in the text. Decrees and letters relating to the land alienation have been documented in the notes to chapter 7; these do not appear in the bibliography.

Personal names of living people in the text are pseudonyms.

Acknowledgments

The original version of this book was submitted as a Ph.D. thesis to the Department of Anthropology, Research School of Pacific Studies at the Australian National University, in June 1983.

My research was made possible by the support of the people of Soroako. Those who helped me are too numerous to name, but they include residents of all sectors of the mining town, as well as a number of the expatriate staff of P. T. Inco, Bechtel Corporation, and Dravo.

The Indonesian Institute of Sciences (L.I.P.I.), Dr. Mattulada, and Hasanuddin University, Ujung Pandang, sponsored my research. The research was funded by a Commonwealth Postgraduate Award and Australian National University research funds.

The final form of this book owes most to the encouragement, comment, and criticism of Christopher Eipper, Douglas Miles, and Richard Mohr. Patsy Asch, Gill Bottomley, Linda Connor, Ann Curthoys, Kirk Endicott, James J. Fox, Margaret Jolly, Marie de Lepervanche, Robyn Mackenzie, Campbell Macknight, Anthony Reid and Adrian Vickers have all provided invaluable comment on parts of the work. Clive Kessler and June Nash provided support and encouragement for the publication of my thesis.

Henny Fokker performed the invaluable service of translating references from the Dutch and German. Pauline Garde proofread the manuscript, which was typed by Kay Hefferan Secretarial Services. John Roberts and Johanna de Roder prepared the diagrams.

The book is dedicated to the memory of the late Chandra Jayawardena, who provided the model of a committed and humanist anthropology.

Chapter 1

Introduction

The village of Soroako is located on the shores of Lake Matano in the mountainous centre of the island of Sulawesi. The rugged terrain gives the region its extraordinary beauty. However, in the past, the mountains and unnavigable rivers kept local communities in relative isolation from their neighbours. The small villages of shifting cultivators, like the population of the New Guinea Highlands, were differentiated by variations in dialect and separated by a high level of warfare, accompanied by headhunting. At the turn of the century, European explorers commented that the region was in a state of war like that of their own Middle Ages (Sarasin, cited by Abendanon 1915–18, vol. 1, p.1352).

The people of Soroako were culturally and linguistically related to the Mori of central Sulawesi, but in the latter part of the nineteenth century they came increasingly under the influence of the Bugis realm of Luwu (centred in Palopo). The Bugis are the dominant linguistic group in southern Sulawesi, known for their pursuit of long-distance maritime trade and their devotion to Islam.

Luwu's political organisation took the form of an Indianized (Coedes, 1968) sultanate, which expanded to incorporate the tribes of central Sulawesi into its domain. The Islamisation of the Soroakans was part and parcel of this process.

Photo 1. On Lake Matano.

The turn of the century ushered in a series of events that brought a new master to the people of central Sulawesi, one determined to exercise a more direct influence on their lives. The Dutch conquest of Luwu, in 1906, brought Soroako into the orbit of the Netherlands colonial system; the villagers ceased to wage war, became more devout Muslims, and began to cultivate rice paddies as an adjunct to swiddening. Their remote lake became the focus of Dutch mineral exploration and, subsequently, a centre for a nickel mining industry. The Japanese occupation (1942–45) and the subsequent struggle for independence by the new Indonesian Republic put an end to Dutch mining and to Dutch influence in the area. Between 1953 and 1965, Soroako experienced another kind of isolation, as part of the territory of the Islamic State (*Darul Islam*) established in opposition to the Republican Government.

But by 1965, the people of Soroako faced a transformation of unprecedented scale: their habitat now became the locale for the operations of one of the world's largest mining companies. There is something poignantly paradoxical in the fact that these people, famed as master blacksmiths in precolonial times, have become unskilled labourers in a multimillion dollar nickel mining and processing venture.

This book focuses on the development of the Soroako nickel project, in particular, its consequences for the lives of the 1,000 indigenous Soroakans whose traditional livelihood was largely destroyed to make way for the project.

Studying Development

The nickel project exemplifies the development strategy adopted by the Indonesian Government: the pursuit of high rates of economic growth through capital-intensive projects, funded largely by foreign investment. Economic growth, it is believed, will overcome the poverty and economic backwardness that characterise under-developed economies (see Mortimer 1973; Palmer 1978).

This strategy has its roots in the analysis of underdevelopment given by the modernisation paradigm, dominant in the sociology of development in the 1950s and 1960s. This equated the poverty and economic backwardness of newly independent postcolonial societies with 'tradition,' and hence identified it as an original state—indeed, *the* original state—of human society. It was as if these societies had

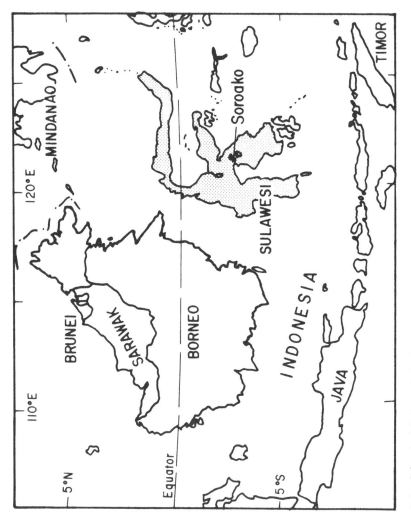

1.1. Island of Sulawesi, Indonesia

been untouched by history until the advent of European colonialism, the historic encounter that became the impetus which pushed them on the road to modernity and progress.[1]

This view of history has become influential in development planning, largely through the influence of the stage theory of Rostow (1960). He prescribed economic growth as the solution to the stagnation of underdeveloped economies, and he recommended infusions of capital and technological knowhow from the developed (modern) world as the way to achieve this end. Such growth would unquestionably lead to development, in the sense of improved well-being for all members of the (now) developing society. This assumption has been challenged in recent years, with critics pointing to the evidence of increasing inequality both within those nations pursuing this strategy and between the developed and underdeveloped world (see Griffin 1981). However, this viewpoint remains influential in the formulation of policy in many underdeveloped countries (including Indonesia) and in the prescriptive statements from such international bodies as the World Bank and such influential leaders as the group responsible for the Brandt report (1980).

Indeed, the rationale for the establishment of the Soroako nickel project derived from this paradigm: the capital-intensive project would engender growth and, hence, be of benefit to the people of Indonesia.

The best known critique of this paradigm is that of the dependency theorist, A. G. Frank (1969). He argued that, far from being an original state, the conditions of underdevelopment (poverty and economic backwardness) were consequences of the incorporation of those societies into a world system in which capitalism was dominant. Foreign investment, the 'medicine' prescribed by Rostow, was identified as the very source of the problem. Capitalist domination was established by colonialism, which was not the benign intervention described by Rostow. Underdevelopment is perpetuated by the structure of the contemporary world economy. Foreign investment has led to the continued extraction of surplus from the underdeveloped world. Unequal economic relations have led to development for the few in the advanced industrial nations and underdevelopment for the many on the periphery. Decolonisation allowed formal political independence, but not freedom from the exploitative economic structures established in the colonial period. Even foreign aid—seemingly altruistic—has been identified as contributing to the process of underdevelopment (see Alavi and Khusro 1970). Within Third World nations, economic ties with the industrial nations bring benefits to local elites only, and poverty and immiseration for the many.[2]

Frank's theory influenced Wallerstein's development of a notion of the 'modern world system' as one that has developed with the expansion of capitalism to all parts of the globe (1974). The basis of this world system is an international division of labour mediated through trade exchanges, without the need for a unified political structure (Nash 1981, p.395).

Anthropologists are centrally concerned with the study of the lives of people in the capitalist periphery. The world economy reaches even to the apparently remote corners of the globe, for example, through integrating petty commodity producers into world markets, or depriving peasant cultivators of their land for mines or plantations. The convention of writing in the ethnographic present has allowed anthropologists to avoid describing the phenomenal reality encountered—the social relations actually observed during field work—by reconstructing an alleged reality through filtering out, using criteria which are not made explicit, all that is deemed modern or new, all those changes arising from the expansion of capitalist markets and the capitalist mode of production.[3]

When anthropologists have made the study of change a central concern, it has been explained in terms of models that maintained the boundedness of the society in question. Forces of change are identified as 'macroprocesses,' external in origin (forces such as 'urbanisation' or 'modernisation'), as opposed to the 'microprocesses' of the local community (Bromley and Gerry 1979, p.4).[4] Another popular paradigm has been that of 'acculturation,' which reduces the question of the relation between the developed and underdeveloped worlds to a cultural phenomenon, of accommodation to Western norms and values (see Magubane 1971).

However, in recent years, there have been a number of studies in which anthropologists, inspired by the insights of such writers as Frank and Wallerstein, have located local communities within the wider social and economic relations of the world system.[5] O'Laughlin stated when studying a local community in the capitalist periphery;

[What] one sees is not the precapitalist sector, but the material expression of two dynamic systems—capitalist and precapitalist modes of production. There is therefore no inner nor outer system: radical anthropology should not consist of showing how exogenous structures of the wider capitalist system impinge on isolated traditional communities or marginal groups, but rather of locating these groups and communities within that structure itself [i.e., wider capitalist system] (1975a, p.366).

Just how to achieve this 'locating' has been a central concern of recent Marxist anthropology. Dependency and world systems theory did not readily provide ways of conceptualising the social relations of the world system that could be transferred to micro field work (Foster-Carter 1978, p.212). Frank and Wallerstein saw the periphery as having been unambiguously capitalist since the beginning of mercantile expansion (about the 16th century). The social structures of peripheral societies were forged in the process of their incorporation into the world system and had nothing in common with previously existing social forms (Amin 1974, p.8). Such blanket prescriptions proved of little value in understanding the social relations of actual local communities (Silverman 1979; Smith 1978).

An early critique of Frank identified the problem in making this shift: for Frank (and Wallerstein), capitalism is defined by exchange relations, not production relations (Laclau 1977). If a society produced goods that ultimately realised profit in markets dominated by the capitalist world, then it could be considered to be capitalist. In his critique, Laclau argued that capitalism, as a distinct mode of production, must be characterised by distinctive relations of production. Thus, for example, goods ultimately exchanged for sale in a capitalist manner could initially be appropriated by a local elite whose relations with the direct producers were of a feudal type and could not be defined in terms of capitalist class relations (i.e., the wage). Frank failed to differentiate between different modes of appropriation at different levels within the world economy. At each level, it is the mode of appropriation that gives social relations their distintive form.

This might seem to be an empty debate over terminology, but without adequate conceptualisation, we cannot understand the nature of social relations in the local community or region, or the mode of its incorporation into, and transformation by, the capitalist mode of production. Most important, without such conceptualisation, there can be no successful strategies to overcome the problems of poverty as a result of incorporation into the capitalist periphery. Indeed, one of the most significant features of the modern world system is the differing nature of class struggle in the capitalist centre compared with the periphery. Workers in advanced capitalist countries have, until now, been able to win material benefits far in excess of their counterparts in the periphery. For the exploited proletariat and semiproletariat, dependency theory offers no way forward (see Smith's critique of Amin [1980]).

This kind of development theory taught in academic institutions and published in scholarly works influences the policies adopted by Third World countries. Nowhere is this more clear than in the pervasive influence of Rostow's stage theory. It is a powerful ideological force, endorsing the continued presence of metropolitan capital in the periphery.

Consequently, many writers have attempted to conceptualise the different nature of capitalist development in the periphery, in particular the difference between societies where capitalism developed autochthonously out of the dissolution of the feudal mode of production and those where it occurred as a consequence of incursion of mercantile capital, or colonial expansion.[6]

Within Marxist anthropology, a central focus is the concept of 'articulation' of the capitalist and precapitalist modes of production. In the periphery, capitalism

> . . . neither evolves mechanically from what precedes it, nor does it necessarily dissolve it; indeed so far from banishing precapitalist forms, it not only co-exists with them but buttresses them and even on occasions devilishly conjures them up *ex nihilo* (Foster-Carter 1978, p.213).

This approach (best known from the work of the French Marxists, Meillasoux and Rey) viewed the social structures of local communities as the result of the complex articulation of capitalist and precapitalist modes of production. It thus allowed for the formulation of models of social relations in specific local communities and regions. It also incorporated a view of those societies as a conjuncture of local and international forces, unlike traditional anthropological models of change (Kahn and Llobera 1981, p.318).

However, Foster-Carter comments that, although this approach allowed the raising of important questions about the nature of social relations in the periphery, it was not able to answer them (1978, p.239). The key concept 'articulation' was imprecisely defined and often amounted to no more than teleological assertion of the functional utility of the precapitalist mode of production to capital accumulation. (See, for example, the discussion of Meillasoux's explanation of the reason for low wages in the periphery, in chap. 2.) Also, writers in this school of Marxist anthropology

> appear to share the view that 'societies' as conceived by traditional anthropology are relevant units for analysis (Kahn and Llobera 1981, p.294).

As a consequence, this approach does not overcome the problem identified by O'Laughlin as the distinction between the inner and outer systems.

Kahn argues for an approach that derives from the world-systems perspective and, hence, locates particular instances within the process of capitalist expansion, and at the same time uses the methodology of class analysis:

> Only by examining the conditions of emergence of particular economic forms in specific regions of the world system in particular periods of time can we hope to understand what is specific and what is general to the world economy. By combining regional class analysis with a world-systems perspective it seems . . . possible to achieve a synthesis of current Marxist debates on problems of development without becoming trapped in the formalism and functionalism in the current debate (Kahn 1981b, p.211).

However, the question still remains as to the meaning of class analysis. Much contemporary Marxist anthropology is heavily 'productionist,' focusing on the formal properties of the modes of production, to the detriment of an examination of the daily lived experience of the people in question (the rich cultural understanding that has been the hallmark of anthropology).[7] Borrowing from E. P. Thompson's critique of Althusser (whose work heavily influenced the 'productionists'):

> The category has attained a primacy over its material referent; the conceptual structure hangs above and dominates social being (1978, p.205).

The overriding concern with the elaboration of the formal model of production relations, as an end in itself, leads to a lack of emphasis on other important categories of analysis, like class struggle. Hence, the marrying of structural Marxism with dependency theory has not been able to overcome what Kahn has identified as a central short-coming of dependency theory: the tendency to see people as passive in the fact of structural change.[8]

Thus, the abstraction of a model of productive relations can only be the first step in a Marxist analysis. This formal model must then be employed in an analysis of the historically and culturally specific situation, to interpret the changing nature of human experience.

> Historical processes do not arise from the machinations of a model; rather, we use models to understand historical processes (O'Laughlin 1975, p.359).

The methodology of participant observation deeply immerses anthropologists in the daily lived experience of the peoples they study, and in the peoples' own apprehension of the nature of that experience. The task of Marxist anthropology is both to 'listen' to that human experience and to abstract from the empirical situation, and then interpret it in terms of abstract categories (see Johnson 1979a, p.62). That is, we must employ the distinction between *phenomenal forms* (the surface forms of everyday life) and the *real relations* (the under-lying processes that explain the surface forms) (Marx 1976, pp.279–80, 1064).

Within contemporary Marxist scholarship, one school represented by scholars like Raymond Williams and E. P. Thompson (the 'cultural Marxists') is suspicious of abstraction, which is seen to be too often the result of analysis, not a part of a method. That is, it can become a form of closure, rather than a way of pursuing a more complex understanding (Johnson 1979a, p.63). They are especially suspicious in this regard of the 'structural Marxists,' in particular Althusser and his followers. Indeed, this school of thought, which has had considerable influence on the new Marxist anthropology, is somewhat contemptuous of empirical analysis, considering it to have no place in the quest for theoretical knowledge.

Richard Johnson, Stuart Hall, and a number of other British Marxist historians have attempted to reconcile these differing Marxist positions.[9] They have found some direction from the work of

Gramsci, who brought a Marxist analysis to bear on the lives of Italian peasants and attempted to deal with what he called the 'commonsense' of their everyday lived experience. In Gramsci, these historians find a way of examining human consciousness (culture and ideology) in the context of class relations, without the functionalist reductionism and loss of historical specificity that characterises the structuralist approach.

'Commonsense,' or everyday lived experience, is taken to be a people's customs and behaviour, the beliefs and values that shape their world and affect their productive lives (for example, patterns of work, forms of marriage and the family, the sexual division of labour). That is, it is very similar to what anthropologists understand by 'culture.'

Gramsci differentiated two other categories of human consciousness. Ideology, or philosophy, referred to an organised set of conceptions produced by intellectuals (those with the function of philosophers), which relate to classes and to the organisation of production, and which have an active and transformative role with respect to 'commonsense' (Johnson 1979b, p.233). He employed the term 'hegemony' to indicate the extent to which 'commonsense' is made to conform to the economic relations of capitalist production and to consent to the corresponding political order (Johnson 1979b, p.233). The working classes do not automatically adopt the ideology of political groups. The conditions of everyday life, of 'commonsense,' are constant foci of political struggle. In contrast to the Althusserian view of the relation between base and superstructure, the two are seen to exhibit 'disjuncture' and 'unevenness' (Johnson 1979b , p.233). Thus, we cannot expect that all features of a society will correspond axiomatically to the dominant mode of production.

In employing class analysis in the periphery, then, attention must be given to aspects of both base and superstructure. It seems a particularly appropriate task for anthropologists to investigate aspects of cultural and ideological change in the context of changing structures of production in the capitalist periphery: questions such as the nature of class consciousness; peasant resistance to change; changes in gender relations, marriage, and the family; and the response to the conditions of capitalist penetration (Nash 1981). The participant observation methodology and local focus of anthropological studies mean that anthropologists can make a unique contribution to the study of the modern world system. Ethnographic studies are a complement to the work of scholars from other disciplines, such as historians, political economists, and political scientists.

In investigating concrete social forms within the world capitalist system, we cannot lose sight of the historical and cultural uniqueness of each instance. The effects of capitalist class relations are powerful and pervasive, but not all aspects of society and culture respond reflexively to their impact. We must describe not only structural change, but the way in which it is apprehended, the cultural form it takes. Richard Johnson has written:

> The working class is not just made by the Industrial Revolution
> . . . but also through political counter-revolution, and a reworking, in the light of new experiences, of inherited cultural traditions (1979b, p.221).

Outline of the Study

The focus of this study is the manner in which proletarianisation has transformed the lives of a community of peasant cultivators. The fundamental change in Soroako has been the loss of the village's most productive agricultural land to make way for the mining project. As a consequence, wage labour for the company has become the principal stable form of livelihood. However, a large proportion of village residents do not enjoy regular employment, and they have been reduced to a semi-proletariat, living by occasional waged work and a variety of activities in the informal sector. For some, agriculture remains the principal source of livelihood, but conditions of agricultural production have also been affected by the company's domination of the local economy. For all village residents, there have been critical changes arising from the general effects of capitalist penetration, through the development of new forms of social relations mediated by the capitalist marketplace. Changes in cultural and ideological forms have been part of the process of capitalist development.

The book focuses particularly on the consequences of the mining project for the indigenous Soroakan. This is the outcome of methodological, not theoretical, considerations. It is not that I see them as a discrete 'society' or 'tribe.' In the mining town of more than 8,000 people, a self-identified group with active social networks provided a suitable focus for a participant observation methodology.

Because of their strong corporate identity, this group might seem to be a 'natural' entity, but I show this category to be a product of human consciousness, formed in the context of particular historical experience (chap. 10).

Chapter 2 describes the mining town as I encountered it in 1977–79. The residents of the town were highly differentiated in terms of lifestyle and status honour. The inequalities were the basis of a status hierarchy, which was the phenomenal form of class relations arising from the mode of capitalist expansion in the periphery.

The historical forces that have shaped changes in both the material conditions of existence and the cultural and ideological forms are introduced in chapter 3. The chapter covers the period from 1880 to 1949, during which the small community experienced progressive incorporation into the world economy. This began with the expansion of European mercantile trade into central Sulawesi and was consolidated by direct colonial annexation in 1906. An interesting aspect of this process is that in the first instance it led, not to a 'Westernisation' of Soroakan society and culture, but to a 'Buginisation'; the expansion of the influence of the Luwu sultanate into the region occurred in association with the penetration of mercantile trade networks as Bugis traders moved into into the region.

This Bugis influence was consolidated in the postindependence period (after 1949) under the influence of the Darul Islam rebels. This is discussed in chapter 4, which also examines the history of the establishment of the nickel project, which was part of the development strategy of the Indonesian Government. The history of the community shows the nickel project to be the latest and most dramatic event in a history of the region's incorporation into a world system in which capitalism is dominant.

Forms of production in the period prior to the project are the subject of chapter 5. The aim is not to establish a static baseline (characterized as a 'traditional society' of a precapitalist mode of production). Rather, I elucidate the nature of the experience of work under precapitalist relations of production and show the ways in which this was affected by the historical processes discussed in chapter 3. An understanding of these historically prior forms of production is necessary in order to understand the Soroakan response to the changes of the 1970s.

Chapter 6 discusses changes in production since the establishment of the project, in particular changes in the nature of work. The capitalist domination of all forms of production meant that even the work experience of those not subject to direct proletarianisation was changed. New forms of social inequality have arisen since the project's development, forms of inequality based on changes in production and mediated through the increased penetration of the capitalist market.

A critical aspect of capitalist domination in Soroako has been the mining company's monopolisation of land use, in particular through the alienation of the village's prime agricultural land. This has only been possible because of the role adopted by the Indonesian state in establishing conditions favourable to the operation of mainly foreign capital. The role of local elites in generating the conditions of underdevelopment for the mass of the people, an important tenet of dependency theory, has been developed in theories of the state in postcolonial societies (see Alavi 1979). Chapter 7 discusses land alienation and two other instances of conflict in which the role of the local representatives of the Indonesian ruling elite was crucial in determining outcomes that were detrimental to the local population. Contributing to the character of these conflicts was the confusion between roles and areas of responsibility of the company and government representatives, on the one hand, and between different levels of the Indonesian government, on the other.

The last three chapters focus on cultural and ideological changes arising from the changes in productive relations. An important aspect of the development of the project has been the massive inflow of immigrant workers, and the corresponding transformation of the rural village into a small town. This new social environment has proven fertile ground for new forms of marriage and household organisation, forms consistent with the trend towards individualism in the development of capitalism. These new cultural forms are discussed in chapter 8. Chapters 9 and 10 deal with aspects of ideology and class consciousness, in particular the way in which racism and ethnicity render the inequalities in the mining town 'natural,' thus masking the ways in which they are generated by the class processes described in chapter 2. However, ethnicity also serves as a way of mobilising against forms of class oppression.

In assessing their fate in the light of the project's development, the Soroakans commonly use a popular Indonesian metaphor: the stepchild. Not only is the word a common figure of speech, the stepchild is also encountered in Indonesian popular culture (films, novels, and drama; see, for example, Peacock [1968, p.129]). In these plots, there is always tension between the stepchild and the step-parent, who never treats the stepchild with the indulgence given a natural child. Frequently, the plot ends with a joyful reunification with the natural parent, the only one who will properly attend to the child's needs and desires.

The Soroakans feel that, as the original inhabitants of the area (referred to in Indonesian as the 'children' of the region, the *anak daerah*), they should have been the prime beneficiaries of the project, entitled to special treatment by the mining company and the govern-ment. Instead, they feel themselves to have been pushed aside and treated like stepchildren (*dianak-tirikan*), while newcomers have re-ceived the fruits of the development.

The book's conclusion takes up the Soroakan evaluation of their changed fortunes since the establishment of the project and analyses the contradictory nature of the change: increased affluence for some, new aspirations and economic hardship for others.

My overall aim is not to present a new theory, but to use a well-established tradition of analysis to provide an interpretation of the historical experience of a particular community. There is little explicit theoretical argumentation in the book, only its application. The real test of theory is the extent to which it elucidates social experience and provides a guide for human action. This book presents an interpreta-tion of Soroakan experience and a test of an approach to the study of development.

NOTES TO CHAPTER 1

1. For critical reviews of the modernisation paradigm, see Gusfield (1967), Tipps (1973), and Taylor (1979).
2. For reviews of Frank and the 'dependency' theorists, see Booth (1975) and Taylor (1979).
3. See Banaji's critique of British Anthropology (1970).
4. See, for example, Schneider's discussion, 'Economic development and Anthropology' (1975). This article makes no reference to the above-mentioned critiques of Rostow and other modernisation theorists. Both Schneider and another influential economic anthropologist, Dalton (1971a), make reference to economic development, but cannot step aside from their debate about the appropriate models to use for analysing economies of 'bounded' small-scale communities (the so-called formalist

versus substantivist debate) in order to address the question posed by dependency and world-systems theory, of the mode of integration of these apparently local economies into a world economy. Indeed, Dalton is explicitly hostile to dependency theory (1971b).

5. See, for example, papers in Idris-Soven and Vaughan (1978), Peoples (1978), and Smith (1978).

6. For example, Amin's attempt at a single model for a specific 'peripheral capitalist formation' (1974) or the debate over a 'colonial mode of production' (Banaji 1972; Barbalet 1976).

7. For example, Hindess and Hirst (1975), Seddon (1978), and Taylor (1979).

8. Some recent studies have discussed forms of peasant response, even resistance, to forms of capitalist domination. See Nash (1979), Taussig (1980), and Kahn (1981).

9. See, for example, the articles by Johnson (1979a, 1979b) and Hall et al. (1978).

Chapter 2

The Mining Town

The nickel project dominated all aspects of social life in Soroako. I felt this from the first encounter. I flew from Ujung Pandang over the densely populated flat land of the southern tip of the Island of Sulawesi. From the air, every inch of soil appeared to be cultivated; it was often hard to discern where the inundated paddy fields ended and the sea began. The rectangular order of the paddy fields was broken only by the meandering rivers. Suddenly, the terrain became mountainous, but even in the highlands there were transformations wrought by human hand. The hills were bare of jungle and there was other evidence of shifting cultivation: small houses alongside swidden fields, and the smoke from fires. The land below gave way to the tropical blue waters of the Gulf of Bone. Occasionally, I spotted a Bugis *perahu* in full sail.

At the head of the Gulf, we again flew over land, but the landscape was very different from that further south. The mountains rose up almost from the shore and were covered in dense jungle, which revealed little sign of alteration by human endeavour. But soon I saw a road, cutting a wide orange swathe through the jungle. It led to a few large, sprawling settlements in the plains between the mountains. Suddenly, the massive grey presence of the nickel processing plant loomed out of the sulphurous cloud enveloping it. Here was a transformation of the environment of a different order from that of

17

Photo 2. Returning from work at Nickel Village.

the southern paddy fields. The plant stood in a compound of red soil bare of vegetation. The hills being mined were similarly bare and took on forms shaped by the strip-mining process.

The plane flew over the mining town. Neat rows of suburban bungalows stretched along the lake shore. As we circled to land, I saw the village, diminutive in comparison with the company townsite that now enclosed it. One end of the village presented a sight we could see anywhere in south Sulawesi: rows of tall timber houses disappearing under a thick cover of coconut palms along the water's edge. The other end presented a hybrid picture: an untidy array of large wooden houses and tiny huts, crowded together. That section was almost devoid of trees. I reflected on the beauty of the wide blue expanse of Lake Matano. Early European travellers to the region had been impressed by the magnitude and extraordinary beauty of the lake. For the contemporary visitor, the grandeur of the natural beauty is overwhelmed by the massive transformation wrought by the project.

I stepped from the plane onto the hot dusty earth of the company airstrip, not a tree in sight. A model of a Torajan house greeted me with the pronouncement, '*Selamat Datang Ke Soroako*' (Welcome to Soroako). The ornately carved house (*tongkonan* T.) is a powerful cultural symbol for Torajans, but not for Soroakans, who, I later discovered, often joked about the irony of this alien image greeting newcomers. It symbolised to them their sense of dispossession, of being pushed aside in their own land.

The original settlement, the Village of Soroako, had been re-named *Desa Nikkel* (Nickel Village), the mining town having usurped its original name. The appropriation of village agricultural land for the construction of the company townsite established firm boundaries to the village's expansion. This inevitably led to overcrowding as people from everywhere in Sulawesi, indeed from all over Indonesia, came seeking work.

In the company townsite, spacious weatherboard bungalows lined wide suburban streets. Each house was surrounded by manicured lawns and well-tended garden beds. The environment the mining company had created for expatriate personnel had much in common with their previous circumstances. The town provided them with such facilities as a supermarket and golf course, running water, electricity, telephones, and air-conditioning. They could import their customary lifestyle from America, Canada, or Australia. There was no need for them to venture outside of the urban niche into the village. Women in Bermuda shorts and with hair in rollers would drive down to the supermarket and buy a frozen pizza, stopping off on the way home for a cup of instant coffee in the air-conditioned, all 'mod cons' (modern conveniences) home of a woman friend. The boundaries of the townsite enclosed a world that was totally alien to its Asian setting. Life was lived in the privacy of the home, and one rarely saw people on the streets.

To visit the village was to enter a world built on a different scale, an enclave of rural Asia in the midst of the suburbs. The houses were smaller, simpler in construction, and built closer together. The streets were narrow and dusty, or muddy, depending on the weather. The dominating presence of the foreign company had not robbed the village of its Asian character. Coconut trees lined the streets, and the houses sat in small, neatly swept yards. Tiny shops and stalls competed for space alongside the main road. The streets were teeming with people. In the early morning, villagers bathed in the lake from jetties built out from the lake shore. However, some of the rhythms of daily life gave this village the flavour of an urban *kampung* (neighborhood). Men left for work each morning in hard hats and overalls, clutching company issue lunch pails. The women stayed behind in the village and spent the early morning at the lake's edge, washing themselves, their children, and the household laundry. Vegetable sellers came among them in canoes, attracting other customers from houses near the shore. Fish vendors arrived from the coast, selling to groups of women who congregated in the street. After the washing was done, women and their inevitable companions, the young children, would stroll to the village market, to buy other requisites for the day's meals.

In the evening, the men bathed and changed clothes after work and promenaded along the lake shore or sat on verandahs or outside their houses to take in the evening air and chat with passersby.

The village and the townsite appeared to be two contrasting worlds, despite their physical proximity, because the lifestyles in the two places were so different, and the inhabitants seemingly spent each day so separately from each other. However, this appearance belied important underlying realities. The suburbs of the townsite enclosed the village, and the connection between the two transcended this physical proximity. Soroako truly was a mining town.

The mining operation physically dominated the landscape as well as forms of economic activity in the vicinity.

The hierarchical structure of the company labour force was the principal determinant of relations within the village as well as the townsite and between the residents of the two places.

Inequality within the Company Labour Force

The powerful influence of the company, and the capitalist organisation of production it introduced, were felt in every aspect of social life. The population of the mining town divided according to their relation to the company. Within the village, a group of nonemployees were differentiated from employees, and the company labour force was internally divided by an unequal distribution of wages and other privileges according to position on the company job ladder. The capital-labour divide exerted the fundamental influence on social organisation in Soroako, but social inequalities within the labour market were crucial in determining the experienced forms of inequality.

The company had 4,000 employees in 1978. It was anticipated that this would be the size of the permanent operation labour force, but by 1980 it had dropped to 3,500, and it is currently (1982) being reduced further, in response to the continued slump in the world nickel market.

Company employees were differentiated by the level of their wages, work conditions, promotion prospects, and stability of employment. Exploitation, in terms of lower wages and less pleasant work conditions (longer hours, dirtier work, and so on) was more intense at the lower levels of the job ladder.

The company represented its manpower structure as a pyramid, most personnel being concentrated at the lower levels (fig. 2.1).

Foreign employees formed a small elite at the apex in professional and managerial positions. The top managers were mostly Canadian, though a few Indonesian employees were also in this category. The Indonesian 'junior' and 'senior' managers worked alongside foreign personnel in all aspects of the operation. Besides the few serving as managers, there were also Indonesians working, for example, as exploration geologists, mining engineers, accountants, and doctors.

However, it was anticipated that the number of foreign personnel would decline (table 2.1) as the company instituted a policy of 'Indonesianisation' in accordance with its contract of work with the national government. At the end of 1978, these management categories accounted for 19% of the work force.

The 'skilled workers,' 26% of the labour force, were all Indonesians. They were, for example, foremen, skilled tradesmen, nurses, and teachers. None of that group had positions equivalent to foreign personnel. Most employees (55%) were 'unskilled labourers.' Their occupations ranged from manual labourers in exploration teams and road gangs to machine operators in the processing plant.

Wages and other emoluments differed greatly for the various categories of employees. Foreign personnel were paid at rates commensurate with salaries in their country of origin. Canadians, for example, received more than Australians who, in turn, were more highly paid than Filipinos or Koreans. Expatriate employees on

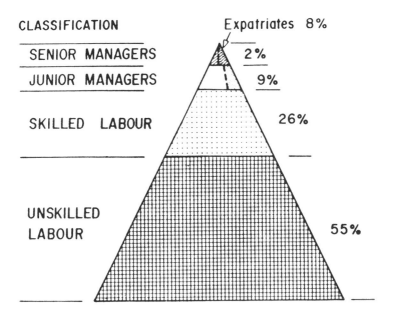

Fig. 2.1. Manpower structure of P. T. Inco, showing percentage in each classification, 1978.
SOURCE: P. T. Inco, Dec. 1978.

average received about four times as much as Indonesians performing the same work (*Tempo* 1977).

It is worthwhile considering the situation in terms of Wright's
analysis of the class structure of contemporary capitalism. He has
argued that managers and technocrats are in a 'contradictory class
location,' that is, a simultaneous position in more than one class.
They have the characteristic of the bourgeoisie in that they command
other workers, but they share with the proletariat a reward in the
form of the wage (1978). However, Braverman argues that the very
high level of management can be regarded as being almost entirely in
the capitalist class, as their very high wages give them, in effect, a
share of surplus value (1974, p.405). This is less so for those on the
lower levels of management, who share with the bourgeoisie only the
control function, which is rewarded by the wage.

The company would not disclose to me the wages paid to
management. However, their differentiation from other workers in
terms of other emoluments was clearly apparent, as was the fact that
they represented the interests of capital. For example, Indonesian
managers controlled the local chapter of the trade union, but they used
this position to ensure that wages remained low for the bottom
categories of workers.

TABLE 2.1.

PERCENTAGE OF WORKERS BY CLASSIFICATION, 1978

(Figures in italics show 1978 projections for future years)

	1978	1979	1980	1981	1982
Expatriates	7.98	*6.64*	*2.80*	*0.94*	*0.57*
Senior managers	2.14	*2.25*	*2.68*	*3.09*	*3.29*
Junior Managers	8.79	*9.28*	*9.76*	*9.86*	*9.49*
Total manage- ment	18.91	*18.17*	*15.24*	*13.89*	*13.35*
Skilled workers	26.41	*25.46*	*26.97*	*27.62*	*27.76*
Unskilled workers	54.68	*56.37*	*57.79*	*38.49*	*58.87*
Total labour	81.09	*81.83*	*84.76*	*86.11*	*86.65*
Total manage- ment and labour	100	*100*	*100*	*100*	*100*

SOURCE P. T. Inco, Dec. 1978.

Wages and salaries of Indonesian employees varied greatly between occupational categories. In late 1978, the average monthly wage for unskilled labourers was Rp.41,000 (US$90); for skilled workers, Rp.82,000 (US$200); and for the managers, Rp.260,000 (US$631) (table 2.2; see note to table 2.2).

Only managers, foreign personnel, and skilled workers (less than 50% of the labour force) were entitled to housing in the company townsite. The type of housing and its location differed according to position in the occupational hierarchy. The managers and foreign personnel lived in luxuriously appointed houses, while the skilled workers were segregated in a suburb with much simpler dwellings.

Unskilled labourers were not allowed company accommodation. The lower standard of accommodation available to them was more costly than subsidised company housing. For example, an Australian skilled tradesman would pay US$20 per month for full board in company barracks, were an immigrant unskilled labourer would pay Rp.15,000–Rp.25,000 (US$36–US$60) to board with a village family, in less comfortable conditions. However, since 1976, unskilled labourers have been eligible for interest free loans to build in Soroako village or the nearby settlements of Wasuponda and Wawandula (map. 2.1).

The categories of employees were further differentiated by their access to other privileges. Only children of employees eligible to live in the townsite could attend the company schools. There were two schools. The 'F school' was a primary school (*sekolah dasar*) for the children of skilled workers. The 'D school' comprised a primary school for the children of managers and foreign personnel, and a

TABLE 2.2.
P. T. INCO MONTHLY WAGE RATES, 1978

Classification	Average	Range
Unskilled labour	Rp.41,000	Rp.22,000–Rp.75,000
Skilled labour	Rp.82,000	Rp.70,000–Rp.100,000
Junior and senior managers	Rp.260,000	Rp.100,000–Rp.1,000,000

NOTE: The figures for the unskilled and skilled labour were provided by the P. T. Inco Personnel Department. They declined to give me either a range or an average for junior and senior managers. I obtained the average for these two groups from a company report (Dagg 1978, p.54), and the range from estimates by Inco employees in those categories.

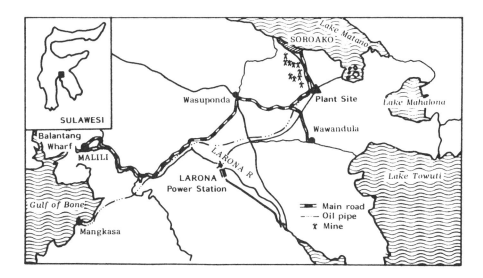

2.1. Major Installations and Population Settlements of the Soroako Nickel Project

junior high schol (*SMP*) for all children of Indonesian employees who were of skilled workers, or higher, status.

Only employees of skilled worker level and above could shop in the company supermarket, where many staples such as coconut oil, soy sauce, and sugar were available more cheaply than in the market. Until mid-1978, there was also a store selling duty-free imported food to foreign personnel. Senior managers also had the right to shop in that store. It was closed when the number of foreign personnel declined at the end of the construction period in 1978. A company security guard manned the door to the supermarket, inspecting identity cards to ensure compliance with the regulations on access.

Employees were also differentiated with respect to holiday entitlement. Foreigners enjoyed paid home leave, as well as rest and recreation leave to Singapore each year (single men were given extra rest and recreation leave). Skilled workers and managers had annual home leave with fares paid to the place of recruitment (for example, Java, Sumatra, Ujung Padang). Senior managers had won the extra privilege of paid isolation leave to Singapore each year. They had fought for this privilege (as well as the duty-free shopping privilege mentioned above), to give them parity with foreign personnel. Their struggles within the company served to gain greater privileges for themselves,not the advancement of the employees, or even the Indonesian employees in general. The inequalities in wages and emoluments served to divide the workers, thus weakening their bargaining power vis-à-vis the company.

Unskilled workers, who were all recruited on site, had a less favourable holiday entitlement. Their two weeks annual leave included no travel expenses. Many of the immigrant workers had not returned home for two or three years, even when the home village was in a nearby region (such as Tana Toraja or Palopo).

The high cost of living in Soroako, relative to wages, left many immigrants with few savings, and they were reluctant to return home without sufficient funds to demonstrate success.

The only facility available without discrimination to all permanent employees and their dependants was the company hospital, whose staff of twelve doctors included a paediatrician, a surgeon, a gynaecologist, and a radiologist specialising in the treatment of tuberculosis, which was endemic to the area. Two of the doctors were foreigners, and the large nursing staff comprised both Indonesian and expatriate personnel. The hospital ran an outpatient clinic five days a week, and the waiting room was always filled to overflowing, especially with women and young children.

The less numerous employees of the catering contractor (Bayu Agung Utama-SHRM) and the plant maintenance contractor (Indomarine-Dravo) were provided with housing and other privileges in a similarly discriminatory fashion.

About one quarter of household heads and about 16 percent of the potentially employed adult male population were neither in fulltime, full year paid employment, nor reliably self-employed. The destruction of the agricultural basis of the traditional economy meant that these individuals and their households were left without a stable source of income. They were dependent on wages from irregular work, for example, as casual labourers for Inco, a local contractor, or a state utility. Some derived irregular income from such informal sector activities as petty trading, sawing timber, or, in the case of women, from prostitution.

Their employment and their income were extremely intermittent, and their standard of living fell below that of the village proletariat. In contrast to company employees, they were ineligible for interest-free housing loans and were asked to meet charges that made the company hospital inaccessible to them. They also lacked the advantages of having the patronage of a boss: goods from the company store, the loan of chairs for a daughter's wedding, a spokesman for their interests in applications for employment.

Residential Stratification and the Segmentation of the Labour Force

The differences between residential areas of the mining town and the differential demographic characteristics of their residents manifested both the inequalities between categories of employees in the company manpower structure and the segmented nature of the labour force. People in Soroako delighted in proclaiming that the mining town had representatives from every island in the archipelago. However, there was no random spread of people from different places of origin throughout the labour force. There tended to be a fit between the occupational (and hence residential) hierarchy and a hierarchy delineated in terms of place of origin and sociocultural identity (fig. 2.2). The differential distribution of rewards and privileges to workers delineated and reinforced a segmentation in terms of place of origin.

Since the company did not provide statistics on the place of origin of employees, I endeavoured to derive some approximation by examining the characteristics of the population in different sections of the mining town (shown in fig. 2.2). I describe both the physical characteristics of each section of the mining town and the place of origin of its residents.

The labour force was highly segmented according to sex, as well as place of origin. Inco provided few jobs for women, except in those occupations customarily considered female in industrial societies (nurses, teachers, and secretaries). The constructon companies had provided some employment for women as waitresses, laundry maids, and so on, in the barracks for single male employees. However, there were never more than a handful of women employed and, by late

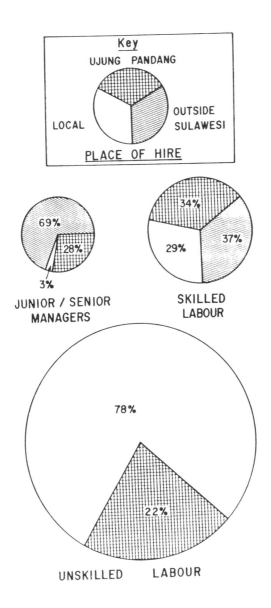

Fig. 2.2. Place of hire of P. T. Inco Indonesian employees, by job classification, 1978.

1980, Inco employed only 206 women out of a labour force of 3,653 (0.06%).[1]

The Company Townsite

The townsite spread out along the shores of Lake Matano, physically enclosing the village of Soroako (map. 2.2). The population of the mining town was about 8,000, almost evenly divided between the company townsite and the village. In spite of its similar population size (although it had been probably two and a half times as large in the mid-seventies) the area of the village was far smaller, giving it a much higher population density (fig. 2.3).

All residents of the townsite were company or contractor employees and their dependents, with the exception of the police and the manager of the commercial bank in the town centre. The townsite population lived in four major residential areas. Three of these were identified by alphabetical labels, reflecting the class of housing (*C*, *D*, or *F*) predominant in each. An attempt to vary this in local parlance, to encourage people to refer to these areas by names, was unsuccessful.

There was only one *A* house, that of the expatriate general manager of the project. It stood in solitude in a quiet bay on the lake shore. This luxurious dwelling, with Italian marble floors and a roof of shingle imported from Kalimantan, was rumoured to have cost one million dollars. Further to the east, under the slopes of Mount Taipa, was the *C* area, comprising 15 *B* houses and 90 *C* houses. These weatherboard dwellings on stilts were luxuriously appointed, with large rooms, netted varandahs, well-appointed all-electric kitchens, air-conditioning and automatic washing machines. All commanded superb views of the lake. The 15 *B* houses were larger than *C* houses and had servants' quarters on ground level. Most households in the *C* area and *D* area employed a maid (or two) and a gardener. There were estimated to be 300 servants working in the townsite, most of them from Tana Toraja (Dagg 1978, p.59).

Most inhabitants of this area were foreigners, but it also accommodated the highest ranking Indonesian personnel and their families (table 2.3, fig. 2.4). All but three of the *B* houses were occupied by foreigners, as were about two-thirds of the *C* houses (table 2.3, fig. 2.4). The town directory indicated that the three Indonesian occupants of *B* houses were from Sumatra, West Java, and Tana Toraja.

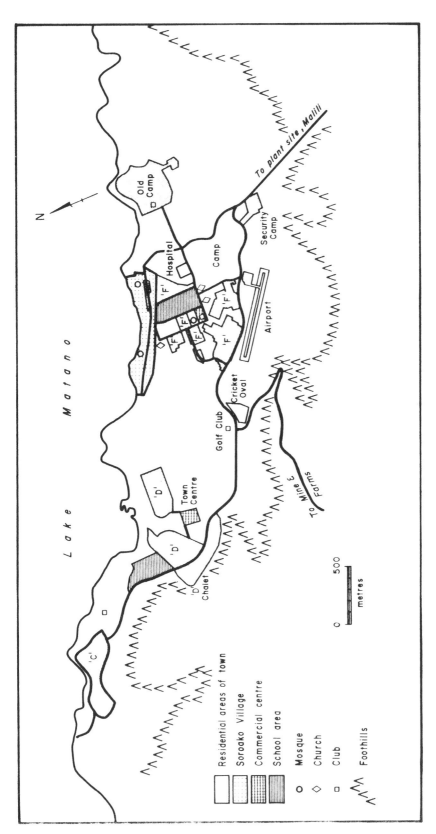

2.2. The Mining Town

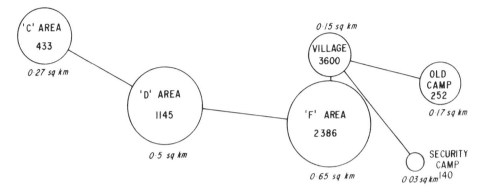

Fig. 2.3. Relative area and population size of areas of the mining town.

The Indonesian occupants of C houses were mainly from Java, especially West Java, reflecting the fact that the Indonesians most evident in high levels of the company were Sundanese from West Java.

The D houses were neat weatherboard bungalows, less luxuriously appointed than the large C houses, and commanding less spectacular views. The D area was planned an an exclusively Indonesian section. But one-third of the 204 junior managerial dwellings were occupied by foreigners whose numbers had exceeded original estimates through expansion in the size of the project.

TABLE 2.3.

TOWNSITE : NATIONALITY OF HOUSEHOLDERS, 1978

Area	Type of housing	No. of houses	Expatriate	Indonesian	Empty
C	B	15	11	3	1
	C	90	58	28	4
D	D	153	54	91	8
	D chalet	51	22	25	4
Old	Inco chalet	5	5		–
Camp	New chalet	53	18	31	3
(D level	Old chalet	25	21	4	–
housing)					

NOTE: This table does not include the inhabitants of single-status accommodation in the C and D areas.

SOURCE: P. T. Inco Town Administration list of householders

The proportion of Indonesian residents in both C and D areas increased as the construction work force left the site (1975–77) and the 'Indonesianisation' of the parent company proceeded (see fig. 2.4*a* and 2.4*b*).[2] For instance, the 51 prefabricated houses known as D chalets originally housed American construction personnel, but as they left, Indonesian junior manager employees moved in. Similar changes occurred in the other area of the prefabricated housing known as 'Old Camp' (the original Inco exploration camp).

The D area had a higher proportion of Sulawesi natives than the C area (including a number of people from Malili and other parts of Luwu Regency). Company figures showed that, of all salaried employees (junior and senior managers), only 37 percent were hired in Sulawesi. But even this percentage overestimated the proportion of Sulawesi natives, since it included people from other islands who came as immigrants to the province and later joined Inco. Also since the figures did not distinguish junior and senior levels of management, they masked an even lower proportion of Sulawesi natives in senior management positions. A notable exception was one Sulawesi-born resident of a B house, the mine manager.

The town centre was located in the D area. It comprised the company store and a number of company-built shops that were rented by mainly Chinese businesses. Nearby stood a post office, a bank, and the offices of the townsite administration. A small garage sold petrol and serviced the four-wheel drive vehicles the foreign and highly paid Indonesian employees hired for private use. The D school and the All Nations Club (*Taman Antar Bangsa*) were nearby.

The difference between the C and D areas was one of degree rather than kind, but the move to the F area was a leap into another world, symbolically indicated by the missing E. The physical distance was greater too, as the golf course formed a buffer zone between them. The F area occupied the plain behind the village and had no direct access to the lake or water views. The tiny houses there were built on stilts in apparent emulation of native Sulawesi architecture, but lacked the traditional large kitchen, which provided the venue for daily life in native villages. Unlike the C and D houses they were not furnished, and tenants even had to provide their own stoves. The smaller yards meant houses were closer together than they were in other townsite areas. The main advantage over village housing was the provision of running water and electricity.

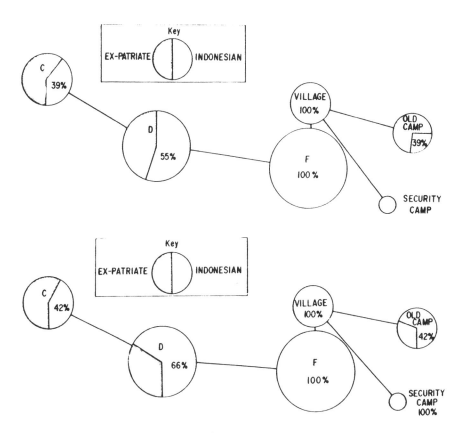

Fig. 2.4. Nationality of residents of sections of the mining town.

The population of the *F* area was greater than that of other parts of the townsite (table 2.4). It was officially 2,386, in 1978, although company officials felt this figure was swelled by a large number of tenants not enumerated in the official figures.

In late 1978, the company estimated that 62% of skilled workers were from Sulawesi, the remainder being 'off island' employees. From a household census conducted by Inco Medical Services, I calculated that 50% of residents of the *F* areas originated off island, the other 50% being natives of Sulawesi, including 5% from the local

TABLE 2.4.
Population of Townsite, 1978

Area	Total Population		Indonesian					Expatriate			
				M	F				M	F
C area	433	181	Adult	38	44	252	Adult	84	55
			Child	54	45		Child	54	59
				M	F				M	F
D area	1,145	753	Adult	204	202	394	Adult	147	106
			Child	163	184		Child	69	72
				M	F					
F area	2,386	2,386	Adult	1020	549					
			Child	401	416					
				M	F					
Security Camp	140	140	Adult	46	33					
			Child	27	34					
				M	F				M	F
Old Camp	252	208	Adult	84	45	44	Adult	15	16
			Child	37	42		Child	7	6
									M	
Camp	34					34		34	
TOTAL	4,392	3,668				724			

Source: P. T. Inco Town Administration.

district (Kecamatan Nuha). The company figures reflected place of hire, while the census recorded place of birth. Also, not all skilled workers had been allocated company houses, because there were too few houses available. The longest-term employees were established in company housing. As time went on, it seemed that more locals and natives of Sulawesi were being promoted to skilled worker status, and the difference in the two sets of figures may reflect this change.

When I first arrived in 1977, the *F* area looked barren compared to the established village, but in time, the occupants established house gardens of both edible and decorative plants. They complained about the low standard of housing in their area, which they compared unfavourably with other sections of the townsite. The Javanese especially disliked the elevated wooden dwellings. However, the *F* residents had a greater sense of community than people elsewhere in the townsite. The area was more like an urban *kampung* (neighbourhood) than the suburban *C* and *D* areas. Only here were there any community enterprises, including sporting activities. It was the only part of the townsite to be organised into neighbourhood associations (*rukun tetangga*), the lowest level of public administration in Indonesia. The local women's organisation (*Ikatan Keluarga Inco*) was most vigorous in the *F* area.

The *F* area had its own school and a company-built market where stalls were rented to people who sold goods ranging from vegetables and spices to motorcycle parts. The traders there were mainly Bugis, not Chinese as in the town centre. In 1978–79, a few local people established themselves in that market. This commercial centre had a recreation hall that operated as a bar and restaurant. The company had also built a mosque and three churches nearby.

The Campsite, which accommodated single male construction workers, was adjacent to the *F* area, but this had closed by the end of 1979. Nearby were barracks for single Indonesian skilled workers, and a nurses' home not far from the hospital.

The townsite was well endowed with recreational facilities, such as tennis and badminton courts, in addition to the golf course. There was an oval where foreigners played cricket and baseball, and Indonesians soccer. By 1980, the company had built a soccer stadium between the *F* area and the village. There was a sailing club, mainly used on weekends by foreigners, many of whom had small motorised boats. A cinema was opened in the area between the village and the Old Camp, in 1979. Most recreational activities were racially segregated. Even the club, generously named the "All Nations Club" (*Taman Antar Bangsa*), did not provide a forum for interracial mixing. It was mainly patronised by foreigners. Even in the mixed residential areas, social contact between Indonesians and foreigners was limited. (I return to this topic in chap. 9.)

Soroako Village

The population of the village decreased from an estimated peak of 10,000 in 1976 (the height of the construction phase) to its 1978 level of just under 4,000. The retrenchment of most construction personnel, coupled with the implementation of a government plan to move immigrants to Wasuponda and Wawandula, accounted for this decline. The 1979 village population almost equalled that of the townsite, but it occupied a far smaller area (fig. 2.3). Here only 45 percent of the inhabitants were company employees or their dependents, compared with almost 100 percent in the townsite.

The village was divided socially and geographically into Old Village (*Kampung Lama*), which roughly corresponded to the administrative division Village Association I (*Rukun Kampung* 1), and New Village (*Kampung Baru*), corresponding to Village Association 2 (*Rukun Kampung* 2) (Map. 2.3).

Old Village was the home of the approximately 1,000 indigenous Soroakans (*Orang Asli Soroako*), whereas New Village was, by and large, a settlement of immigrants. The first newcomers had obtained

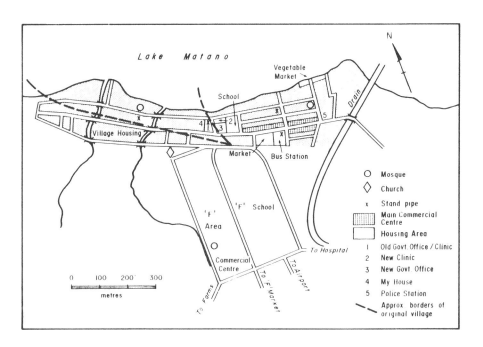

2.3. Soroako Village

permission to build there, in the early 1970s, on land the indigenous Soroakans had used for cultivation and pasture. The village school, the market (built by the village government in 1974), as well as all of the large stores, were located in New Village. A new school (constructed under the *Inpres*[3] scheme) was built there, in 1980.

When I first arrived in 1977, the contrast between the two areas was marked. Old Village formed the permanent core of the settlement, characterised by large, well-established wooden dwellings built in the style common throughout South Sulawesi. The houses were on stilts, about two metres off the ground, and comprised two buildings; the front was divided into one section for receiving guests and another for sleeping. A separate kitchen was attached at the back. Houses were roofed with sago-leaf thatch or more expensive corrugated iron. Previously, yards were extensive, with fruit trees, coconut palms, cassava, and vegetable plots, but since the land shortage caused by the construction of the townsite, many of the yards had become house sites. Also, many houses had recently been boarded in underneath, to provide space for a small shop, or a room for renting to immigrants.

The houses of the immigrants (and the new dwellings of some of the indigenous Soroakans) spread out from the central core of of original housing, mainly into New Village. The immigrants, on the whole, originated from rural areas, arriving with no resources with which to begin their new lives, and so built their makeshift and tiny dwellings from whatever came to hand, usually a combination of jungle materials, such as sago-leaf thatch, and cast-off company packing crates. The houses in New Village were not built on orderly streets off the main thoroughfare; they were built cheek by jowl, haphazardly connected by lanes and muddy tracks.

Amid this jumble was an occasional well and many piles of rubbish. For most of the village inhabitants, the lake served as the source of water for drinking, cooking, washing, and bathing, as well as for the disposal of human waste. Sanitation services—drains, wells, and garbage collection—were not provided by the village administration, which had neither the revenue nor the personnel to do so. This was an urban settlement with the administration of a rural village.

By contrast, the company's Town Administration provided all these services to townsite inhabitants, i.e., to half the work force only. Such discrimination established fundamental inequalities between categories of company employees in everyday experience and life changes.

The village underwent a transformation in 1977–78 with the implementation of a plan from the Provincial Government to reorder the settlement. In New Village, substandard houses were demolished. Many were bulldozed when their inhabitants refused to move voluntarily (see chapter 7). A grid structure was imposed by the construction of roads, and permanent dwellings were built alongside them. Older houses were moved to conform to the new plan. Many of the houses were built end to end; one village resident complained that the main street looked more like a train than a village.

Many of the original homes in Old Village have been refurbished (often with the aid of housing loans from the company) in order to conform with modern taste. Windows have been glazed and the thatched roofs replaced with corrugated iron, which is both more durable and more prestigious. Some occupants have built an extension (*petak*). The most affluent have laid cement floors downstairs and installed interior bathrooms and toilets (pit latrines). Because the iron roofing makes the upstairs areas hot in the middle of the day, many houses have spaces for sleeping downstairs.

In the past, construction was by cooperative labour, of neighbors and kin. These days, the common practice of engaging tradesmen, many of them Bugis immigrants, indicates the decline in self-sufficiency in the village economy. The refurbishing of houses, and the building of newer, bigger ones, has proven to be the most public manifestation of differential wealth in the village. Those households with wealth from trade or long-term stable wage labour lived in more luxurious style than their neighbors whose employment had been short-lived or irregular and whose houses remain relatively unchanged from the precompany period. On my return visit in 1980, these differences were sharper than in 1979. There tended to be a concentration of wealth in certain neighbourhoods, poverty in others.

From late 1978, the village was electrified. The state electricity authority agreed to sell the power, which they received from the company's hydroelectric scheme on the Larona River. (The changes in the village are further discussed in chapter 7.)

Population of the Village

Prior to the establishment of the project, just under 1,000 indigenous Soroakans and a few Bugis settlers-by-marriage lived in the village. A dramatic transformation in the social composition of the population accompanied the subsequent increase in population.

By 1978, fewer than half the inhabitants were indigenous Soroakans (fig. 2.5). Many others came from the immediate locality (the districts of Malili and Nuha). Overall, two-thirds of the population (including the indigenous Soroakans) originated in Kabupaten Luwu. The vast majority of the remainder came from other parts of South Sulawesi, including 10% from Tana Toraja, where land shortage forced many to emigrate (figs. 2.5 and 2.6).

It is surprising that only 4.5% of the village population came from other provinces of Sulawesi, given that the borders of Central and Southeast Sulawesi are not far away. Only 5% originated outside Sulawesi. The project attracted mainly immigrants from the province of South Sulawesi, in particular from Tana Toraja and Palopo.

Productive Activities in the Village

Before the establishment of the project, all Soroakan households engaged in subsistence agricultural production. A few derived additional income from trading. This situation changed radically with the development of the project, not only because of new employment opportunities, but also because of the appropriation of the paddy fields, which had been the mainstay of the village economy. Changes in productive pursuits of the indigenous Soroakans are dealt with in detail in chapter 6; here I present a broad picture of economic activities in the village.

Since the coming of the project, the largest occupational category has consisted of those in Inco's permanent employ, or the employ of one of the contractors (table 2.5). Almost all were 'unskilled labourers,' though a few were 'skilled workers' who had not been allocated company housing. According to company estimates, 12 percent of unskilled labourers were from Malili-Nuha, about 40 percent from Tana Toraja, and the rest from other parts of South Sulawesi. The proportion of Torajans was not reflected in the residential census of Soroako Village, probably because Wawandula had become a predominantly Torajan settlement. Also, the Bugis population of the village was swelled by the large number who were attracted to Soroako by retail and trade opportunities, rather than by paid employment (see chap. 6).

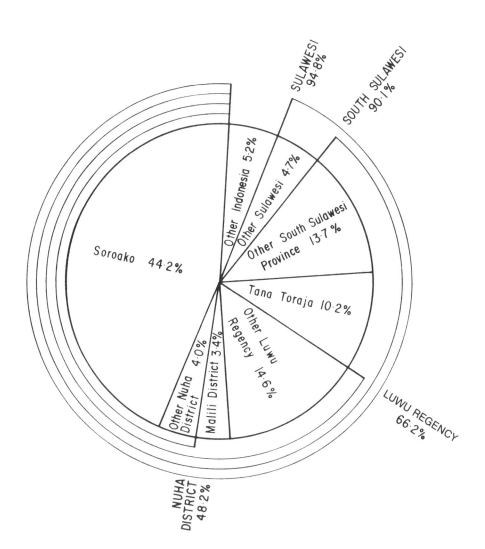

Fig 2.5 Birthplace of residents of Soroako Village
SOURCE: Population Census by P. T. Inco Medical Services, 1978.

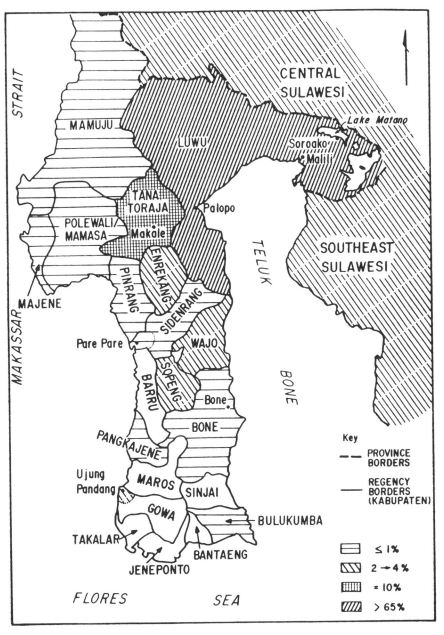

Fig. 2.6. Proportion of Soroako Village residents from region of Sulawesi.
SOURCE: Population Census by P. T. Inco Medical Services, 1978

TABLE 2.5.
PRIMARY OCCUPATION OF RESIDENTS OF SOROAKO VILLAGE, 1978

Occupation	%
Inco and contractors	16.3
Other waged work	2.9
Government and public service	1.0
Sales	6.1
Self-employed (tradesmen and contractors)	1.9
Farmers	6.1
Dependents of Inco and contractor employees (mostly women and children)	30.0
Other dependents (mostly women and children)	27.0
Unemployed	8.7
TOTAL	100.0

NOTE: The census tended to under-report female work. Many of the people in the two 'dependents' categories would be women who also are farmers, or in sales.
SOURCE: Census by P. T. Inco Medical Services, 1978.

Some waged work was provided by a number of small businesses which, for example, made rattan furniture for sale to foreigners, ran minibuses between Soroako and Malili, or provided sawn timber to the company. In 1978, the company began divesting itself of some of its service activities, including running a local bus service, the provision of vegetables to the company store, and mowing lawns in the townsite. These activities were taken over by local contractors, but the number of jobs thus created was small and the work was usually on a casual basis. The pay was less than for employment in the company, and these workers were not entitled to free treatment at the hospital.

Inco was also retrenching employees and taking on casual labour. Their daily rate of Rp.1,000 provided them with a lower monthly wage than the average 'unskilled labourer.' They were not entitled to treatment at the company hospital, except for illness or injury contracted in the course of work, and they received neither holiday pay nor interest-free housing loans. Employment was on a daily basis, so people in casual employment—whether for the company or one of the small local contractors—were subject to greater intensity of exploitation in the form of less security of employment and lower pay.

Soroako was truly a company town in that Inco provided the principal source of regular employment, and other job opportunities ultimately derived from its activities. The fortunes of the citizens of Soroako rose and fell with the fortunes of the company.

There were a number of wealthy traders, who brought rice and other goods from Palopo each month. Most of these people had been small traders in the early days of the project, and they made great profits in the construction period. There were a few indigenous Soroakans among them, but the majority were Bugis immigrants. In addition, there were a large number of small shops; 146 small shops and businesses in 1978 (see chap. 6). The small shops, however, especially those in Old Village, served more to circulate income among kin than to make great profit. Some of the other small businesses served the population of the townsite and the village, for example, tailors, beauty salons, and photographic studios.

The presence of a large number of single men in the camp had led to the establishment of several bars and restaurants in New Village. These were all owned by immigrants. Their customers were principally foreigners, though some of the young Indonesian workers enjoyed frequenting the bars, often sharing only a single bottle of beer, in order to enjoy the attention of the hostesses.

The village market was situated on the road leading to the townsite. Most of the large shops were located nearby. The market was built by the village government, a rough construction of timber and thatch. Inside, it was dark, close and low-ceilinged. Most of the vendors also lived there, bedding down amidst their wares and cooking in makeshift kitchens. At the end of the month, the market would swell with traders bringing wares to sell to workers after pay day. Indeed, the rhythm of life in this community was set more by the monthly cycle of pay days than by the calendar of the agricultural year.

However, for a small proportion of the villagers, all of them indigenous Soroakans, agricultural production still provided the principal form of livelihood. The loss of the paddy fields meant it was difficult for them to live exclusively by farming the remaining available land, suitable only for slash and burn cultivation. The conditions of agricultural production have been dramatically changed by the company's presence (see chap. 6). These people were always seeking paid work in order to make ends meet, as casual labourers for Inco or one of the smaller contractors, or by performing a day's work for a fellow villager.

Those villagers whose income derived from agriculture and from casual employment, as well as the small shopkeepers, formed a group differentiated by poverty and uncertainty from those fortunate enough to be in stable wage employment.

A small number of village inhabitants were government employees. They included the school teachers and the men in the village administration. At the time of my arrival the village headman was an outsider who received a government salary. The other indigenous government officials received only a monthly honorarium of Rp.1,000 (US$2.40) or less in some cases.

The low level of pay was predicated on an assumption that village officials' income would basically derive from agriculture, but this was no longer possible in Soroako. All the village officials had supplementary income, from agriculture, trade, and rent.

The post of village headman had always been held by a Soroakan, chosen from among a few influential families. However the low level of remuneration for village government officials meant that the incumbent headman was easily lured by the promise of higher wages to work for one of the contractors, in 1973. The post was then filled by an outsider appointed from the regency capital (Palopo). It was not a successful appointment and he was moved in 1977, to be replaced by another outsider, regarded as a temporary appointment until the matter could be resolved. Eventually, in 1978, the former headman, having been retrenched from the construction company, was persuaded to take up his post again. The disputes between the indigenous Soroakans and the immigrant village headman are discussed at greater length in chapter 7. They exemplify the conflicts between the Soroakans and outsiders over the loss of indigenous control and influence, following on the development of the project.

Labour Market Segmentation and the Company Work Force

The inequalities in Soroako, manifested in the differences in wage levels and distribution of other resources, can be understood by reference to the class basis of capitalism. Capitalist development is based on capital accumulation, through the appropriation of surplus value. An important aspect of this is the differential exploitation of workers in various categories, based on what Braverman has called the division of labour in detail (1974, p.72):

> (T)he labour process . . . may be divided into elements some of which are simpler than others and each of which is simpler than the whole. . . . (L)abour power capable of performing the process may be purchased more cheaply as dissociated elements than as a capacity integrated in a single worker (1975, p.81).

This process is at the basis of the company job ladder. The division of labour within the capitalist enterprise allows for the creation of a segmented labour force in which the bottom segments are subject to greater intensity of exploitation through lower rates of pay, a longer working day, less pleasant working conditions, and less stability of employment.

In advanced capitalist countries, groups with particular ascriptive characteristics (for example, blacks, women, immigrant workers) tend to cluster in the low-paid jobs, irrespective of their skills or of the level of skills required for the jobs (see Collins 1978). In the context of the internationalisation of capital, the low-paid segments of the proletariat are increasingly to be found in the capitalist periphery. The compliance of national governments seeking foreign investment at any cost means that wage rates are kept attractively low, and there is often legislation limiting trade union activity. Hence, the product of the workers' toil is distributed between labour and capital in such a way as to ensure higher profits.

Orthodox labour market theory explains different wage levels among the proletariat by differences in marginal productivity and skills. This type of explanation was echoed in the company's 'view'—the lower wages of Indonesians resulted from their lower productivity and low education standards. However, many of the jobs needed only short, on-the-job training. Those construction companies with less time for recruiting an already trained, skilled labour force were adept at this, turning men with little or no formal education into electricians, welders, blasters, or equipment operators. (The training was specific to the tasks at hand.) These trained personnel were still paid the same low wages as unskilled labourers. Indeed, even skilled Indonesian personnel were paid at rates less than foreigners, even though they had comparable training (often degrees from the same Australian and American universities).

In Soroako, racial and ethnic differences were used to legitimate wage differences between groups, who were concentrated in different parts of the job ladder; these differences were used to legitimate the generally lower level of Indonesian wages and the particularly low wage paid to 'unskilled labour.' (This is discussed at greater length in chaps. 9 and 10.) As we have seen, indigenous people tended to be concentrated at the low level of the company hierarchy.

In addition, the division of labour in detail, and the related segmentation of the labour force, served as mechanisms of control. We have seen how the Indonesian managers fought to win privileges giving them parity with foreigners. This seemed to strengthen their identification with the company management rather than an identification with other workers. Braverman has written of the way in which the division of labour in detail divides the labour force between the few with special knowledge who can command the whole process, and the majority (albeit a segmented and hierarchically ordered majority) whose tasks involved simple labour and no knowledge of the overall production process (1974, p. 82–83). This is a facet of management control, as well as separation of interests between management and the mass of workers.

There are several explanations for the differential rewards to labour under capitalism. Orthodox labour market theory sees them as the outcome of the shortcomings of individuals (in lower skill levels and lower productivity). Marxist theory attributes low wages to the nature of capitalist class relations, and to the existence of an 'industrial reserve army' or 'relative surplus population.' This argument is applicable to the lower pay of workers in the periphery, compared with workers in capitalist centres.

Marx defined the industrial reserve army as a 'population that is in excess as regards the average needs of capital for self expansion' (Tracy 1981, p.2). It is an ever present feature of capitalism. Every worker under capitalism is part of the industrial reserve army whenever he/she is unemployed or partly employed. The important force in the growth of the industrial reserve army is the increasing organic composition of capital, as capital replaces labour by machines.

> It is capitalist accumulation itself that constantly produces, and produces in direct proportion to its energy and its extent, a relatively redundant population of workers (Marx 1930, p.694, cited by Tracy 1981, p.2).

The latent relative surplus population, which is located in the countryside, comprises the rural proletariat or agricultural wage workers who are always on the move to join in the urban proletariat. In Marx's study of the development of capitalism in Britain, the English and Irish rural populations were an important source of industrial labour. In the conditions that pertain in the periphery of capitalism today, there is a constant pressure on agricultural producers, forces that tend to separate them from their land. These forces include population increases leading to fragmentaton of land holdings, new technologies requiring money inputs, consumerism that drives people off the land in search of off-farm employment.

The stagnant relative surplus population comprises those proletarians whose wage labour is extremely unstable. They provide an inexhaustible source of available labour power. Their working conditions fall below those of the class as a whole; they tend to work long hours for a low wage. In Soroako, this group was represented by those villagers who had only casual employment with Inco or one of the contractors, and those whose main occupation was eking out an existence in agriculture, supplemented by intermittent paid employment.

The relative surplus population provides a constant source of labour for the expansion of capital. Because all its members are potentially employable, it exerts a regular pressure on the wages and working conditions of all workers, enabling greater intensity of exploitation. There is a constant supply of labourers waiting in the wings, willing to work at any price.

> During the periods of stagnation and average prosperity, the industrial reserve army presses on the army of active workers; and during the periods of overproduction and boom, the former holds the claims of the latter in check. . . .Taking them as a whole, the general movements of wages are exclusively regulated by the expansion and contraction of the industrial reserve army (Marx 1930, p.706, cited by Tracy 1981, p.4).

The concept had been eclipsed in contemporary Marxist writing, but it has recently resurfaced in studies of the situation of segmented sections of the labour force in advanced capitalist societies (blacks, immigrants, women). However, it has not been resurrected in contemporary studies of imperialism, perhaps because it was dismissed as having no relevance by Baran (Tracy 1981, p.1), whose work has been influential on contemporary theories of underdevelopment. However, it is highly relevant to studies of the movement of capital from the centre to the periphery. High wages in metropolitan capitalist countries, coupled with new technologies and new forms of transport making relocation possible, have led to a search for new labour markets (which are submissive and exploitable) in the periphery.

Besides putting pressure on the wages of the proletariat in the periphery—and therby intensifying their exploitation—the size of the relative surplus population in the periphery puts pressure on the wages and conditions of workers in advanced industrial societies—for example, the threatened relocation of industry to areas where wages are lower, or the recent controversial plan in Britain to pay young unemployed workers to work in factories at wages commensurate with wages in Third World countries, to make their products more competitive.

The level of industrial development was so low in South Sulawesi, and paid employment in such short supply, that people would travel long distances in search of work. Many villages with economies based on agriculture and fishing are extremely poor (Makaliwe 1969; Hafid et al. 1981). In particular, people from the overpopulated area of Tana Toraja have flocked to Soroako. For many of them, their natal villages could no longer support them or their families. They have not wished to return home and have moved on to seek further employment when job opportunities have dried up.

The poverty of rural villages in Sulawesi, like rural villages elsewhere, is being exacerbated by the expansion of capitalist markets into the countryside. New aspirations are created by advertising and by the diffusion of new consumer values from the urban areas, e.g., through popular culture and by the example of urban lifestyles. These desires can be met only through seeking off-farm employment, which provides the cash necessary to buy clothes, kitchen utensils, watches, radios, television sets, and motorcycles. (see McGee 1982).

The question of the low wages paid to the proletariat in the periphery has been taken up as a key element of the articulation of capitalist and precapitalist modes of production in contempory peripheral capitalism. Meillasoux argues that the capitalist mode of production actively preserves the precapitalist 'domestic community' in order that the reproduction of labour power can be carried out within the precapitalist mode of production. Labour is cheap in the periphery because the proletariat does not have to be paid a living wage/family wage that is sufficient to meet the costs of reproduction of labour power (1981, p.92). This view is evident in the work of a number of authors writing in the 'articulation of modes of production' paradigm (see, for example, Taylor 1979, p. 224; Deere 1979).

This argument leads one to think of a process whereby capital makes rational calculations about the minimum wage necessary to provide for the reproduction of labour power and so calculates a lower wage in the periphery by taking into account the inputs from the precapitalist mode. This fails to take account of the fact that capital always seeks to maximise the rate of profit, by minimising the wage bill. Higher wages in the metropolitan capitalist countries have been achieved by the workers' struggle, not freely given by capital in order that the workers can be maintained, and the labour force reproduced. In addition, struggle over wages concerns minimum wages determined by historically changing cultural expectations about standards of living, not minimal biological needs.

In many peripheral economies, however, the wage does not even meet these minimal needs for food and shelter (see Borkent et al. 1981). Many of the proletariat no longer have economic ties to the countryside and are totally dependent on the wage. Many urban dwellers supplement a wage that is less than a living wage through economic activities (by themselves and/or with other household members) in the so-called informal sector. (Can this also be considered a precapitalist mode, preserved by capital in order to meet the costs of reproduction of labour power?) It is clear that many proletarians in peripheral economies are inadequately fed, and so face disease, starvation, and death. This is of no concern to the capitalist: if the workers or their offspring die, or become unfit to work, there are plenty more potential workers to choose from. The moribund state of the agricultural sector in peripheral eocnomies means that there are always people who will take any work in their struggle to survive. This is the way in which the relative surplus population puts pressure on the wages and conditions of other workers.

There is no doubt that, for some peripheral proletarians, the inputs from the rural sector are important in helping them to survive, whether it be through inputs of food parcels to the urban worker, the survival of a male worker's wife and children through her own labour in agriculture, or through providing for the worker when he/she is no longer employed. It is teleological to say that these inputs are the cause of low wages in the periphery. The capitalist firm will pay the lowest wages it can get away with. The large industrial reserve army means that there is a pressure to keep wages down that originates from other oppressed people. The excess rural population cuts in to the bargaining power of the proletariat as a whole.

Meillasoux does not discuss the notion of relative surplus population in relation to low wages in the periphery. He rejects any discussion of low wages being related to the supply and demand of labour (1981, p.92). It is as if Meillasoux (and others writing in that paradigm) are so concerned to find features peculiar to capitalist development in the periphery that they overlook important features of the development of capitalism in Europe, which historically can be shown to be features of capitalist development in general.

An examination of the relevance of the notion of relative surplus population and its effect on wages is indicated by an examination of the wages paid to the highly segmented labour force in Soroako. At the running down of the construction phase, there was a reduction in size of the permanent labour force and an increase in the number of casual employees. On the other hand, in order to comply with the government's ruling on 'Indonesianisation,' the company had to attract highly skilled Indonesian technical and managerial staff. To do this they paid higher wages and provided better conditions than, for example, the Indonesian government-owned mining company at Pomala, in Southeast Sulawesi.

Status—the Cultural Evaluation of Inequality

The unequally distributed reward for employment, and the different lifestyles they supported, divided the population of the company town into status groups in the sense used by Max Weber. They were

> stratified according to the principles of their consumption of goods as represented by special 'styles of life' (Weber 1970, p.193, cited by Barbalet 1980, p.404).

Differing degrees of status honour were afforded individuals according to their position in the company and their place of residence.

In daily social interaction, people constantly asked questions concerning the occupational and residential categories of others, in order to place them in the social system generated by the company job ladder. It was analogous to the situation Geertz described in Java where two strangers will try to place each other by establishing their relative social status (1960, p.243).

However, in Soroako, the language used to evaluate relative status was a creole derived from the English used in the company and the jargon of company parlance. For example, the term 'expat' was used by Indonesian and English speakers to mean 'expatriate employee' (except that it really had the connotation 'white,' as the Filipino and Korean employees were not termed 'expats' by the Indonesians). 'Boss' was another word in common parlance. Place of residence was identified by the class of housing. The Indonesian inhabitants of the village spoke of the *tonsait* (townsite), *B haus* (B house) and *D haus* (D house). Status in the company was identified, for Indonesians, by references to the abbreviations (in Indonesian) of titles for classes of employees, so people were identified as PT (*pegawai tinggi*, senior manager), PS (*pegawai staf*, junior manager), PM (*pegawai menengah*, skilled worker) or PB (*pegawai biasa*, unskilled worker). Place of work was also identified by creolised labels, for example, *werhaus* (warehouse), *proses* (process plant), *mining* (mining).

So, not only were new forms of identity being imposed by a foreign-dominated set of class relations, but the language for establishing one's place in the new social system was foreign and imported.

From the point of view of the villagers, bosses (Indonesian and expat) deserved deference and respect, and the bosses in turn constantly expressed their moral superiority to the common folk (see chaps. 9 and 10). Villagers who were in the company's employ earned respect, not only because of their relative wealth (especially for those who had been in long-term stable employment), but also because of their identification with the power, wealth, technological sophistication, and modernity of the company. They expressed their pride in this identification by wearing company-issue hard hats, safety glasses, boots, and overalls outside of working hours.

Within the village, government employees and wealthy traders were afforded high status. In particular, those traders who had made the pilgrimage to Mecca were highly regarded. Their prestige in the village, however, had no currency in the company town, where they were regarded as low in status, along with all village residents.

For those villagers in the company's employ, prestige in the eyes of the villagers was somewhat offset by their low status on the company job ladder. They felt denigrated by their low position in the job hierarchy and their low status in the eyes of townsite residents. They and their wives constantly complained that their wage was not enough (*tidak cukup*) no matter how well paid they were in relation to other villagers. Their concern was that the income was insufficient to allow them to live in the manner of the bosses.

This was a consequence of both newly created aspirations and the significance of the very public nature of the differences in the lifestyles of different groups. Privileges such as better housing and telephones and company cars, and the different lifestyles that wage levels afforded, gave rise to envy in the community. Status envy rather than class consciousness was the phenomenal form of consciousness of inequality (as well as race and ethnic consciousness, disussed in chaps. 9 and 10).

For Soroakan employees, their relegation to low status underlay their sense of dispossession. For the population generally, they all came from societies that had particular ways of expressing and evaluating social status. These cultural forms were overwhelmed by the dominating hierarchy deriving from the company job ladder. There were attempts to graft indigenous symbols of prestige onto the existing hierarchical structure. For example, a Sundanese who had been promoted to senior manager and as a result moved to the C area, tried to validate his new higher status and earn top respect through the staging of an expensive and elaborate circumcision ceremony for his young son. The ritual took place in the D school, before an audience of of several hundred people. I describe a similar process among the indigenous Soroakans, through the staging of weddings, in chapter 8.

Conclusion

This chapter has described the physical structure of the mining town and the attributes of its population. In doing this, I have attempted to show that the initial impression of the village and the company townsite as separate entities belies the true nature of this community. By virtue of the scale of operations of the company and the dominating force of capitalist class relations, both are integrated into a single social entity in which the operations of the company are dominant. In particular, I have shown the importance of the company hierarchy, manifested in its job ladder, in determining lifestyles and forms of social interaction, which are interpreted in the consciousness of the people as differences in status.

I have argued that these status differences are in fact manifestations of the class structure in this peripheral capitalist society, where the magnitude of the relative surplus population provides conditions for a highly segmented work force, and differential wage levels allow for maximum extraction of surplus value. Such strongly hierarchical job ladders are also common in mining enterprises in developed countries (see, for example, Williams 1981).

However these forms become exaggerated in Third World countries where the structure of the labour force represents the new international division of labour. The top levels of the work force (involved in management and technical operations) are from the advanced industrial home countries of the transnational corporations, and the lower levels are recruited under conditions where the intervention of the state prevents worker agitation for higher pay and better conditions.

In Soroako, company managers claimed that the hierarchical forms of the townsite were to meet the cultural expectations of Indonesians—'they liked it that way.' However, attitudes expressed by Indonesians at the bottom of the hierarchy did not reflect such uncritical acceptance of the situation in which they were always the worst off.

In the next chapter I turn from the Soroakan present to the past, in order to develop an understanding of the forces that have created contemporary social forms.

NOTES TO CHAPTER 2

1. The following table shows the distribution of Inco workers according to sex, in each of the categories of employees. I have noted the characteristic jobs of women in each of the categoreis.

DISTRIBUTION OF INCO EMPLOYEES BY SEX, NOVEMBER 1980

Classification Level	Male	Female	Female Jobs
Senior manager	80	2	dentist, manager's secretary
Junior manager	266	19	nurse, administration (esp. accounting)
Skilled labourer	1,147	113	nurse, teacher
Unskilled labourer	1,954	72	cleaner, tea girl
TOTAL	3,447	206	

SOURCE: P. T. Inco

2. By the October 1980 Indonesian national census, Indonesian citizens comprised 70% of the population of the C area, 86% in the D area, and 83% in the Old Camp.

3. *Inpres* refers to development programmes carried out in Indonesian villages with funds disbursed directly from the President, rather than by way of local and regional government

Chapter 3

The Village of Soroako: Its People and the Beginnings of Their Incorporation Into the Modern World

This chapter investigates the history of the village of Soroako, its people, and their relation to that history. I begin with the most distant events in both their oral traditions and in the few written sources available. The discussion then considers the period prior to the assumption of sovereignty by the new Indonesian Republic.

Introduction

The rugged interior of the island of Sulawesi is characterised by high mountain ranges and a lack of navigable rivers. This has led to a dispersal of the sparse population and to a considerable degree of linguistic diversity in the region (Lebar 1972, p.124; see also Mills 1975).

In contemporary Indonesia, Soroako is part of the province of South Sulawesi, and as I will discuss below, the indigenous Soroakans have been profoundly influenced by the Bugis, the dominant linguistic group in southern Sulawesi.[1] However, they are culturally and linguistically related to the people of the contemporary province of Central Sulawesi. The indigenous language (*Mepau Soroako* S.) is a dialect of Mori, one of the Bungku-Laki group of languages spoken in

55

Photo 3. Villagers at their field hut.

central and southeastern Sulawesi[2] (J. Kruyt 1919, p.328; Esser 1927, p.5; Mills 1975; J. Kruyt 1977, p.22). Indeed, according to J. Kruyt, a missionary-linguist, the indigeneous Soroakans spoke the same dialect as the Mori rulers, who were based in Tinompo (J. Kruyt 1919, p.329).

The people of the mountainous centre of Sulawesi (map 3.1) were, before the turn of the century, principally swidden cultivators and foragers in the jungle. In lowland areas, villages comprised thirty to fifty houses, while in the mountains, they would include only ten to twenty houses (A. C. Kruyt 1900, p.458).

European visitors to Soroako at the turn of the century commented on it being larger than neighbouring villages (Grubauer 1913, p.69). This was the result of its favourable location on the shores of Lake Matano, which gave it an advantage both in food production and in inland trade. The indigenous Soroakans were well-known as blacksmiths, smelting iron ore and fashioning it into knives and agricultural implements. This small commodity production probably also contributed to the larger size of the village (see chap. 5).

Until the latter part of the 19th century, the central region of Sulawesi had attracted little attention from the Dutch colonisers, although the trade in such jungle products as dammar resin and rattan (Allen and Donithorne 1954, pp. 302–3) stimulated by Dutch mercantile activities, had drawn Bugis traders from the southwest peninsula to the region. The internal trade of central Sulawesi, especially the trade in iron, had apparently long attracted the rulers of the Bugis domain of Luwu (centred in Palopo) to the region around Lake Matano.

The Bugis form the numerically largest linguistic category in the southwestern peninsula of Sulawesi. They have long been known as seafarers and traders, and for their strenuous identification with Islam. They are what H. Geertz has called a 'centripetal society,' constantly throwing off members who go in search of new economic opportunities (1963, p.69). They have had, since at least the 14th century, more elaborate, centralised forms of political organisation than the swidden cultivators of central Sulawesi. These political forms aided in their annexation of central Sulawesi. The expansion of Bugis influence in that region went hand in hand with the development of trade in jungle produce, in the late 19th century.

The people of Soroako have little sense of the ways in which their own past relates to the wider history of either the region they inhabit or the Indonesian nation. Nor has this remote locale figured promi-

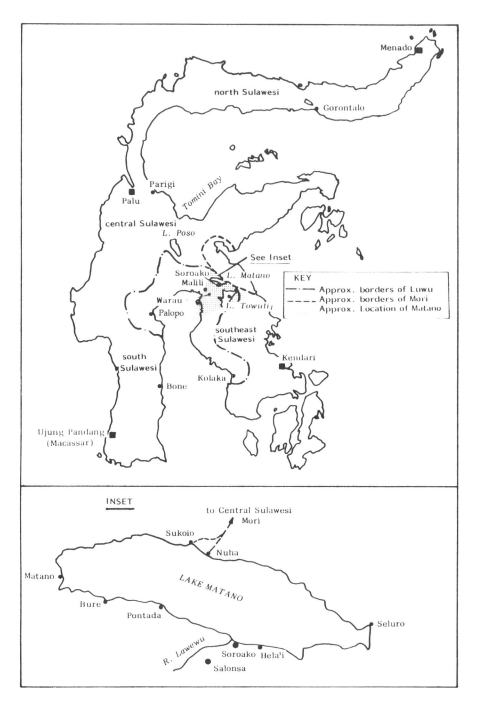

3.1. Sulawesi in the 19th century

nently in the historical records of either the domain of Luwu or of the Dutch. I have consulted the few available written sources that throw light on events in the region around Lake Matano, fleshing them out with the oral history of the people themselves. This procedure has enabled me to describe the dramatic events of the last 100 years. The depth of the history, then, is given by the extent of the oral and written sources. It should not be assumed that this represents a baseline beyond which we can assume life in Soroako was static, unchanging, or 'traditional.'[3]

With respect to their own history, the Soroakans have a truncated oral tradition. Many people had little or no memory of many of the events discussed below. However, in a profound way, their identity has been shaped by a sense of themselves as formed by past events. Soroakan identity in the 1970s was crucially concerned with ties to place, validated by a widely known story of the founding of the village. This was related to the strong ideology of indigenous Soroakans as people sharing a common descent. Islam was another crucial element of contemporary sociocultural identity, as were the popular beliefs about the nature of the conversion. Finally, the Soroakan view of historical processes revealed their parochial mentality, their lack of understanding of the world beyond Lake Matano. This aspect of their relation to historical events is crucial in understanding their response to the mining project.

This chapter records the ways in which the Soroakans have become incorporated into the domains of larger, more powerful indigenous political entities, the expansion of mercantile trading networks into the region, the incorporation and establishment of direct colonial control in the early 20th century, and events of the Indonesian struggle for independence. These processes have effected important changes in forms of production and production relations within Soroako. It becomes clear that these changes have been part of a generalised process of the incorporation of the village, the region, (indeed the whole archipelago), into a world economy in which capitalism is ultimately dominant. In this process, the villagers have lost control over certain productive processes that sustained their independence from extracommunity economic relations. The development of the mining project can be seen as the culmination of this process of incorporation, rather than as a sudden and cataclysmic transformation of an isolated precapitalist society.

The Story of the Founding of the Village

The story of the founding of Soroako on its contemporary site was an important statement of the view the indigenous Soroakans had of themselves and the way in which the Soroakan identity was formed from historical processes. Most people, including the young, could tell at least a truncated version of this story. Indeed it was often the only history they knew. It stressed the identification of the Soroakans with the current site of their village and established this tie to place as a central feature of Soroakan identity, as expressed in the modern world. Also, although the Soroakan version of the story related only to the village itself, it contained elements that enable us to locate the village in supralocal historical processes.

The story begins when an enemy force conquers the ancestors of the contemporary Soroakans. Their village, then located at Hela'i (the area known as Old Camp in the mining town), was burned to the ground. This unfortunate occurrence caused the people to abandon the old village site (see map. 3.1). A warleader (*tadulako* S.) named Tosalili set off in a boat, in order to seek a new site. He was accompanied by the Opu Bintao Wita (the Lord who left his land), the title (*Opu* B.) identifying him as an aristocrat from Luwu. The two men followed the lake shore until they reached the River Lawewu (in the centre of what is now Old Village). Their dog began barking at some bushes. The Opu pointed to a tree growing there and asked Tosalili, "Do you know the name of that tree?" Tosalili replied that he did not. "I know," said the Opu, "it is called 'Serewako' (sic)." The dog then caught a deer in the bushes. "This is a good sign," said the Opu. "You should build your houses here." Tosalili agreed, but said that the Opu should build his house on that particular spot, and the rest of the population would build on the other bank of the river. The Opu planted a pole (in some versions ordered Tosalili to plant a pole), which is sometimes said to be the branch of the Serewako tree. In the 1970s, people could indicate where the Serewako tree had grown, even describe it, but the tree no longer existed, nor could they identify a similar specimen.[4] Nevertheless all Soroakans insisted that it was this tree which gave the village its name. According to the story, the survivors of the battle of Hela'i regrouped with people from the enemy force to establish the new village. The current day residents of Soroako and Nuha are their descendants. Since then, four generations of their descendants have lived in Soroako and Nuha. The descendants of both Tosalili and the Opu Bintao Wita have had a special role in the history of the village, which is discussed below.

Supravillage Political Relations

This oral tradition was concerned only with events as they occurred within the village. There was no speculation as to the motives of the invaders, or the way these events related to forces operating outside the village. However, the founding story contains hints that, when pieced together with other information, allow us to interpret something of the nature of political relations between the region around Lake Matano and the domain of the Datu (ruler) of Luwu.

The people of Lake Matano were subjects of the petty ruler (*Makole* S.) of the domain of Matano, who resided in the village of Matano. Matano's territory was said to have covered the area around Lakes Matano and Towuti (Document 8 1933)[5] (see map 3.1). According to a memoir of one of the last of these petty rulers, the people of the villages around Lake Matano, including Soroako, were incorporated into the realm of the Makole as directly ruled subjects (*ihi inia* S., literally 'contents of the village'). In further outlying areas, control was exercised through an alliance between the Makole and a local rule (Document 8 1933). Ties to the petty ruler were loose in these outlying areas. One informant, a descendant of the Makole, described the directly ruled subjects (*ihi inia* S.) as 'closer to the Makole,' (*lebih rapat dengan Makole*). It was a characteristic of these precolonial political forms in Southeast Asia that they centered on the person of the ruler, who was a magical centre and a source of power (Anderson 1972; Matheson 1975). Writing of the Sulu sultanate, Warren says:

> Traditional states were defined by varying relationships to the centre, rather than fixed geographical frontiers (1979, p.227).

However, as indicated above, at any time the extreme boundaries of the ruler's terrain could be conceived of as geographical frontiers. Incorporation into the realm of the Makole required Soroakans to pay tribute to the petty ruler, in the form of products from the smith's anvil, at times of important court rituals (weddings, funerals, and investitures). However, it does not seem that the power (or the will?) of the ruler to exact tribute from his/her subjects was very great.

It appears that the village community, as elsewhere in Southeast Asia, remained the basic unit of social organisation, land management, and conflict resolution (Reid and Castles 1975, p.vi). The connection between the history of the domain of Matano and the oral history of the Soroakans was given by the common presence of the Opu Bintao Wita. This was the death name[6] of one of the Makole Matano, according to the memoir referred to above (Document 8 1933).

In that document, the Opu Bintao Wita figured in a story of rather sordid political intrigue. He came to the office after forcing a rival to flee to central Sulawesi (Mori). After years in exile, the rival returned with a massive force, and decimated the village of Matano. The memoir records the version of the ruling elite and makes no mention of the fate of the subjects living around the lake. However, the common presence of the Opu Bintao Wita in the two stories, and their similar genealogical depth, supports the inference that they refer to the same events. The Soroakan oral tradition ignores the story of the decimation of the ruler's power. These days, the indigenous Soroakans do not recognise that they were once subjects of the Makole Matano, although they acknowledge the claims to royal blood made by members of the Matano royal line living among them.

In a manner characteristic of the political organisation of Southeast Asian 'segmentary states' (Warren 1979, p.224) the ruler of Matano was, in turn, a vassal of the Datu (ruler) of Luwu, whose court was in Palopo. As a contemporary descendant of the Matano ruler put it, 'The Datu of Luwu had authority over our domain (*Datu Luwu yang perintah kerajaan kita*).' As is also typical of those polities, the incorporation of Matano into Luwu was formalised through the intermarriage of the daughters of the Makole Matano with the royal line of Luwu. (In such alliances, wife-givers usually were of lower status.) The memoir of the last Makole, the offical genealogy of the ruling line in Palopo, and the genealogies of living people all attest to these connections. (The Opu Bintao Wita also indicates the connection with Luwu, as Opu is a title used by Luwu nobility.)

The ruler of Matano was expected to organise his/her subjects to deliver tribute to the envoys of the Datu. This was requested at times of festivities in the royal court. The envoys were received by officials of Makole's court, in a hut built especially for the purpose, on the borders of his domain.

At the time of the request for tribute, the Datu made a small presentation to the allies (*palili* B.), giving the transaction the formal character of an exchange. The allies were urged to ensure that the tribute was adequate, in order that the festivities would fully attest to the prestige of the Datu. The memoir of the last Makole cites the Prime Minister (*Pabicara*) of Matano making the following customary speech, at the time of the payment of the tribute:

> This is to symbolise that we are under the authority (*kuasa*) of the Datu of Luwu. We live in the land of the Datu and so we are under his gaze. For this reason, we collect the product of the land and fill his chest, as a symbol of the strengthening of the custom (*adat isti adat*) to which we hold (Document 8 1933).

However, Matano was also keen to stress its independence from Luwu. As mentioned, the envoys were received on the borders of the Makole's domain. The memoir emphasises the autonomy of Matano in internal matters.

> Regulations could not be imposed from outside, the allocation of office could not be disturbed, nor could its people be enslaved. The envoys of Luwu could not uproot plants on Matano's soil (Document 8 1933).

The relations between Luwu and Matano replicated on a larger scale the relations between Matano and its vassals, with power being concentrated at the centre of the realm, the ruler's authority being strongest for the directly ruled subjects. Matano was at the furthest reaches of Luwu's domain and, in a manner characteristic of the segmentary state, she could thereby stress her relative independence from the centre.

It seems probable that the alliance between the local Makole, or ruler, and the Datu of Luwu provided a model in terms of which the Makole could formalise the organisation of the court and its authority over its subjects. A. C. Kruyt asserted that such a process had occurred with the indigenous ruler of Mori. He had been a vassal of Luwu, but asserted his independence. Kruyt commented that Bugis custom was gradually being incorporated into the 'housekeeping' of the realm (1900, p.455).

Officials of the Matano court held titles identical to those of the Bugis court in Luwu. The members of the Matano royal line made (and still make) claims to 'white blood,' the sign of aristocratic birth in Bugis realms. Matano also boasts a *To Manurung* story. All Bugis realms have versions of this myth, which describe the descent to earth of divine beings who gave rise to current dynasties (see Andaya 1975; Mattulada 1982). The Matano version claims that, not only did the ruler of Matano come to earth at the source of Lake Matano, but he was accompanied by six other divine beings who spread out over the land. They included the Datu of Luwu and the Arumpone (ruler) of the mightly realm of Bone. The people of Matano have used the form derived from Bugis culture to deny the derivative nature of their higher level political institutions; indeed they use this Bugis myth of origin to assert their own prior possession of those cultural forms.

What was the impulse behind Luwu's annexation of outlying territory? The Datu and his/her court did not interfere much in the daily lives of his/her subjects, and the amount of tribute demanded was not great. Adriani commented:

> The Datu is more like a fetish (*djimat*) who, with the regalia safeguarded the existence of the realm, rather than being a mightly monarch (1901), p.156).

A number of writers (Andaya 1981; Macknight 1981) have commented on the connection between external trade and the development of the centralised polities of South Sulawesi. Macknight makes a contrast with the Indianized polities of Java, where wealth and power was based on the control of agricultural surplus (Macknight 1981, p.5). Andaya laments the paucity of material dealing with internal and external trade in Sulawesi prior to Dutch control of commerce (after 1667). However, he makes a plea for a study of the connection between trade and political development, similar to Warren's study of the Sulu sultanate (1979, 1982).

In the case of Luwu, much of the hinterland contained communities having economies dependent on swidden cultivation, or on exploitation of the sago palm. It is difficult to envisage such production providing sufficient volume of tribute to support the centralised polity. It sems that the main object of the Datu was to extract tribute to support the staging of court rituals. The successful completion of a ritual in which a large amount of tribute was consumed, and a large number of participants satisfied, served to demonstrate the prosperity and prestige of the ruler. This in turn was of benefit to the peasants, who basked in the ruler's prestige and prosperity. The control of the following necessary for such a ritual performance was the worldly manifestation of the ruler's spiritual power. The structures of domination did not arise from the economic system itself, as under capitalism. The peasants remained owners of the means of production of their own subsistence.[7] Because the producers were not tied to the ruling class (who appropriated surplus labour as tribute) as a consequence of ties based in the organisation of production, there was a need for extra-economic coercion. According to G. A. Cohen, this accounts for such highly elaborate ideological forms as are found in the precolonial polities of Southeast Asia (1978, p.196).

It appears that, as in Gowa (Andaya 1981), the principal source of Luwu's wealth was trade, probably not only from private trade by the rulers and officials but also from levies and 'gifts' from the trading activities of others (see Andaya 1981, p.7). However, Andaya writes:

It is difficult to discover anything about how trade actually functioned (in Makassar) and of the direct impact it had on Gowa society. There is even less known about the other South Sulawesi States (1981, p.5).

There are numerous references in historical sources to the nickeliferous iron ores of central Sulawesi, which were used in manufacturing the ceremonial daggers (*kris*) of the Javanese kingdom of Madjapahit (see Reid 1981, p.6). Reid states that Lake Matano was the principal source of iron ore in Eastern Indonesia (1981, p.12).

There was good reason, then, for Luwu's interest in the domain of Matano. The valuable iron, and iron tools produced by Soroako's smiths, were traded through the market at Sukoio, on the opposite shore of Lake Matano (see map. 3.1). It was situated below a pass in the mountains that was a gateway to central Sulawesi, an important inland trade route. At the turn of the century, this market operated every ten days, providing a venue where agricultural produce and bark cloth from central Sulawesi were traded for products from Lake Matano (Sarasin 1905, p.305; Grubauer 1913, p.59).

Goods destined for the European-controlled trade networks only began to be exported from central Sulawesi in the 1880s. Prior to this, the trade internal to the archipelago, in goods destined for other parts of Sulawesi, or even Java, was more significant than the dammar (resin) and rattan of later years (see below).

The power of Luwu waned in the region around the lake after the sacking of Matano (and the decimation of Soroako). Most of the remaining members of the royal line fled to Palopo. With the demise of the court of the Makole, the power of the Datu waned and the payment of tribute ended. The connection to Luwu was re-established only with the direct annexation of central Sulawesi by the Dutch in 1905–1906. They sought a descendant of the Makole to establish as the indirect ruler of Nuha district (discussed below).

Sociocultural Identity

In contemporary Soroako, the question of who was regarded as an indigenous Soroakan (*Orang Asli Soroako*) was a contentious one. In chapter 10, I argue that the form of assertion of that identity in the context of the mining town has to be seen as a response to class relations in the modern world. However, the cultural content of the identity derives from the unique historical and cultural tradition of the Soroakans, and here I wish to investigate the forms of identity that pertained in an era of different productive relations, different social forms. These provide the cultural basis of the forms of identity in the contemporary period.

In the contemporary situation, Soroakan identity was based on an assertion of common descent, which also entailed a tie to the village site. It was also salient that all indigenous Soroakans shared the Soroakan language (*Mepau Soroako* S.), which they held to be distinct from the languages spoken in neighbouring villages (except for Nuha; the people of Nuha were regarded as sharing common descent with the Soroakans and as speakers of the same language).

Cognatic reckoning of descent, coupled with a tendency to forget genealogical connections beyond one or two generations, allowed that every Soroakan could be regarded as a kinsperson. 'There are no outsiders,' (*tidak ada orang lain*), was the most common statement of collective ideology. In practical terms, it was clear that one was deemed to be a kinsperson because one was identified as an *orang asli Soroako*, as a member of the collectivity, rather than that identity being an entailment of actual genealogical connections.

Few people could account for actual genealogical connections to other Soroakans. One worked out the correct form of address by remembering the term of address used by one's parents for a particular individual. All people who were not members of one's immediate family could be addressed by a term stressing generational relation. Everyone else was a grandparent, aunt or uncle, or a cousin. People were rarely clear on the degree of lateral relationship. The vagaries of address underscored the 'genealogical amnesia' and supported the ideology of common descent. The common use of teknonymous terms (as well as a generic term for age mates and one for older people)[8] were important in this, too.

The oral tradition of the founding of the village indicates that it was established on its present site about 100 years ago, the founding population being the remnants of the village of Hela'i and the enemy force. Abendanon reported that at the time of his visit, in 1903, as a consequence of the preceding state of war the population comprised Bugis and *To Bela*, the latter being a Bugis term meaning 'inland peoples,' commonly used to refer to all of the people of the interior of Sulawesi (1915–18, p.1352.)

The village-based identity, supported by an ideology of common descent found in the contemporary situation, would seem to have roots in the forms of identity in the past. Discussing the culturally related peoples of Poso (see map 2.1), J. Kruyt wrote that the members of each village shared a feeling of unity based on a notion of common descent and from living together and sharing a common fate (1977, p.25).

However, he also identifies supravillage groups:

> We can identify a number of groups amongst the people of Poso. Each has its own name and distinguishes itself from others by means of its own territory, its own dialect and small differences in custom. However, they do not have a name for 'ethnic group' (*suku*) in their language (1977, pp. 24–5).

In the writings of the early missionaries, the people of the villages around Lake Matano are attributed such a supravillage identity, sometimes being called the *To* (people) *Nuha*, the *To Matano* or the *To Rahampuu* (this being an old name for Matano). In the memoir of the last Makole, the nonroyal people of the lake are called the *ihi inia* S., which I have glossed as 'directly ruled subjects.'

This memoir also contains an indigenous Soroakan word, which is glossed in Malay as *suku* (ethnic group). The word is *gau* S. which has the other meaning of tribute.[9] It becomes clear from reading that document that these supravillage entities, at least in the context of Matano, were the constituted tribute-paying groups. Groups of village communities were organised around the person of a leader who was a vassal of the Makole Matano. Hence the list of *gau* gives us, on the one hand, the *ihi inia* S., or directly ruled subjects and, on the other hand, lists groups identified by tribal or ethnic group labels, for example, the *To Karongsi'e* or *To Padue*.

In contemporary Soroako, the ideology of village unity based on undifferentiated common descent prevailed in spite of a contradictory modern tendency; a subgroup of the indigenous Soroakans asserted their membership of a *fam* (a group sharing a patronym), rights to use the name being defined by patrilineal descent from a common ancestor. The common ancestor was Tosalili, the man credited with the founding of the village on its current site. The principle entailment of the use of the term *fam* Tosalili was the right to leadership in the village, in particular the right to hold office in village government. A contemporary descendant of Makole Matano said that the village headmen of Sorsoako were 'all descendents of Tosalili. There has never been an exception (*Semua keturunan dari Tosalili. Tidak pernah lepas*).' This group claimed high status in the village; another indigenous Soroakan described them as being 'like the nobility' (*seperti bangsawan*) of Soroako. They regarded themselves as equivalent in status to the other prestigious families in the village, who claimed descent from either the Makole Matano and the Datu of Luwu, or both. The Tosalili *fam* had intermarried with both those groups. They had also begun to practise first-cousin marriage, a custom of high-born Bugis. According to Soroakan custom, this was an incestuous union, and it still caused moral abhorrence to some people, including reputedly in one case, the mother of the one of the first-cousin grooms. There was an apparent attempt on their part to emulate Bugis custom in asserting their status. There was a general tendency for Bugis cultural forms to become vehicles for claims to prestige in this community (chap. 8 considers the matter further).

While the claims by the Tosalili *fam* were generally accepted by other Soroakans, they did not go unchallenged. One old man, whom I was questioning about the founding myth of the village, said in exasperation, that he was sick of recounting the version of the story that made Tosalili the founder.

> We are all kinsmen (naming some prominent members of the Tosalili *fam*). My grandfather was the one who founded this village, but my father was very poor. Only [the people named above] were rich, so that's the way it goes. Whoever is rich, that's whose name is always mentioned.[10]

In his view, the origin myth served to justify, in terms of descent, domination by a group whose power was in fact based on control of wealth. The character of social relations in the precompany period will be further explored in the discussion on precapitalist economy.

Dutch Annexation of Central Sulawesi

At the turn of the century, the Dutch presence in Sulawesi was concentrated in the southwestern peninsula, and in Minahasa in the far north. Relations between the Dutch East India Company (later the government of the Netherlands Indies) and the rulers of the southwestern peninsula had always been uneasy. Gowa and its allies had been defeated in a military campaign in the 1660s, and the resulting treaty of Bongaya (1667) supposedly regularised relations. The Dutch occasionally claimed that this treaty marked the beginning of their control over south Sulawesi. However, even in Gowa, this established a commercial monopoly, rather than political control (Harvey 1974, p.47). Dutch relations with the indigenous rulers remained ambiguous, complicated by their continued jockeying for power among themselves.

In north Sulawesi, there had been a constant, if low-key, Dutch presence since the Governor of the Moluccas concluded an alliance of free will with the local rulers, in 1679 (Vlekke 1965, p.205). The more harmonious relations with northern leaders paved the way for missionary activity. However, further south, in Gorontalo, the Dutch presence was less firmly established (Klerck 1938, p.381). The central part of Sulawesi was outside of the orbit of Dutch control, though areas of Bungku and Mori were nominally under the suzerainty of the Residence of Ternate in the Moluccas (Klerck 1938, p.459).

The lack of a Dutch presence in central Sulawesi was, according to de Klerck, the consequence of the Dutch policy of noninterference in the outer possessions (1938, p.430). However, this was felt to have led to a lack of respect for the Dutch in those areas not under direct control. De Klerck, himself a colonial official, reported that there was anxiety that the Dutch Government could not guarantee the safety of foreigners in central Sulawesi. The Governor of Celebes (Sulawesi) himself went from Makassar to Palopo, in 1902, in order to negotiate safe passage for the explorers, the Sarasins, before their expedition to the central regions. It did not please the Dutch that the Governor was kept waiting for several days in Palopo, and then was received only by court officials, rather than the Datu herself (Klerck 1938, p.431).

At this time, there was an increase in economic interest in central Sulawesi. The Sarasins and a number of subsequent exploration teams investigated the potential wealth of the region. The Netherlands administration showed anxiety when a pair of Australian gold seekers gained access to central Sulawesi without permission from any Dutch authority. One of my informants unequivocally saw the Dutch interest in the region around Soroako as deriving from a desire to exploit its wealth.

> It is written in the *lontar* [ancient palm leaf books] that the wealth of Luwu is in Nuha, and they came looking for that wealth.

The last decades of the 19th century also saw the opening up of trade in junge produce from central Sulawesi. Makassar was an important market for a variety of gums and for rattan creepers. Both dammar resin (used in the manufacture of paints and varnishes) and rattan are found in the jungles of central Sulawesi. The growth in importance of this trade attracted Chinese and Bugis traders to the region (see Allen and Donithorne 1954, pp.303–4) and, consequently, the attention of the Dutch. A colonial official remarked at the time that the Indies Government should recover a share of the tax on this trade through Palopo (Document 2 1904).

At that time, colonial rhetoric expressed an increasing concern for the well-being of the native populace, seen to be at the mercy of despotic 'feudal rulers.' The following comment, for example, was made by a Dutch official, when advising the Government of the need to intervene in Luwu:

> Our policy has always been such that there has been a minimum of interference in the Outer Possessions and this

has been particularly the case with Celebes and the Dependencies and nowhere has this policy had such a bad effect as here: slave hunting, slave trade, head hunting and bad treatment of people by the kings and chiefs. There should be an end to this situation, for humanitarian reasons and also because it is our duty as the rulers of this archipelago (Document 2 1904, p.3).

European commentators constantly labelled the situation in central Sulawesi as 'feudal' (see, for example, Abendanon 1915–18, p.1352; Klerck 1938, p.389). J. Kruyt described the Matano-Malili area as being under the despotic rule of the Datu of Luwu, the local population being mere slaves of the foreign dynasty (1977, p.24). James Boon comments, with respect to a similar characterisation of Bali by Europeans, that it gave a justification for Dutch intervention in that they were liberating peasants from 'a vestigial Dark Age' (1977, p.6).

This rhetoric was important in the context of the philosophy of Liberalism, which was gaining ascendancy in the determination of colonial policy. This asserted that despotic rulers should be curbed by placing them under the supervision of humane and rational European rulers. This

would bring improved welfare to the native population at the same time that it increased the profits of the capitalist (Harvey 1974, p.48).

To this end the Netherlands Indies Government appointed a Controleur (District Official) to Tomini Bay, in 1901. He had problems in dealing with Luwu; he had been appointed from north Sulawesi, and Luwu, being one of the southern states, would have dealings only with Makassar.

In 1904, the Dutch Government, resolved to 'cleanse the Augean stables of Celebes' (Klerck 1938, p.456) with a military campaign against the southern rulers. They were forced to sign short declarations (*korte verklaringen*) avowing loyalty and obedience to the Queen of the Netherlands and her deputies and, further, agreeing to have no contact with other foreign powers (this idea was devised by Snouck Hurgronje) (Harvey 1974, p.50). However, the native rulers were to be autonomous with respect to internal matters (Vlekke 1945, p.315). So much for the rhetoric that intervention was to end despotic rule!

The military campaign began in 1905 and, by August, most of the southern rulers had surrendered. Luwu, however, refused to capitulate, so troops were despatched to Palopo in late August. Although de Klerck writes that Luwu was captured without resistance (1938, p.457), an historian of Luwu claims that the Dutch encountered pockets of resistance until 1906 (Mattata 1962, p.81). J. Kruyt also reported resistance (1977, p. 146).

In 1908, the Dutch civil administration was established in south Sulawesi, including the former territories of Luwu in central Sulawesi. By 1910, the retiring Governor could write:

> During this government, peace and order have been estab-
> lished, and although local disagreement may arise here and
> there, I don't think there will be any resistance of much im-
> portance. . . . The population is generally co-operative and
> usually obeys our commands. In most regions our officials . . .
> travel without protection and only accompanied by the chiefs
> of the districts they travel through (Document 3 1910, p.31).

The people living around Lake Matano were not involved in the events leading to the defeat of Luwu, and their oral history has no mention of these events. However, the consequences of the establishment of Dutch administrative control were profound for the social and economic organisation of the community.

Changes in Government in the Colonial Period

In accord with the principles of indirect rule proposed by Snouck Hurgronje, the Dutch sought an heir to the Matano 'throne' to install as District Chief (*Kepala Distrik*). Bypassing an heir living in Matano, they brought an appointee from Palopo. An informant said to me, they had to bring someone from Palopo because the local contenders were all ignorant (*bodoh*) in that they could not speak Bugis, let alone Malay (which was one of the official languages of the colonial administration). Andi Cabo was installed as District Chief and Makole Matano (the old title), in 1906. She was replaced by her daughter, Andi Halu, in 1908.

The indirect rulers took their place in a state bureaucracy that exercised more power than the traditional polities and that intervened far more directly in the lives of its subjects. Through participation in indirect rule, the power of local rulers with respect to other villagers was increased. Adriani and Kruyt commented that the village leaders, who had been *primus inter pares*, had to learn to rule in Dutch style, passing orders down to the villagers (1969, pp.236–7). Their power increased at the expense of their autonomy (Sutherland [1979] discusses this process in Java).

According to J. Kruyt, the population of central Sulawesi did not expect Dutch rule to be any more onerous than that of previous authorities. He recounts the shock of the people at the far heavier demands to which they became subject, and the greater regulation of their lives (1977, p.153). The son of Andi Halu commented to me that the number of orders coming from the colonial government was greater than the number coming from precolonial rulers.

The Dutch Government immediately banned a number of customary practices that were held to be 'heathen.' Most notable of these were headhunting and warfare, both of which had been connected with customary religious practices. This brought peace and stability to the region. However, the beneficial consequences of some of the prohibitions were less obvious. Secondary burial was prohibited and village shrines were not allowed to be maintained.

To facilitate control of the population, villages and homesteads were moved from locations high in the mountains to sites closer to new roads (the villages of Wasuponda and Wawandula date from this period). The people were not allowed to rebuild shrines in the new villages. After a few years, many of the old shrines could be found decaying in the jungle, monuments to the abandonment of customary religion (J. Kruyt 1977, pp.148–9).

The requirement of paying taxes in cash propelled men into the monetary economy. In central Sulawesi, the only source of cash was through collection of rattan and dammar resin. J. Kruyt commented on the negative social consequences of this activity, with men spending much time away from the village. In particular, he noted the hardship for women forced to carry out agricultural production on their own (1977, p.153).

The obligation to participate in forced labour (*rodi*) was even more onerous. This labour was used in the construction of roads to link the interior to the coast, thus facilitating administration and trade. The people saw this work as a form of slavery, as the hours of work were dictated to them, and they laboured under the scrutiny of a foreman (J. Kruyt 1977, p.153). Though Kruyt was writing about Poso, his comments mirrored those offered to me by older Soroakan informants, who spoke both of their hatred of forced labour and of their need to collect jungle produce to pay tax.

Changes in Agriculture

The Dutch enforced dramatic changes in forms of production. Under the Ethical Policy, intervention in peasant agriculture was seen as a way of improving village welfare (Penders 1968). In Luwu, the government banned the burning of the forests (Document 4 1918), a regulation that, if enforced, would have meant the end of swidden cultivation, which in the view of the Dutch was destructive of the environment. In August 1921, a further regulation was passed requiring the population to establish paddy fields (Document 5 1921).[11] The attempt to enforce settled cultivation was part of the strategy to bring the population under firmer government control by moving them down from the mountains.

In Soroako, the plain behind the village was divided up and the District Chief appointed a *mantri sawah*, a kind of agricultural extension officer, to teach cultivation techniques. The people of Soroako remembered at first being reluctant to cultivate wet rice fields. It was hard work: some of them, owning no buffalo, had to work the land with hoes.[12] However, they were impressed by the higher yields and, after a few harvests, became committed to the cultivation of paddy fields. (By the time of the development of the nickel project, the paddy fields had become their principal source of livelihood.)

People said that they liked not having to move each year, as with swidden fields. The proximity of the paddy fields to the village allowed them to spend more time there and less in the cultivation hamlets. Also, they soon perceived that paddy fields, unlike swiddens, could be sold.

Adriani and Kruyt reported a similar initial reluctance on the part of the people of Poso to cultivate paddy fields. The resistance was exacerbated by the arrogance of the Javanese agricultural extension officer there in dealings with the local people (1969, p.10). This was not a problem in Soroako, where the extension officer was Daeng Masale, a Bugis from Balanipa, Sinjai. He was quickly accepted by the villagers and brought profound changes to their lives.

Islam

The agricultural extension officer (Daeng Masale) came from a long line of *imam*; he introduced the Islamic religion to the people of Soroako. Islam has become an important aspect of Soroakan identity.

The view widely held in Soroako was that they chose to become Muslims. They say they were told by the government that they would have to choose a religion (that is, a proper world religion, not their own 'heathenistic' belief in animistic and ancestral spirits). Some versions of the story allege that Christianity was offered, but they were not interested. Only when offered Islam did they convert.

The descendants of Daeng Masale unequivocally credited him with the conversion of the village. Seeing his responsibility for both their material and spiritual needs, he converted them to Islam as he converted them to wet rice cultivation. Two generations of his male descendants subsequently became *imam* in Soroako.

The lineal descendants of Tosalili, the alleged founder of the village, had a different story. They said it was Magani, a former village headman and grandson of Tosalili, who was the catalyst to conversion. He converted to Islam while away on a trading mission, and the rest of the village followed suit. This version fits with their view of the role of village leaders. The ordinary people take their lead from a benevolent leader.

Both families remembered that the Imam and Magani were detained by the Dutch, for allegedly forcing people to adopt Islam (rather than Christianity). There is no doubt truth in both stories, but the historical record holds some clues that lead us to doubt the assertion that conversion was instant and all-encompassing.

It is an interesting question why the Soroakans became Muslim rather than Christian. Christian missionaries had been active in the area around Tomini Bay since 1893 and had made many converts among the natives of central Sulawesi. Indeed, they were so successful that, today, the people of Lake Matano form a tiny island of Islam in a sea of Christians who constitute the majority of the population from Poso to Mori.

What special factors in the history of Lake Matano led the people to become Muslim? The connection to Luwu is presumably significant. Luwu had been Muslim since the 17th century. According to

Adriani and Kruyt, officials of Luwu made no effort to spread Islam, although chiefs who were vassels of Luwu would claim to be Muslim (1969, p.309). In this regard, it is interesting to note that the village headman at the time of Grubauer's visit was called La Salima (1913, p.69), part of his name being a Bugis prefix, the second part being an Islamic name. Yet he was the father of Magani, the man credited with effecting the conversion. As for Magani himself, it is likely that his name was derived from Mohamed Gani, also an Islamic name. From this slender evidence, perhaps we can question the idea that the conversion to Islam was so sudden. Perhaps the indigenous elite had some commitment to Islam as part of their links with Bugis aristocracy.

The connection between trade and the conversion to Islam is well documented in the Malay world (see, for example, Dobbin, 1980). Adriani and Kruyt make a similar observation of central Sulawesi. They wrote that Bugis traders spread the religion (1969, p.303) and that their obvious great wealth made the religion attractive (1969, p.308). They first converted people along the coast (1969, p. 311), but then their influence spread inland along trade routes. Soroako, with its involvement in inland trade, was open to such influence. A similar account was given by Salvation Army missionaries of the same era (Kow 1949, p.59).

In 1979, I asked the District Chief, himself a Christian from Wasaponda, why the Soroakans had become Mulsim. His answer was: 'Because of their connection to the outside. Before that Islam was concentrated on the coast (*pantai*).' Indeed, the local story said that Magani converted to Islam while on a trading journey.

Once converted, links with Bugis traders on the coast, as well as intermarriage with Bugis villages in the vicinity, served to keep the Soroakans within the ambit of Islam. Simultaneously, the link with Islam tied them to the pan-Bugis world. This led to changes in Soroakan society and cultures as they assimilated to Bugis models.

Sociocultural identity was also significant in conversion to Islam. The people of the lake had been more closely linked, as directly ruled subjects, to the petty ruler of Matano, who was also descended from the line of the Datu of Luwu. The groups that converted to Christianity were those regarded as more distant vassals. Moreover, it can be speculated that in becoming Muslims rather then Christians there may have been elements of an anticolonial stance.

In the years following their conversion, their adherence to tenets of Islam was seemingly not notably strict. They retained practices contrary to the tenets of Islam, such as drinking grain wine (*pongasi* S.) and slaughtering buffalo at elaborate mortuary rites. Grubauer commented with respect to the inhabitants of Lake Matano, 'In his heart he has remained a heathen, though outwardly he had become a Muslim' (1913, p.77). It was probably similar to the situation of converts on the coast south of Poso. They had little knowledge of Islamic doctrine and law, and abstention from eating pork was the main sign of their new faith (Adriani and Kruyt 1969, p.311). It was only with the rule of the Darul Islam rebellion in the 1950s and 1960s that the Soroakans became more orthodox in their practice of the faith (see chap. 4).

Education

Resistance to Christian conversion is even more remarkable because of the continued presence of Christian missionaries in Soroako, from 1915 to 1956. Under the auspices of the Netherlands Missionary Society (Nederlandsch Zendingsgenootschap) in Menado (North Sulawesi), Minahassan teachers established a school in Soroako. They built a church in the Village of Karongsi'e, two kilometers away, on the present site of the golf course. The Karongsi'e had been resettled from the mountains. Most of them were Christian converts. A few Soroakans converted to Christianity, but they later followed the majority and became Muslims.

Though the Soroakans were not attracted to church, they were enthusiastic about the school that taught up to sixth grade. Attendance sems to have been almost universal for both boys and girls. In contemporary Soroako, I was surprised that all but a handful of the old people could speak Indonesian, a legacy of their childhood instruction in Malay. This impression was confirmed by a population census conducted by P. T. Inco Medical Services in 1978, which showed almost all the indigenous Soroakans to be literate. A teacher from Lake Towuti, who was a native of Soroako, confirmed that Soroako had a higher rate of literacy than other villages in the area. In fact, the people were also literate in their own language, which had been taught in the lower school grades. (People would correct my

transcription of Soroakan words.) However, at that time the importance of education was not altogether clear to them. One old friend
said to me, 'If only I'd known that this (project) was going to happen,
I would have paid more attention in school and not run away.'

The religious influence of the missionaries was slight, but their
pedagogical impact was far reaching. This was due mainly to the efforts of one missionary, known to the villagers as Guru Tua (Old
Teacher). He came to Soroako as a young man, in 1911, and became a
loved and respected member of the community and confidant of the
village headman, Magani. He and his family remained in the village,
despite his lack of converts, until his death at the hands of Muslim
rebels, in 1956.

The most dramatic changes in Soroako during the colonial period
were the transfer of political authority, the transition from shifting to
settled cultivation, the greater involvement in the money economy,
and the conversion to Islam. However, the beginning of the search
for minerals also began in this era. The impact was small at that time,
but it paved the way for the establishment of the Inco project, with
which this book is centrally concerned.

Early Mining and Exploration

Apart from the missionaries, the first foreigners to visit Soroako
belonged to geological expeditions. It is not surprising that my
informant should deduce that the Dutch came to Nuha seeking its
legendary wealth. The first European explorers were the Sarasins in
1896, followed by Grubauer in 1902 and Abendanon in 1909 (who first
alluded to the possibility of nickel deposits in the region). The
Soroakans spoke of the area's being opened up by the Germans in
1916. This refers to a team of three mining engineers employed by the
Dutch government who were based at Warau on the Larona River.
They had a small work force, including a few Soroakan employees.
However, the foremen were from Palopo (ter Braake 1978). They
made some excursions into Soroako in the course of their explorations. The grade of nickel-bearing materials was too poor and the price
of nickel at the time too low to make exploitation of the deposits feasible. The project was abandoned after a few years (ter Braake 1977a).
Exploration resumed only in 1941, when the Celebes Mining Com-

pany (Mijnbouw Maatschappij Celebes, hereafter MMC) began to work in the area.

This company established the centre of operations in the region now known as Old Camp, building housing for the 'handful of Dutchmen' (ter Braake 1978) and the skilled Indonesian workers (mostly Javanese and Menadonese). Their facilities included offices, a laboratory, and a clinic. The small clinic was open to the local community, and villagers often contrasted this with the restricted access to the Inco clinic today. Villagers attended movies, a football competition, and other social activities organised by the company.

The company engaged mainly in exploration, plus a little mining and surface collection of ore. It probably accounted for the small amount of nickel exported from Sulawesi in 1942 (Harvey 1974, p.73). The simple tools used contrasted with the high-technology mining of today. Most employment was on a piece-work basis; for example, after digging a hole of a certain dimension, a man was free to collect his pay and go home. One informant estimated that half the men in the village had worked for MMC. Their land was not alienated, and the organisation of work left them free to pursue agricultural production. Wages earned were additional to subsistence cultivation. A small number of people, including four women, was in permanent employment, in the office and laboratory.

The presence of MMC was short-lived. In 1942 the Japanese began their invasion and occupation of Indonesia. As part of their strategy of channeling the natural resources of Indonesia to the war effort, the Japanese began exploiting the nickel mine that had been abandoned by the fleeing Dutch. A few of the Soroakans worked for the Japanese, but with little enthusiasm. There was a shortage of consumer goods, as the economy was mobilised for the war effort. Trade with the coast stopped. The main complaint about this period, apart from the authoritarian behaviour of the soldiers, is that, although they received plenty of money from the Japanese, there was nothing to spend it on. However, their agricultural produce was not appropriated to feed troops, as in other parts of Indonesia.

The End of Colonial Rule

Soroako has been something of a backwater with respect to the main events of Indonesian history. The population has been affected by the major changes of the last 100 years, but it has not experienced the violence and drama associated with them. Throughout the Japanese occupation of the Second World War and the subsequent struggle for Indonesia to assert her proclaimed independence in the face of Dutch efforts to reestablish their authority, no fighting ever took place in Soroako. Malili was bombed and Palopo was the nearest battle site, when Australian troops supporting the Dutch confronted the Nationalists, in January 1946. However, these events were of no immediate consequence in Soroako. Indeed, the history of this period was vague in most people's minds. For example, I asked one woman in which period a particular occurrence had taken place. 'Well, I didn't notice whether it was under the Dutch, or the Japanese, or under the federal state. I don't know,' she said. 'They were changing all the time.' Later she added, 'I think the Dutch ruled here on two occasions, but then I'm not really sure.'

The second occasion of Dutch rule was the period of the NICA (Netherlands Indies Civil Administration). The Dutch established the federal state of Eastern Indonesia as a ploy to reassert control of Indonesia after the Japanese were defeated. At this time (1946), the personnel of MMC returned, and operations resumed for another three years.

If the sequence of events at that time was unclear to Soroakans, the political significance certainly evaded them. The Dutch, the Japanese, NICA and the *pemuda* (independence fighters) are spoken of in a detached way, as if they were characters in a play being enacted around them, but not involving them. The attainment of Indonesian independence was hazy in their minds, no one being quite sure how it grew out of those turbulent yeras. For Soroakans, these years were overshadowed by the drama of the first years of the new Republic, when they found themselves in the centre of a territory in rebellion against the central government (see chap. 4).

Conclusion

The people of Soroako were parochial in their view of the world and knew little of events outside of their own village. Nonetheless, in spite of their lack of historical knowledge, the events of their own history were of significance in shaping their view of themselves. Their oral tradition asserted the significance of their tie to the site of their village as a centre of Soroakan identity. Their connection to Islam and the Bugis world have similarly become important elements of their view of themselves.

They also saw themselves and their village as parochial, and for many, one of the main benefits of the mining project was that it opened them up to new experience, lifted them out of 'rural idiocy,' and set them on the centre stage of national events. However, their sense of tie to place was threatened by the way the project developed. 'We Soroakans will be pushed into the lake. There is nowhere else for us to go.'

The past 100 years has seen the increasing incorporation of the Soroakans into a world system in which capitalism is dominant. This began with the expansion of trade networks, fuelled by European mercantilist expansion in the 19th century, and has culminated in their direct proletarianisation by the establishment of the nickel project in the 1970s.

The next chapter examines their fortunes in the period since independence: their greater incorporation into the pan-Bugis world, under the influence of Darul Islam, and the establishment of the nickel project, bringing even more fundamental change under the impact of capitalist class relations.

NOTES TO CHAPTER 3

1. The Dutch defeat of Gowa, aided by the Bugis kingdom of Bone (which led to the Treaty of Bongaya, in 1685) brought about Buginese ascendancy in the politial, social, and cultural life of Sulawesi (see Mattulada 1982).

2. Soroako falls within the province of South Sulawesi (*Sulawesi Selatan*) in the contemporary Indonesian nation-state. However, geographically and linguistically it is part of what the Dutch termed Midden Celebes. I use the terms south, central, southeastern Sulawesi, etc., to refer to the geographically defined regions, and the capitalised forms (South, Central and Southeastern) to refer to the administrative divisions of the modern state.

3. No history of the region has been published. Apart from missionaries' and explorers' reports, I have relied on documents from the Indonesian National Archives, in Jakarta and in Ujung Pandang. The main published historical sources that refer to South Sulawesi are de Klerck

(1938) and Vlekke (1965). De Klerck, a colonial official, gave a partisan version of Dutch annexation of central Sulawesi.

The main indigenous source, a history of Luwu written by a local scholar (Mattata 1962), pays scant attention to Lake Matano, one of the remotest parts of the domain.

4.   It is interesting to note here that in pre-Islamic south Sulawesi, a banyan tree stood at the centre of each Bugis village. It was a sacred place, believed to be the birthplace, or site of incarnation, of the founder of the village (Mattulada 1982, p.7).

5.   This document is a memoir of one of the last heirs to the title *Makole Matano*. It was recorded in 1933 by another member of that lineage, Haji Ranggo of Soroako.

6.   Aristocrats from Luwu are given a title by which they are known after their death. The name commemorates some significant event or aspect of their lives. This practice was adopted in Matano, for members of the ruling house.

7.   The specific class nature of Asian societies (i.e., their differences from feudal and capitalist societies) was explored by Marx in his concept of Asiatic Mode of Production. There has been much debate about the defining features of the Asiatic Mode (see, for example, Anderson 1974a, pp. 462ff.; Bailey and Llobera 1981). However, it seems to me that the critical feature distinguishing this social form from feudalism is the ownership of land by the peasant cultivators (see Bailey 1981).

8.   Old people were known as *baloki* S., and age mates called each other *silow* S.

9.   In Toraja, *gau* means work in the context of ritual, specifically to slaughter buffalo (Toby Volkman, December 1981, personal communication). Similarly, in some dialects of Malay, *gau* is a synonym for *karya*, meaning work (Leclerc 1972, p.81.). In High Balinese, *karya* has the meaning of ritual (Adrian Vickers, January 1983; personal communication).

10.   The context in which he made this statement is interesting. He had, on a previous occasion, served as an interpreter when an old man who spoke no Indonesian was telling me the version of the founding of the village, recorded above. I had gone to visit him one evening to ask for clarification of aspects of the story, and he made this outburst in the privacy of his home, after asking me to turn off the tape recorder.

11.   Further regulations banning the firing of jungle and grasslands were passed in 1922 (Document 6 1922) and in 1932 (Document 7 1932).

12.   It is common for new paddy fields to be prepared with hoes. Plough cultivation is often established after a few years, when the stumps and burned timber have rotted away (see, for example, Furukawa 1982, p.43; Tanaka 1982).

Chapter 4

Political Independence:
The Village in the New State

In the first decades following independence, the people of Soroako were subject to violent swings in their fortunes, as a consequence of the turbulent politics of the new Indonesian Republic. Between 1950 and 1965, South Sulawesi was in the grip of an Islamic rebellion that opposed the central government and aimed at achieving the proclamation of the republic as an Islamic state. This rebellion, which won fervent support from the rural people of South Sulawesi, led to great privation and suffering, as they retreated into the jungle havens beyond the reach of the central government's military forces. There, daily life was characterised by simplicity and hardship.

The defeat of the rebellion occurred simultaneously with the change of government from the fervently nationalist Sukarno regime to the technocratic New Order Government of President Suharto. This government consolidated strong centralised control over the outer provinces and introduced new policies that greatly affected the lives of Indonesia's populace. Nowhere was this more manifest than in Soroako, where new policies led to the establishment of the foreign-owned nickel project. Within five years of the end of rebel rule, the Soroakan people had returned from their life of privation in the jungle refuge (*penyingkiran*) and were at the centre of the largest mining project and one of the most modern towns in Indonesia.

Moreover, the political rule that brought in these changes was the unknown, distant and impersonal central government, a marked contrast to the revolutionary style of the Islamic rebels. This chapter deals with rebel rule and the history of the development of the nickel project, discussing the ways in which the Soroakans were caught up in these dramatic political events of the new republic.

The Darul Islam *Rebellion*

The rebellion, aimed at the establishment of an Islamic state (*Darul Islam*), was led by Kahar Muzakkar, a low-ranking aristocrat from Luwu. He had served with the independence fighters in the war of independence against the Dutch (Mattulada 1977). He declared a Muslim Republic in 1950, and by 1956 the rebels controlled all but the cities of South Sulawesi (Harvey 1975, p.15). In 1958, South Sulawesi was declared a province of the Islamic State proclaimed by Kartosuwirjo, the leader of a similar *Darul Islam* movement in West Java (Caldwell and Utrecht 1979, p.95). This was guerilla war, played out in the jungle, needing and demanding the support of the rural populace.

The rebellion had the stamp of the politics of the troubled 1950s, the first years of the new Indonesian Republic. It contained elements of the competition in the national arena between Islamic groups and the Indonesian Communist Party (P.K.I.), on the one hand, and the conflict between Java and the Outer Islands, on the other. While acknowledging that the rebellion was fundamentally about centre-region relations, Barbara Harvey, who has written a comprehensive history of the revolt, sees the immediate precipitating cause as the exclusion of the freedom fighters of Sulawesi from the new professional army of the Republic. This fed more general fears of Javanese domination (1974, p.15).

However,

> Within two years the leaders of the rebellion sought a more substantial ideological foundation for their protest, both to provide justification for it and as a means of attracting popular support. Communism was considered, but rejected in favour of Islam (Harvey 1974, p.15).

The banner of Islam had great appeal in rural South and Southeast Sulawesi, which soon came under rebel control. The old independence fighters, who formed the core of the rebel army, recruited new blood from among the populace. The daily affairs of the people were regulated by a rebel administration that dispensed justice in accord with the prescriptions of the Koran. The peasants were required to provide sustenance for the rebel troops.

The conflict spread to the area around Soroako, in the early 1950s, as the rebels annexed the region. The rebellion was the first event of national politics to have really engaged the interest and concern of the Soroakans, perhaps because it was the first whose import they felt they understood.

In 1953, following a battle near Lake Matano between rebel troops and the Indonesian army (hereafter TNI), the people of Soroako evacuated their village and fled to more securely controlled rebel territory on the oposite shore of the lake. After the engagement, the village was showered with pamphlets from a government aeroplane, which advised them, 'If you wish to stay alive, go to Malili.' They were very frightened, but preferred to evacuate with the rebels rather than flee to the safety of the town. Following their departure, the village was burned to the ground by rebel troops.

The rebels' logic in urging evacuation was that, if the people were living far from roads and were inaccessible to the army, they could not be forced to provide food and shelter to the government troops.

The new village site was Seluro, a farming hamlet at the southeast corner of the lake (see map 3.1). The people built houses under tree cover, so as not to be visible from the air, and established gardens, similarly hidden by jungle cover. Indeed, this period is always characterised as 'living in the jungle' in the dual sense of not living from settled agriculture and living beyond government control. The land at Seluro was not suited to paddy field cultivation, so they established dry fields, mainly for cassava and sweet potato. At the time of evacuation, they had been about to harvest the rice. There were food shortages, especially in the initial years at Seluro, although some of the large landowners managed to take rice stored from former years. Commenting on the privation of those years, one man said;

> We had lots of food, just very little rice. You don't need much cassava—a few mouthfulls and you're full.

The rebels forbade all contact with the towns (on the whole still under government control) and enforced this rule by destroying bridges and roads. The disruption to trade led to a shortage of the manufactured goods that had become important in the daily life of the villagers.

Envoys of the rebel administration were charged with obtaining limited supplies of even the simplest commodities (for example, cloth, sugar, and salt) from the towns. A trader from Soroako who had performed this role told me that, apart from there being an absolute shortage of such luxury items as sugar, cigarettes, and canned milk, the rebels did not want people to use these 'foreign' products lest they should get a taste for them and run to the towns (see Van Dijk 1981, p. 191). (Indeed, in the contemporary situation, the desire for such goods is one of the major factors encouraging people to seek off-farm employement, thereby joining the industrial labour force.)

Nevertheless, some of the customary forms of trade continued. Villagers took jungle produce and metal goods (such as *parang*, large swordlike knives) to trade centres on the coast, to exchange for rice and salt, which was manufactured from sea water. To overcome shortages, some goods, for example, sugar and bark cloth (*fuja* S.), were again produced locally.

The shortages of consumer goods were felt as extreme hardship by the people of Soroako, attesting to the crucial role these goods had come to play in the local economy. The lack of salt, as well as patent medicines, was cited as the reason for many deaths. The dead had to be wrapped in woven mats (*tikar*) instead of the white cloth decreed by Islamic custom. A school teacher told me he had often worn a sarong to school, as he owned only one pair of trousers. This traditional dress was regarded as inappropriate for the classroom and he felt great shame. Food shortages were in part overcome by more intensive exploitation of stands of sago, but this often meant trips, under military guard, into areas not under firm rebel control. On one such trip, a group of Soroakan men were fired upon by government troops. One was killed and a number of others wounded. The survivors fled, and on their return the next day, the body had been removed. On other occasions villagers were captured by the army and held in the town until the end of hostilities.

School continued, but under difficult conditions. There was a shortage of teachers, so clever primary school graduates (including the current village headman) were pressed into service, after a special course at a rebel teacher's college near Lake Towuti, under the instruction of a Christian teacher who had been kidnapped by the rebels. Because paper was in short supply, pupils wrote on banana leaves with pens made from the ribs of coconut leaves (*lidi*). Since the image would fade in three days, pupils were pressed to memorise the lesson.

There was no school beyond the primary level in rebel areas. A number of the trading families from Soroako had begun to send their sons to Makassar (now Ujung Pandang) for high school education. These boys were trapped in the city for the duration of the rebellion, but all showed amazing initiative in still achieving a high level (in some cases, tertiary) of education. These men now all have prestigious positions in Jakarta and other urban centres. They later played an important role in intervening in the land appropriation, discussed in chapter 7. Their younger brothers, including the man who became the primary school teacher, missed the opportunity for postprimary schooling, and these men often reflected on how different their lives might have been if they had had the opportunity for further education.

The rebels proscribed many traditional Soroakan customs on the grounds that they were contrary to the prescriptions of the Koran. They enforced an orthodoxy in the practice of Islam that was new to the Soroakans, thus propelling them further into the orbit of Bugis culture. Both Islam and Bugis custom have subsequently become important elements of contemporary Soroakan cultural identity (see chap. 10).

Extramarital relations, and social mixing between the sexes in particular, were proscribed by the rebels. It seems that previously there had been quite free mixing between men and women. Unmarried adolescents had many opportunities for flirting. Young men had often sat in the kitchen, both in the public world of the day and the privacy of night, to chat and flirt with girls. At night, such flirtation could eventuate in the young men's creeping into girls' beds. 'One pillow, two heads (*satu bantal, dua kepala*) was the poetic way one old man described such exploits. Under rebel rule, men could not enter the kitchen, let alone sit with the women, unless they were sufficiently closely related to preclude the possibility of marriage (*muhrim*). Work in the fields and festive occasions also provided opportunities for flirtation. At festivals, the Soroakans—like people from other parts of central Sulawesi—had formerly staged a *madero*.[1] Dancers held hands to form a circle, men and women alternating. They danced in unison and sang to the beating of a drum and a gong. Between each chorus, individual dancers composed *pantun* (quatrains). There were many opportunities for flirting, whether dancing beside different partners or composing romantic *pantun*. Old men reminisce nostalgically on the joy of tickling the hands of beautiful girls during the *madero*. It was banned by the rebels, as the degree of licentiousness was held to be in opposition to the teachings of Islam. An old friend said to me, wistfully, that flirting was wiped out (*hapus*) by the rebellion (see Van Dijk 1981, p. 192).

The freedom of movement that women had enjoyed was drastically curtailed. They were forced to adopt the custom of covering their faces with a veil and to remain more within the confines of the house.

In contradiction to the concern for the protection of women expressed in these rules, many of the rebels forced young women to marry them, against their will and contrary to the wishes of their families. Many people said they had assented to such proposals out of fear. One woman told me how her sister-in-law had regarded her rebel husband (who had long since left the village and had never supported the child of the match); soon after the army (TNI) arrived, he came home one night to find she had pulled up the stairs inside the house. Many of these men already had wives in their natal villages, and after pacification they fled, leaving behind Soroakan wives and children. Such behaviour was at variance with Soroakan ideas about marriage; among Soroakans polygamy is rare, and a long-lasting stable monogramous union is the ideal.

Many customary rituals were affected by rebel proscriptions. There was a ban on staging ritual feasts with large quantities of food and on the slaughtering of buffalo for festive occasions. This affected all the major public ceremonies in Soroak: weddings, funerary rites, agricultural festivals, and celebrations of births. The slaughtering of buffalo at the time of a death was held to be contrary to the teachings of the Koran. Expenditure on weddings was limited, so that, at best, people could provide their guests with tea and fried bananas. The shortages of food and luxury goods in rebel territory also limited outlays on feasting.

According to the Imam of Soroako, at first people resented these provisions, but the villagers later came to realise that the provisions were directed as much at the troops as at the common folk. There was fear that the troops might use their guns to force the villagers to provision their own elaborate feasts; therefore, the rebel commanders decided to ban such practices absolutely.[2]

The period of rebel control hastened the process begun under co-lonial rule, whereby the customary practices of the people of Soroako were replaced by Bugis cultural practices under the banner of Islam. Customs like the *madero* came increasingly to be identified with the Christian people of central Sulawesi.

Everyone in the rebel area had to become Muslim. Many Chris-tians in villages neighbouring Soroako converted, but may others fled. Whole villages were deserted and have never been repopulated. Prior to the rebellion, there had apparently been a friendly enough modus vivendi between Christian and Muslim villages in the area, for exam-ple, with mutual visiting for ceremonies, and to *madero*. The period of rebel rule brought an element of hostility to Muslim-Christian rela-tions, still evident today.

The attitudes Soroakans expressed towards this period reflected the parochial limitations of their understanding of events, but also their fatalism with respect to the vicissitudes of history. Most people in contemporary Soroako said they had followed the rebels because they had no choice. They were frightened of the rebels and frightened of the army: caught (*terjepit*) between the two. 'Whoever was strongest could take us, so we just had to follow.' They spoke of their powerlessness and the hardships of the period with characteristic fatalism. I asked one old man if he missed the entertainments pro-vided by MMC in this period. He replied,

> We had no time to miss it. What was the point of longing for it (*Rindu, ya rindu*)? All we had time for was to think what our luck would be tomorrow!

Others told stories that led one to question the degree of helpless-ness. Some claimed there were many opportunities to run away to the town (as indeed many did). Many people related an occurrence in 1957, when a group of TNI soldiers came to Seluro and ordered the population to follow them back to Soroako. The people (in boats) followed part of the way, and then slipped back. Whether this in-dicated fear of, or support for, the rebels, I could not say.

However, it seems that in the first instance there was a lot of sup-port for the rebels. When I asked people what the aims of the rebellion had been, they always replied 'To advance the cause of Islam.' If one loved one's religion, it was natural to follow the rebels. Only once did someone allude to an understanding that the politics may have been more complex:

We saw it as a struggle to promote our religion. I have heard that there may have been other politics involved, but we people did not know about such things.

This expressed the parochialism of the Soroakans. The only world they really knew was their own, and they had little knowledge or understanding beyond their immediate experience of events.[3]

However, it seemed that, once people had experienced the privation and the arbitrary nature of rebel rule, they became less enthusiastic in their support. There was little actual fighting in the vicinity of Soroako, and only a few villagers were shot. Most of the victims of the rebellion were people who died as a result of the privations. As one woman described it:

When they first came, we were happy, but things got difficult. The road to town was closed. We pitiful Soroakans (*Kasihan orang Soroako*). Some of us had to make clothes of bark. We (meaning her family who were wealthy) wanted to help the less fortunate, but we had run out of goods, too. I used to have a lot of gold, but it was taken by the rebels. They said that they only wanted to borrow it, and that I'd be compensated, but to this day—nothing.

This supports Harvey's analysis that, whereas the popular appeal of Islam led to powerful support from the people of South Sulawesi in the first instance (1974, p.262), by 1956 the honeymoon was over and the rebels ruled by terror (Harvey 1974, p.268). The reliance on Koranic law in the jungle seemed to leave an open door for abuse of power. Troops used their power backed by arms to force their will on the people. 'They knew no rule of law. They had only one law—cutting your throat,' one man said. I was repeatedly told that, under rebel rule, thieves had their hands cut off. However, I only knew one man who claimed to have witnessed it. Others would always say 'not in this area.' The threat of this draconian punishment may have been a powerful sanction in controlling the population. The possibility of violent action on the part of the rebels was never in doubt: many villagers reported seeing enemy heads impaled on posts.

The rebel movement was on the wane all over South Sulawesi by the early 1960s. Since many of the regional-based grievances had been solved, much of its impetus was lost (Harvey 1974, p.423).

At this time, the people of Soroako were making frequent trips back to their former village, and were constructing temporary huts (*pondok*) there. During a cease-fire in 1962, a group returned to Soroako to gather coconuts for a feast. They stopped to rest in a covered bridge, and found themselves surrounded by TNI troops. One of the captives was delegated to return to Seluro, his companions being held hostage. He was instructed to convey the message that, unless they all returned voluntarily to Soroako, the soldiers would attack them at Seluro (cease-fire notwithstanding!). On hearing this demand, the people consulted a rebel officer stationed at Seluro. He was reported to have said 'I'm not telling you to stay, nor am I telling you to go. You must do what you think best.' So the people loaded their boats and returned to Soroako the next morning.

They began to rebuild houses, cultivate the paddy fields, and recapture the buffalo, which had run wild. The road to Malili was reopened. By 1963, their fortunes had improved (*rezeki sudah naik*). However, the cease-fire was short-lived. The leader Kahar did not get the guarantees he sought; consequently, he returned to the jungle and was again declared an enemy of the state.

During that period (1963–64) the Soroakans again evacuated to Seluro, though this second period of exile was less trying than the first. In August 1964, TNI paratroopers landed in a village near Lake Towuti, and the rebel control in that region was broken.

In 1965, Kahar was shot, and the remaining support for his cause collapsed. Over the next few years, the remaining rebels slowly emerged from the jungle and surrendered—although Kahar still remained a hero in the eyes of many, and the most faithful supporters refused to accept his death on the grounds that they had not seen the body.

On their return to Soroako, the people again began building temporary houses and cultivating their fields. In the absence of buffalo (which had been impounded by the rebels, or allowed to run free by their owners, to avoid that fate), many had initially to cultivate paddy fields with hoes. Trade was reopened with Malili, though under more difficult conditions than in the colonial period, as the roads and bridges had been destroyed by the rebels, and there was no longer any motorised transport. Also, the traders were short of draught animals—buffalo and horses—the latter having also been impounded by the rebels.

Those who had been traders before and during the rebellion continued to perform that role. The same influential families provided village leadership, too, when the Republic of Indonesia reasserted control in 1965. Kahar's egalitarianism and dislike for traditional authority relations (Van Dijk 1981, p.192) had not penetrated to Soroako. Even so, the descendants of the Makole did not reassert the control at the district level of government that they had held under early Dutch colonial rule.

The years of the rebellion brought about a more rigorous practice of Islamic orthodoxy by the Soroakans: many of the non-Islamic cultural practices declined during the rebellion and were never reinstated. For example, they never returned to the elaborate feasting associated with mortuary rites.

They continued to mourn in the customary Islamic way, with great simplicity. I found the people of Soroako to be devout in their observance of Islam, performing the ritual prayers (*salat*) punctiliously, and attending to the other four pillars of Islam. They no longer made and drank palm wine, for example, which their nominally Muslim forebears had done. The greater attention to Islam was part of a generalised accommodation to Bugis culture. While asserting an autonomous identity as the indigenous people of Soroako (*orang asli Soroako*), they were simultaneously taking on Bugis cultural practices as part of the assertion of that identity. The process of 'Buginisation' began with their incorporation into the political sphere of Luwu, and it was given impetus by the limitations of pre-Islamic cultural practices under the Pax Nederlandica. Rebel rule gave force to the process of incorporation of Bugis culture along with Islam, the Bugis religion (see chap. 10).

These cultural changes have had a lasting impact on Soroakan culture, they endured long after the rebellion. For example, the prescriptions regarding the freedom of movement of women were rigorously followed in the years immediately following the rebellion. Many of the first immigrant workers in the community (who arrived in 1969–70) spoke with amusement of the ways in which Soroakan women concealed their faces and hid themselves away from the stranger's gaze. These practices were beginning to fade only at the time of field work, under the countervailing influence of the immigrants, especially the urban elite in the company townsite.

However, it was clear that, in the contemporary world, the Soroakans were part of the pan-Bugis world. In their daily lives, they were more like the Bugis than they were like the neighbouring and linguistically related peoples of Central Sulawesi, who have experienced a corresponding accommodation to the more Europeanised norms of Indonesian Christianity.

Throughout this century, the people of Soroako had been incorporated into a world extending far beyond the region of Lake Matano. They had begun to accommodate to that wider world, in establishing trade links, and sending children from the village to school in Makassar, for example. The rebellion interrupted those processes, taking them into a world with a different kind of isolation from the simple village community. Those changes reinforced a sense of powerlessness to affect the course of events originating beyond the lake. That feeling of powerlessness was further reinforced by the experience of the greater intervention by the Indonesian central government after 1965 with the implementation of the New Order's development policies.

The New Order Government's Foreign Investment Policy

The economy of the new republic did not appear to be faring well in the first two decades of independence. In particular, the first years of the second decade were characterised by 'stagnation in production and trade, breakdown of the economic infrastructure and galloping inflation' (Mangkusuwondo 1973, p.28). Mangkusuwondo presents the view accepted in Indonesia and abroad, that the economic chaos was a product of the mismanagement of the Sukarno era, when economic aspects of development were neglected for ideological programmes directed at fostering national unity.[4]

The coming to power of the New Order governent in 1965 ushered in a radical change in government policies, leading to a change 'in Indonesia's operational motto from Revolution to Development' (McDonald 1980, p.68). The economic disorder was alleged to be so great that redressing its effects was taken as a major concern of the new government.

> It is no wonder that they put heavy emphasis on economic measures, with almost total neglect of the other (i.e., social) aspects of development. The major concern was how to halt the runaway inflation as soon as possible and how to get the economy rolling again after years of stagnation and neglect (Mangkusuwondo 1973, p.28).

The immediate aim of the government's economic policy became the achievement of sustained high rates of economic growth—and a shelving of a primary concern with equitable distribution of the national income. This was the form of 'Development' intended in the government's slogan (*Pembangunan*).

There was also a change in attitude towards foreign investment. Sukarno's nationalism had led to a turning away from foreign intervention in the economy, and the nationalising of the assets of foreign companies already in the country. The New Order government resolved to seek out such investment, as a major part of the strategy of pursuing high rates of economic growth as the major instigator of economic development. The Foreign Investment Law of 1967 served this end.

> In contrast to the uncertainties before 1965 foreign companies were given pledges against nationalisation and their freedom to repatriate capital was guaranteed. Exemptions from taxes and charges were liberally awarded, and the few provisions for local equity and recruitment were not rigorously applied (McDonald 1980, p.80).

The Law provided that investment should take the form of joint ventures between Indonesian and foreign capital. The pragmatic optimism with which such arrangements were viewed is well exemplified in the following editorial from an influential Indonesian business journal:

> To Indonesia such form of joint enterprise is not without risks. Due to lack of capital, skill and technology, chances of foreign domination always present themselves. Yet we may limit defects through various regulations and taxation. For our industrial development, we have only two alternatives: First we can develop Indonesian undertakings through our own institutions and guidance, with the risk of growing very slowly, because of lack of capital, skill and technological know-how. Secondly, we may do so through foreign capital investments in which we do not play a decisive role but through which we can gain know-how and technical experience and thus achieve faster progress. In our opinion this is no longer a matter of prestige, but a choice of how to develop our economy swiftly to enable us to provide employment to those who need it (*Business News* 1967, cited by Arndt 1967, pp.32-3).

By 1970, *Business News* had a change of heart about the economic strategy of the government, and in particular the possibilities of development through foreign investment. Their expressed doubts were shared in wide sectors of the Indonesian society in spite of the successful performance of the economy in terms of indices of growth:

> The technocrats say 'Production has gone up'. What production and who owns it? Giant industries . . . foreign owned and joint . . . ventures. And the rest? The national and people's businesses? Oh, they are flat and empty. But that is not really the question. The main thing is—production has gone up. Full stop!

> The technocrats say 'Per capita income has gone up! Whose income? The income of the corruptors and other money kings. But that is not the question. The main thing is per capita income has gone up.

> For the ordinary people, it's only high blood pressure which can go up (*Business News*, 26 January 1970, cited by Polomka 1971, pp.115–6).

This mirrors the disenchantment felt by the indigenous bourgeoisie at government policies that favoured foreign investment at their expense (see Robison 1978). However, it also mirrored the disappointment in other sectors that the hoped-for benefits of such investment were slow in coming.

Foreign Investment in Mining

It was felt that the mining sector had suffered from the economic policies of the Sukarno government. According to one observer, as a consequence of the expelling of foreign companies, coupled with inexperience, poor administration, inflation, and corruption, the mining industry was severly disrupted, and in some cases severed from world markets (Hunter 1968, p.74). The government view was that Indonesia's natural resources, in particular oil, could play an important role in achieving the desired rates of economic growth. At the time of the change of government, mining was 90 percent state owned and operated, under the control of the Ministry of Mines (Hunter 1968, p.80). According to Hunter, all but a few of these state enterprises were characterised by inefficiency and corruption. One of the

enterprises regarded as efficient however, was the P. N. Aneka Tambang nickel mine at Pomalaa, in Southeast Sulawesi. A reorganisa-
tion of the ministry was aimed, on the one hand, at giving more
autonomy to the local mining units (such as Aneka Tambang at
Pomalaa) and, on the other hand, at seeking out private, mainly
foreign, capital to develop mineral resources. Although foreign
capital had formerly been used in exploiting oil deposits, it had not
been used in metal mining (Hunter 1968, pp.82–3).

The government tried out a number of different strategies for
attracting foreign investors to metal mining. The first contract under
the provisions of the new Foreign Investment Law was signed in
1967, with Freeport Sulphur, to exploit the copper deposits in West
Irian. Of this contract, the then chairman of the Foreign Investment
Board (who later became the Minister for Mines) said:

> When we started out attracting foreign investment in 1967,
> everything and everyone was welcome. We did not dare to
> refuse. . . . We needed a list of names to give credence to
> our drive. The first mining company virtually wrote its own
> ticket. Since we had no conception about a mining contract
> we accepted the draft written by the company as a base for
> negotiations, and only common sense and a desire to bag the
> first contract were our guidelines (Dr. Mohammad Sadli,
> quoted by Palmer 1978, p.100).

This 'first generation contract' allowed Freeport a tax holiday and
other concessions on normal levies, freedom from royalties, a lack of
any requirement for Indonesian equity, and a wide leeway on the use
of foreign personnel and goods (McDonald 1976).

The contract was subsequently renegotiated, to waive part of the
tax holiday and make provision for Indonesian equity. Nonetheless,
despite the massive capital investments in infrastructure, Freeport
was operating profitably within a few years of beginning operations
(McDonald 1980, p.82).

In subsequent mining ventures the government adopted a new
approach. In an attempt to secure the most favourable terms on new
concessions, the Mines Department resolved to call on international
tenders. A large number of foreign mining companies were invited to
submit bids based on initial exploration, and the foreign investment
committee of the department awarded the contract to the most
favourable tender (Panglaykim 1968, pp.17–8). The so-called second

generation contracts were signed under new regulations implemented in 1968. These allowed no tax holiday, set varying levels of
royalties, and stipulated the taking up of 20 percent equity by the Indonesian public in the first ten years of the project's life. Sixteen contracts were signed under these regulations and ten were still in operation in 1976. The contract with International Nickel of Canada for the
exploitation of the lateritic nickel ores of South and Southeast
Sulawesi was the first and largest of these 'second generation' contracts.

In 1972, the regulations governing the award of contracts for the
exploitation of nonenergy minerals were rescinded, and over a four-
year period the government attempted to formulate new ones. Their
original plan insisted that:

> all foreign exchange earnings from mineral sales be converted
> back into rupiah through the Indonesian central bank [and it]
> sought to impose a general 10% tax on mineral exports in line
> with levies on other commodities and to make mining com-
> panies subject to local government taxes and charges
> (McDonald 1976).

These new regulations would have resulted in increased
revenues from mining projects and increased foreign exchange earnings. However, objections from foreign companies who were potential investors led to the issuing of new regulations in 1976, which
were more favourable to the companies (McDonald 1976). Further
changes in the legal framework governing foreign investment were
made in 1980, mainly concerning the attainment of Indonesianisation
in joint ventures (Healey 1981).

Exploration in Soroako

It had long been known that there were rich lateritic nickel
deposits in Sulawesi, as a consequence of the exploration and mining
during the colonial period. The Indonesian government began exploration in the Malili area as early as 1965, under the auspices of the
Mines Department and its subsidiary, P. N. Aneka Tambang.

The early exploration geologists ventured into the area at a time
when the government was only beginning to reestablish control after
the defeat of the Darul Islam rebels. Communications between Java
and Sulawesi were still poor. The roads into Sulawesi's interior were

still impassable in places, following their destruction by the rebels.

An exploration geologist told me of his initial journey to the region, in 1966, to get from Palopo to Malili:

> We were at the mercy of the army, as only the army had landing craft (there was no commercial shipping). In the beginning, of course, the army was quite eager to land us. They even forgot the charges, you know, basically because the chief of the army in Palopo came from the same area (West Java) as I came from; it's always the regional or religious element that makes things go. So, you know, we crossed the bay on a landing craft taking our Nissan Patrol (vehicle) with us.

They explored the area from a base camp near Malili. They had to proceed on foot, following buffalo tracks, ,as the Malili-Soroako road (built by MMC in 1939) was still impassable. They encountered remnants of the rebel army on their journey.

> They were still around and even the night we were in [the district capital] there were reports that the rebels were coming. I kept saying, 'Look, we are here on a peace mission. Don't be afraid; I can explain things.' Anyway, nothing happened at the time except someone came to the house of the District Chief (*camat*) to ask what the strangers were doing here and we explained we were on a mission to develop the area for the sake of the local people, and so on.

Even in these early days, then, the project was represented as being developmental, and for the benefit of the local people. Modern technology and modern goals would bring them out of the backwardness and isolation they had experienced under Darul Islam.

The geologists walked on to Soroako, where they were met by the village headman.

> They were surprised [to see us] but as soon as they looked at the gear, they knew what we were up to. They saw the compass, and that means business for Magani (the Village Headman, who had worked as a foreman for MMC). We hired him as our guide. Next morning he gave us lesson number one in nickel laterite. He took us to Hela'i and Samasang and showed us the ore, and even told us what the grades were. Later on I took samples and checked with the lab in Malili and they were correct.

As a consequence of these explorations, tenders were called to explore and develop the nickel ores believed at the time to be potentially the richest metal deposits in Indonesia. The contract was awarded in July 1968, to International Nickel of Canada (Inco), the world's largest nickel producer. In 1950, it had accounted for almost 90% of the non-communist world's nickel production, and it has pioneered many of the new uses of nickel that have led to a growth in the world market (Swift 1977).

By 1976, the company still controlled 55% of this expanded world market. Before their venture into Indonesia and the simultaneous establishment of another project in Guatemala, in 1971, all their nickel had been produced from the sulphidic ores mined in the Sudbury area of Ontario, Canada. To comply with Indonesian law, Inco incorporated P. T. Inco as a wholly owned Indonesian subsidiary of the parent company, in July 1968.

The proximity to the growing Japanese market was one of the factors that attracted Inco to Indonesia. Most of Japan's supplies had come from New Caledonia, from the mines of the rival, Le Nickel. By 1972, Japan was importing a quarter of its nickel from Indonesia, and Inco hoped to tap that lucrative market (Swift 1977, p.92). Also, it was reported that the Sulawesi deposits would rank as 'one of the world's principal sources of nickel' (*Toronto Financial Post*, 19 April 1975, cited by Swift 1977, p.92), and Inco could not ignore such developments, for fear of losing her preeminence in the world nickel market.

The Contract of Work

The contract, signed by the chairman of Inco and the Indonesian Minister for Mines, on 27 July 1968, empowered the company to explore an area of 6,600,000 hectares in South and Southeast Sulawesi, and to establish and operate the project. They were allowed five years for investigation (surveying, exploration, and evaluation) at the end of which they had to relinquish at least 75% of the initial area. The contract ran for 30 years from the date of commencement of full production of the processing plant, but the term could be extended, subject to the company's making a new investment.

The company was required to pay land rents, royalties, and corporate taxes to the central government. These payments were to begin after full production. It was estimated that revenues to the Indonesian state would be around $8 million annually for the first decade of operations, with an increase of $20 or $30 million annually in the remaining twenty years of the contract (Swift 1977, p.97).

Swift pointed out that, at the end of the thirty-year contract, Inco should have sustained sales of $6 billion (calculated at then current prices) and the Indonesian nation would have received at most $840 million. He calculated out that the thirty year's revenue would not have been adequate to service Indonesia's current foreign debt for any one of those thirty years (Swift 1977, p.97).

The only revenues accruing to local levels of government from the project were royalties on sand and gravel used in construction of the project's infrastructure, paid to the Regency (*Kabupaten Luwu*).

The contract contained a stipulation that the company must employ Indonesian personnel wherever possible, and that 75% of all positions over the entire job ladder had to be held by Indonesians within five years of the construction of the processing plant. (This clause was later renegotiated, allowing the company to extend the period within which it had to 'Indonesianise' the work force.)

There was also a provision for the taking up of Indonesian equity: 2% of shares were to be held by Indonesian nationals in the first year, the figure rising to 20% after ten years. Neither the contract nor the regulations governing foreign investment specified how this was to be achieved (*Australian Financial Review*, 1977). It was not until 1979, with the opening of the Jakarta stock exchange, that a mechanism was established. Inco anticipated that ten years after beginning construction fo the project, equity would be 29% Indonesian, 4% Japanese, and 77% Inco Ltd. (Jessup 1977, p.4). Six Japanese companies signed agreements entitling them to minor shares in P. T. Inco, in 1972. The agreements included undertakings by three of them to take most of the nickel production in the first fifteen years of production. This apparently guaranteed market for the product was instrumental in the decision to expand the size of the processing plant (Jessup 1977 p.3). Unfortunately, these companies later went bankrupt or reneged on the contracts, exacerbating the difficulties faced by the plant after commencement of full production in 1977.

The contract contained a number of other clauses aimed at ensuring that the project contributed to the government's development programme. The company was urged to maximise the benefits of the project for regional development through coordination with regional government and to ensure that all needs of the project and its employees were met.

This was more an exhortation to good works than a requirement for specific action. However, Inco did agree to undertake the training of Indonesian nationals, either through its own programmes, or by sponsoring employees at educational institutions, both in Indonesia and abroad.

From the point of view of the people of Soroako, the most significant clause of the contract committed the government to resettle any indigenous inhabitants whose removal was necessary for the project's operation. The company would be obliged to pay reasonable compensation for dwellings, cultivated land, or any other permanent improvements on the land that were damaged or taken over by the company. This allowed for the appropriation of the village's prime agricultural land. The consequences of this are discussed in chapter 6, and the struggle for adequate compensation, in chapter 7.

Establishment of the Soroako Nickel Project

Inco began exploring, from a base camp in Malili, to select a target area, both for mining and building the processing plant. From the accessible coastal regions, they later moved to the more rugged inland terrain.

Exploration began in the Soroako area in 1969. The labour force at that time was small, with a few foreign and Indonesian geologists and a small number of unskilled Indonesian workers. After initial air reconnaissance, these teams began ground exploration, drilling holes and digging test pits and trenches. Work conditions were tough, the teams often spending weeks away in the jungle. Inco's employment of many Soroakan men, and some of the long-term immigrants, began at that time.

Samples were tested at laboratories in Malili and in Canada. By mid-1971, the company was satisfied that the Sulawesi deposits could sustain a major nickel-producing plant, and that it would be best situated at Soroako. However, from the outset the project was beset with problems arising from the volatile nature of the world nickel market. One of the long-term expatriate employees said to me that, in 1972,

there was a terrible nickel slump, and the bottom fell out of
everything, and morale was very low. We didn't know if we
had a project because like now (1977) nickel prices were down
and everything was delayed. . . . It wasn't until the latter
part of 1973 that things started to brighten up.

The decision whether to proceed was delayed. Many of the men
working for the exploration contractor were laid off.

However, by 1973, the economic climate seemed brighter. Inco
had developed a refining process suited to the lateritic ores of the
region, and they were satisfied as to the engineering and financial
feasibility of the project. The company notified the Minister for Mines
that it would proceed with the project. Exploration indicated reserves
in the area to support a processing plant with a capacity of 45,000
metric tons annually for the thirty-year contract period (P. T. International Nickel n.d.).

In April 1973, Inco engaged Dravo, an American construction
firm, to design and construct the project. Necessary facilities included
roads into the mining areas, upgrading the Malili-Soroako road, and
the construction of the refining plant, which would employ the
technique developed by Inco in Canada. Plans included the townsite,
and a wharf at Balantang, near Malili, to bring in materials needed for
construction and eventually, to ship out the ore. At that time there
was still no access to Ujung Pandang by road. A pipeline was also
built from the wharf to Soroako, carrying the oil necessary to generate
electricity for the project (see map 2.1).

The processing of lateritic ores is energy intensive, using four to
five times the energy necessary for processing sulphidic ores. The rise
in oil prices in 1973 created a new crisis for the project. The company
resolved to build a hydroelectric plant on the Larona River (map 2.1)
although, to make this feasible, they needed to expand the capacity of
the plant. The undertakings they received from Japan to take the product from the plant (see above), seemed to make the expansion possible. In 1974, plans for Stage Two, entailing two more production
lines, and the hydroelectric scheme were submitted to the government. These plans were agreed to early in 1975, with the proviso that
5 megawatts of the 165 megawatts produced at the Larona plant
would be given to the state electricity authority (PLN), for electrification of villages in the area.

The expansion in the size of the project, coupled with unforeseen production problems, led Inco to engage an additional construction subcontractor in 1974. Bechtel Corporation undertook the construction of all infrastructure other than the processing plant, that is, the roads, townsite, port, airstrip, and so on. The engaging of the second contractor and the increased size of the project led to a massive increase in the labour force. At the peak of construction, Inco and the two contractors employed a combined labour force of more than 11,000 people.

The construction of Stage One of the plant was completed at the end of 1976. Stage Two, begun in late 1975, was completed in 1978. This increased the capacity of the plant from 35 million pounds of nickel matter per year to 100 million pounds per year (International Nickel Co. of Canada Ltd. Annual Report 1976). This capacity made it one of the major nickel plants in the world (P. T. International Nickel n.d.). The first nickel matter was produced in February 1977, and in March of that year President Suharto officially opened the project. Stage Two came into production in 1978, and the plant went into full, as opposed to experimental, production in December 1978. This marked the beginning of the thirty-year contract period.

Early operations were dogged by production problems—stemming mainly from the experimental nature of the new process—and a glut on the world nickel market. The glut on the nickel market stemmed from the depressed state of the world steel industry (*Mining Journal* 1979, p.422). The low price of nickel and the difficulty of finding markets caused anxiety to Inco management. Much of the product sat on Balantang wharf for many weeks awaiting a buyer.

These problems led to constant reformulation of plans for the operation of the project, mainly concerned with saving money. This has usually involved retrenching workers, restructuring the labour force, and cutting expenditures on services not directly concerned with the production of nickel. These changes have led to anxiety and uncertainty on the part of employees, and indeed all the local inhabitants who have come to depend in some way on the continued success of the project. Soroako was always rife with rumours, in the highest levels of management and the lowliest village household, about possible future changes. Indeed, at the commencement of production, it was anticipated that the company would have a permanent operational labour force of 4,000. This has been subject to constant revision: for instance in October 1982 500 people were sacked from a labour force that had already shrunk to just over 3,000 (*Kompas* 1982c).

Inco's Involvement in 'Development'

The low level of development of economic infrastructure in the Malili-Nuha region meant that Inco had to undertake construction of even the most basic facilities necessary for its operation. In 1976, they reported that 15 percent of funds deployed up to that time had been used in the construction of roads, bridges, the port, and airstrips (Tjondronegoro 1976).

In its publications and press releases, Inco has made frequent reference to its contribution to the development of the region.

> For hundreds of years Buginese ships have sailed the seven seas from Sulawesi ports, carrying the island's products to market. Today, in the mountainous interior of this lush, green island, the space age metal nickel is being mined and processed for shipment to market, contributing to the progress of the world and to the island's economy (Inco publicity pamphlet, cited by Swift 1977, p.96).

A representative of P. T. Inco told a conference on the Indonesian mining industry, in 1977, that

> as a responsible mining company and a foreign investor, Inco has been concerned with the local and regional economic impact of its project in Sulawesi (Jessup 1977, p.4).

He argued that, apart from the direct effects of improved communications and the provision of employment in the area, the project served as a 'pole of development.' There were 'multiplier effects,' including the creation of new industries, to meet the project's demand for food and services (Jessup 1977, p.9). He made similar claims in the speech at the official opening of the mine in March 1977 (Swift 1977, p.96).

In the same speech, Inco's managing director argued that the facilities constructed by Inco in Malili and the townsite—schools, clinics, and stores, as well as the water supply, sewerage, and bus services—brought benefits to the area. He cited the company's contribution to public health through the spraying campaign to eradicate malarial mosquitoes, and the aid given to government health clinics. A future benefit would be the electricity distributed to the villages, after the completion of the Larona Hydroelectric Scheme. He argued that the Indonesian government benefited from the taxes (personal income tax, sales tax, and royalties) that the project generated (Jessup 1977, p.11).

The speech, which I read before going to Soroako, gave a picture of an ideal, responsible corporate citizen. This view was only partly sustained when I arrived there and came to realise that many of the facilities mentioned were available only to employees, or employees or a certain rank. Also, the company's practice of importing the necessary food and most of its workers, eschewing any active effort to involve local people in either training or food production, seemed to limit the possibilities for spinoff effects.[5]

The company was especially proud of its record in community development. In the speech cited above, the managing director mentioned three new housing developments. Apart from the townsite, the company worked with the provincial government to establish two model towns to house the workforce. Inco spent US $1.8 million to build schools, water supply, and clinics in these towns. Many employees received interest-free loans to build there. A similar plan for the reorganisation of Soroako village is discussed in chapter 7.

Inco also stressed its training programmes as a development effect of the project, as is indicated in the following comment by a company engineer.

> This (project) allows the native people of Sulawesi to study technology, thus improving their social status (*Tempo* 1977).

His statement mirrors the technocratic view of the Indonesian government.

A degree of social planning specified in the Contract of Work was necessary because of the remote situation of the project and the undeveloped nature of government services in the area. Inco could not have attracted a skilled work force without providing schools, medical care, and housing, for example.

Although the company publicly asserted its concern regarding the social aspects of the project, it is clear that these considerations were always secondary to the main task of nickel production. Expenditures in areas not directly related to the production, such as the town bus, clean water for the villagers, or even training personnel, were the first to go when costs were being cut. Also, the immediate effects on the local economy of loss of jobs were not considered when employees were being retrenched.

However, the convictions expressed by company managers about the positive developmental effects of the project fit well with the ideology of development espoused by the Indonesian government: the belief that capital investment would be the motor of development and facilitate the desired goal of modernisation. For example, one of the early exploration geologists claimed that he presented the exploration for nickel as part of the development process to benefit the Indonesian people, rather than foreign investors or the Indonesian elite. Similarly the mining engineer quoted above stressed the importance of understanding technology for the improvement in the social status of his countrymen. The statements of the Candian general manager also stressed this.

The Indonesian managers formed part of the dominant class in contemporary Indonesia, which is reaping benefits from the operation of foreign capital in the country (Robison 1978). Their interests were close to those of the military-bureaucratic elite, and they often acted simultaneously as spokesmen for that group, as well as for the foreign corporation. Indeed, they played an especially important role in the performance of public rituals that used the ideology of the state to establish legitimate authority for the company.

The Company's Cooption of the Legitimating Ideology of the State

The company always sponsored rituals celebrating major national holidays, like Independence Day (17 August) or major religious festivals, like the end of the Muslim fasting month (*Hari Raya Idul Fitri*). National days were never celebrated as purely Indonesian events, in contrast to the major Islamic rituals. Expatriate managers always played a prominent role in them. For example, on Independence Day 1977, the foreign manager of the project delivered a speech, prepared for him by one of the Indonesian managers, which he read in Indonesian. (He did not himself speak Indonesian.) When it was published in the company magazine it was not translated into English, although every other article in the magazine, including the paragraph introducing the speech, was written in English. Clearly, the message was intended for the Indonesian employees, the ones for whom the message had meaning and authority. Among other things, the speech declared:

> Thirty-two years ago, the Indonesian people declared their independence and immediately confronted many paths. Today, development (*pembangunan*) is in progress. Sulawesi has already begun to develop and P. T. Inco is one of the industries which is helping in the development of Sulawesi.
> . . . All difficulties in the former era were faced with full confidence. We hope that you will all show similar confidence and perseverance (now) so that the development of this project can be completed in the shortest time and in accord with plans. . . . The P. T. Inco project will be of direct use in fulfilling Indonesia's independence in the present era and in years to come (*Berita Soroako* 1977).

The speech compared the struggle to achieve independence with the effort necessary to complete the plant, implying that the sacrifices individuals should make in achieving the completion of the project were analogous to the sacrifices of the people who fought for independence. The completion of the project was presented as having the same consequences for the general good of the community.

The following year, the same manager read a similar speech at the Independence Day celebrations held at the district capital (*Kecamatan*). In that speech, he stated that the company and its interests could not be distinguished from the interests of the people of the district (Nuha), or the people of Indonesia (*Berita Soroako* 1978b).

Most interesting of all was a speech delivered by one of the Indonesian managers at a farewell to the Canadian managing director of P. T. Inco. Here again the Indonesian revolution is mentioned.

> For the Indonesians who are very proud of their history, heritage and culture, and who honour the heroes who fought for independence, the contribution of an International Lawyer, P. C. Jessup Sr. . . . who played a unique role in the forum of the United Nations in the birth of the Republic of Indonesia, was of very great significance, therefore P. C. Jessup's son, the managing director, has occupied a very special place in the heart of the 1945 generation, and this has had a direct bearing on the development of P. T. Inco (*Berita Soroako* 1978a).

The revolution and the men who fought for independence (the generation of 1945) are powerful symbols in Indonesian political culture. The use of these symbols was an attempt to identify the company with the achievement of independence and nation building, now being expressed through the ideology of development. There was an attempt to link loyalty to the state and the ideals of the new republic to loyalty to the (foreign owned) enterprise. There was no corresponding assumption of loyalty by the company to its employees.

Even though expatriate managers did not participate in Islamic festivals, the company also identified itself with Islam, the religion of the majority of its employees and the majority of the Indonesian people, through its sponsorship of mass rituals on important feast days. On the holiday celebrating the end of the fasting month (*Hari Raya Idul Fitri*), in 1978, Inco sponsored a visit by Hamka, one of the best known religious leaders in Indonesia. He was flown in to deliver the address (*khotbah*) at the open air ritual, where all Muslims in Soroako were gathering to pray.

In the early years of the Republic, devotion to Islam had led the people of South Sulawesi to join a rebellion in opposition to the central government. In the contemporary world, Islam too was serving as one of the ideological forces assuring their loyalty to the military bureaucratic elite and the development projects they were sponsoring.

This chapter has described the establishment of the Soroako nickel project out of the chaos associated with the Darul Islam rebellion. The next chapter investigates forms of work in the preproject economy and the way in which these changed with the beginnings of the incorporation of Soroako into the world economy.

NOTES TO CHAPTER 4

1. *Madero* is the dance that became most popular during the colonial period. The Soroakans formerly performed a number of similar circle dances, the most distinctly Soroakan being the *monsado* S., now forgotten by all but a few old people.

2. These interventions in social and economic life were to accord with the Makalua Charter, the constitution of Kahar's Islamic State. It stipulated

that marriage should be in accord with Islamic law, proscribed purchase and ownership of cattle, land, shops, factories, and so on, and forbade the ownership and use of luxury goods, such as clothes from expensive material, or imported food (Van Dijk 1981, pp.192–4).

3. Caldwell and Utrecht argue that:

> (t)he local population supported Kahar, not from sympathy to the idea of an Islamic State, but because Kahar's resistance to the central government in Jakarta was an advantage to their economic interests (1979, p.95).

In particular, they mention the interests of exporters of copra and rice. This may have been true for some sectors of the population, but for the Soroakans, Islam had strong ideological appeal.

4. J. S. Kahn presents an alternative perspective on Sukarno's economic policies, arguing that the isolation from the world economy provided a situation in which indigenous capitalist forms could develop among petty commodity producers (1980, pp.190–7).

5. An article by Aditjondro (1982) rejects the idea that Soroako (or Tembagapura, in Irian Jaya) serve as 'poles of development.'

Photo 4. Early morning on the lake shore.

Chapter 5

Land, Labour, and Social Relations in the Preproject Economy

The contemporary social system in Soroako manifests not only features common to all societies based on capitalist class relations, but also features that derive from its historical specificity.

> Any historical moment is both a result of prior processes and an index towards the direction of its future flow (Thompson 1978, p. 239).

In order to interpret contemporary forms of social organisation and their corresponding cultural and ideological forms, it is necessary to understand the Soroakan past. The preceding chapter viewed that past in the context of regional history. This chapter focuses on forms of production in the predominantly agricultural economy of the village prior to direct domination by industrial capital.

In chapter 3, I argued that, in the precolonial polity, social inequality was manifest in differential social status, although the payment of tribute to the rulers was not a fundamental organising principle of village economies in the region. Inequalities did not rise out of differential access to productive resources in the peasant economy. However, mercantile trade and Dutch colonial domination brought about forms of ownership of productive resources that allowed highly organised exploitation. The character of this change cannot be

111

understood simply by reference to formal characteristics of changing production relations. For example, the mode of organisation of the domain of Luwu provided the cultural form for the expression of emergent class relations. The social relations established during the period of colonial rule, and their cultural form, have had consequences for the response to the domination by industrial capital in the contemporary period (see Bradby 1975).

Because of the difficulties involved in reconstructing the past, it is easy to fall into the trap of characterising prior social forms as 'traditional' society, constantly reproducing itself without change. This is not only a problem for structural-functionalist analysis: it is a problem that has plagued much recent Marxist anthropology,[1] which makes the object of analysis the characterisation of the structure of the precapitalist mode of production, rather than using the analytic constructs of class analysis to analyse the historically and culturally specific situation (O'Laughlin 1975, p.344).

Consequently, rather than focusing on the formal characteristics of production in Soroako, my aim is to understand the nature of work in Soroako prior to the establishment of the project. The character of the labour process is an outcome of the relations of appropriation between people, based on relations to the means of production. In discussing work in Soroako, I begin with the question of access to productive resources, in particular, land, the fundamental means of production in the predominantly agricultural economy. Next, I describe the organisation of the labor process, through the division of labour in deatil.

Methodology

It is not easy to describe economic organisation in the period prior to the establishment of the project. Inco's domination of all economic activity in the area, and the influence of capitalist class relations in all spheres of economic life, make impossible any simple extrapolation to economic processes in the past, from observations in the present.

In December 1979, I interviewed fifty-three indigenous Soroakan households, comprising a 25 percent systematic sample: every fourth household from a population census that I had commissioned. The interview schedule covered past and present economic activities. The systematic sample ensured that I interviewed households from all strata, including the poorest; thus I located poor households that I had not met through the social networks employed in participant observation. The interview situation provided the opportunity for wide-ranging discussion on economic matters. The results of the survey were supplemented by further interviews and the collection of detailed biographies from nine indigenous Soroakans.

The Organisation of Production

Prior to the establishment of the nickel project, the people of Soroako formed a community of subsistence cultivators, with some involvement in supralocal trade.

They cultivated the hills surrounding Lake Matano as well as the plain behind Soroako Village. In addition to this settlement, the Soroakans established temporary hamlets near fields distant from the village, many of them accessible only by boat. They gave easy access to the jungle, which provided both land for swidden cultivation and a wide range of edible products (including palms, fruits, fungi, and leaves) as well as deer, which they hunted, and the dammar resin and rattan that, since the end of the last century, could be exchanged for commodities, or in emergencies, rice. Furukawa commented with respect to a community of swidden cultivators in contemporary Luwu; 'Rice is just one of the "crops" they get from the forest' (1982, p.41). The comment could well apply to the Soroakans prior to the establishment of permanent field cultivation.

The Soroakans were previously well known as blacksmiths, a skill differentiating them from other people in the area (see Abendanon 1915–18, p.1352–4). They smelted iron from locally obtained ore and fashioned it into a wide range of agricultural, household, and war implements. The iron ore and the metal tools were important in inland trade (see chap. 3).

At the turn of the century, Grubauer commented that Soroako was larger than neighbouring villages (1913, p.69). In this region, characterised by swidden cultivation, villages were tiny settlements. In some cases, they were not nucleated settlements but homesteads scattered over their territory next to their fields. The Soroakans maintained both a nucleated settlement and field huts. P. and F. Sarasin noted that the Sororkans 'enjoyed a certain well being' which they attributed to their wealth from dammar, and from smithing (1905, p.313).

Miles (1967) has argued that, in Kalimantan, involvement in trade has enabled some shifting cultivators to establish larger, more permanent settlements and this would seem to be borne out by the Soroakan case. The village's favourable location for agriculture on the edge of the plain, which Grubauer described as a 'fertile cultivated valley' (1913, p.77), and the ready accessibility of other land via water transport would also favour a larger settlement. The expansion of European trade networks in jungle produce into the interior, at the turn of the century, would also have favoured the development of the village.

Land: Swidden Cultivation

'From our forbears, we have cultivated swiddens.' Thus the Soroakans viewed their past. For as long as anyone can remember, they have been dry field cultivators, clearing and burning the jungle cover, to plant numerous varieties of rice, as well as corn and Job's tears. (One old man claimed that their ancestors had not cultivated rice, but foraged in the jungle.)

Even after the establishment of paddy fields, they continued to cultivate rice in swiddens. Only three households out of the fifty-three surveyed said that they had not done so. All three had owned extensive paddy fields. Prior to the establishment of the paddy fields, swiddens had provided the basic subsistence of the villagers. (They have never been basically dependent on sago, as are other people in Luwu. However, sago has been a supplement to rice.)

In the majority of households surveyed, the bulk of rice production came from the paddy fields, swiddens providing a supplement (see below). However, for those households without permanent fields, there was no difficulty in obtaining land for dry field cultivation.

Land was plentiful, given the low population density of the region. Access to land for dry field cultivation was limited only by one's ability to clear it. 'People owned wet rice fields, but not swidden land,' was a typical statement. 'You just went out and used it: there was plenty of land.' In discussing the disputes that have erupted over rights to land in the contemporary situation (see chap. 7), one woman said to me:

For what purpose would our forebears have been concerned about rights to land? There was plenty of land.

Land was possessed during the time it was under cultivation.[2] These rights lapsed when it reverted to fallow, except when rice fields were also planted with permanent tree crops that were still producing. In such cases, it was necessary to ask permission of the owner of the trees, before clearing and cultivating the land.

The various sites around the lake differed not only in the number of years of continuous cultivation possible, but also in the length of fallow period necessary. The optimal fallow period was determined by the size of the regrown jungle, rather than by counting a number of years. A cleared field was abandoned when the labour-intensive task of weeding became more onerous than the task of felling trees to clear new terrain (in some areas, after only one year's cultivation). This points to a crucial feature of swiddening: labour, not land, was the scarce commodity.

Use of Tools in Swidden Cultivation

Cultivation was carried out with the aid of simple tools; an axe for clearing the tree cover, a weeding hook, and a finger knife for harvesting.These iron tools, all of local manufacture, were readily available. For planting, a dibbling stick, a stake cut from the jungle, was used. The style of cultivation ensured minimal disturbance of the soil. The felled timber was fired but the stumps and incompletely burned logs were left on the steeply sloping fields. Corn and other vegetables (beans, spinachlike leafy greens, and gourds) were planted and helped to protect the soil before the rice sprouted. The weeding hook was designed so it barely disturbed the topsoil.

In conditions of low population density, this system was a stable one, not subject to the ecological devastation seen in swidden systems where population pressure forces the farmers to overcultivate the fields through too many years of continuous planting and shortened fallow periods. Even so, some of these negative features could be seen in the 1970's (see chap. 6).

At the time of the establishment of the project, many households also cultivated tubers (cassava and sweet potatoes), bananas, and other fruits and vegetables in dry fields at the foot of the mountains behind the village. Because they were under continuous cultivation, these plots were permanently owned by the cultivator.

Land: Paddy Fields

The introduction of paddy fields at the behest of the colonial government (see chap. 3) was an important innovation: the introduction of a form of production based on private ownership of land.

The original distribution apparently provided an equal amount of land to each cultivating household. Some households later established more paddy fields on their own initiative. 'Everyone had some paddy fields, even if it was a small amount,' one respondent claimed. All households surveyed reported they had formerly had access to paddy fields, even though not all had a member who was listed as an owner (see below).

> In the past our main source of subsistence was from farming, from paddy fields and dry fields, planted and harvested at different times. The yield was for consumption; it was not sold.

Most village households consumed rice from the two harvests, one from the paddy fields and one from the swiddens. However, informants constantly repeated that the bulk of their needs was met from wet rice production. Thus the new form of rice cultivation, introduced at the behest of the colonial government, came to be the mainstay of the village economy.

One of the most often heard statements about the preproject economy is that the village was self-sufficient in rice. 'We never bought rice (*tidak pernah beli beras*),' people were always saying. A contrast was always made with the contemporary situation, in which the purchase of rice is the single largest item in the household budget. A few households in the survey reported that they had bought (or bartered) rice at times in the past, usually from fellow villagers in return for goods, for example, fish, or services, such as help during the harvest.

This self-sufficiency in food production contrasts markedly with the situation since the establishment of the project, in which the paddy fields, which provided the bulk of the rice yields, as well as many of the dry fields, have been alienated by Inco (see chap. 7).

The villagers' insistence on their former self-sufficiency in rice production is borne out by the picture of land holdings that emerges from the list prepared for the land compensation payment, in 1972. One hundred and thirty-six holdings were listed, accounting for 120 hectares of wet rice fields and 240 hectares of dry and wet holdings. This was in a community with an estimated population of fewer than 1,000 people.

The land lost to the project included almost all the wet rice fields belonging to the Soroakans, but only some of the land cultivated as dry fields. For that reason, the following discussion of land holdings is concerned only with the paddy fields. Also, although there were 136 land holdings listed, information was incomplete in some cases, so I have calculated the figures on the basis of 125 land holdings.

The average size of paddy field holdings was 0.93 hectares. This compares with a figure of 1.14 ha for the average *total* land holding in South Sulawesi in 1973, which in turn is almost twice the average total land holding in Central and East Java (Kristanto 1983). The average holding of wet and dry land, in the list prepared for compensation, was 1.74 ha. This figure underestimated the total amount of land, since a small amount of cultivated land (now part of the village) was not alienated. According to these figures, the Soroakans were indeed well endowed with land, especially wet rice fields, compared with other Indonesians. An even more dramatic contrast can be made by comparing ownership of wet rice fields for the nation as a whole (these all-Indonesian figures including the land-poor areas of Java and Bali). The results are presented in table 5.1.

The table shows there were proportionately fewer landless households and fewer really large landowners in Soroako. The situation was more egalitarian than for the nation as a whole; in addition, the average holding exceeded that for the rest of Indonesia.

The picture emerges of a community with social inequality in that there were some landless and some large landowners, but one in which the majority were apparently well-off.

Whereas swiddens, established in the jungle end regarded as a free gift of nature, were not owned by any individual, paddy fields were property. They were permanent fields, representing congealed labour in their establishment and in the construction and maintenance of irrigation channels. But ownership in societies where production relations were embedded in kinship relations did not mean the same as it does in capitalist societies. Ownership of this pro-

TABLE 5.1.
AREA OF WET RICE FIELD HOLDINGS:
SOROAKO 1972, AND ALL-INDONESIA 1976

| Area operated (ha) | Agricultural Holdings (%) | |
	All-Indonesia	Soroako
0	30.5	13.6
0.01–0.10	8.5	0.8
0.20–0.30	11.5	8.8
0.30–0.40	6.7	9.6
0.40–0.50	9.2	5.6
0.50–0.60	2.7	4.0
0.60–0.75	4.6	8.0
0.75–1.00	7.3	8.8
1.00–2.00	5.0	20.8
2.00–3.00	1.0	5.6
3.00–4.00	0.3	9.8
4.00–5.00	0.1	1.6
5.00 +	0.5	0.8
Total	100	100

SOURCE: All-Indonesia—Sundrum and Booth 1980 (based on Sakernas, Sept.–Dec. 1976); Soroako—Revised list of landholdings for compensation, Dec. 1979 (based on 1972 data).

ductive resource did not entail rights to the social surplus product of the land.

Although all of the respondents to the survey stated that they had previously cultivated paddy fields, not all of them were formally regarded as owners. In the majority (76 percent) of cases, households had worked on land regarded as belonging to both sets of parents of the conjugal pair. I soon realised that I was asking questions about *ownership* of productive resources, but was being answered in terms of *access*. In those cases where the land belonged to the parent of only one spouse, the partner was an immigrant. In several cases, the immigrant spouse had bought land in his or her own right. For example, a man told me:

> I came from Maholona. I had my own paddy field (in Soroako), but I had to work in order to buy it from other people.

The common picture was that children worked the land of their parents, in cooperation with their parents and siblings. Postmarital uxorilocal residence and a coterminous period of bride-service (Goody and Tambiah 1973, p. 1) also established economic ties between sons-in-law and parents-in-law, which could endure beyond the period of common residence (which usually ended with the birth of the first child). This underscored the importance of households—embedded in networks of kin relations that were also ties of economic cooperation—as fundamental producing units in that peasant society. Marriages served a crucial role in constituting the household units and the ties of interhousehold cooperation. Clearly marriage was important in the reproduction of economic relations as well as in the reproduction of labour power (see chap. 8).

Paddy fields, as property, were inheritable, but it is difficult to characterise a system of inheritance in Soroako because paddy fields, the most important owned resource, had existed for a period spanning only two, at most three, generations. At the time of the land alienation in 1972, some old people were still cultivating the fields they had themselves initially established, probably in the 1930's, when the directive to establish paddy fields was announced.

In theory, land was divided equally among all children after the death of both parents. People told me of situations in which ageing parents had distributed land among their children prior to their death. In the case of the death of one parent, the estate remained intact under the custodial care of the living, (usually a widow). Land divided up after both parents' death had to be distributed in accord with their expressed wishes 'to avoid fighting.'

Although female children ideally received an equal share with their male siblings, in practice there was a bias favouring male children. As one old man put it:

> We gave preference to male children in disposing of land because we hoped that female children would have the good fortune to marry a man with his own wealth.

The preference was justified as arising from a consideration of practical matters, of the children's different access to other land or other sources of livelihood. If a good marriage had been contracted for a daughter, this was regarded as discharging the obligation to provide for her.

A different bias, in favour of males as land proprietors, was evident in the preparation of the list of people to receive compensation for land alienated for the mining project (which included almost all the village's paddy fields). Of the 136 individuals listed as entitled to compensation, only 4 were women. It seemed from the list that land ownership was vested mostly in individual males. But this impression was at odds with both the views of informants in the household survey referred to above and villagers' discussions concerning disputes about land or the division of the compensation payments. Just as there were conflicting views on inheritance, there were also conflicting views on land ownership, often simultaneously held by the same persons.

I asked the village headman why the compensation list recorded mainly males as landowners, and he replied, 'Indeed, we men have greater rights than women' (*kita laki-laki lebih punya hak dari wanita*). Yet his ageing mother was usually regarded by the community as the owner of his family's land, even though the compensation list recorded only her male children as such. Similarly, the household in which I lived had all of its estate listed under the name of the oldest son still residing in the village. However, other Soroakans always referred to the land as belonging to his mother.

The same people, then, simultaneously held conflicting views about land ownership. This led to an apparent lack of clarity on Soroakan principles of land ownership. It was clear that these views were changing with the development of capitalist class relations (see chap. 7). Perhaps too, the values of Islam and the urban bourgeoise (for example, the bureaucrats who oversaw the land compensation) were responsible for conceptualising land ownership in terms that were in apparent contradiction to those expressed by Soroakans in everyday life.

Paddy fields, unlike swidden fields, could be bought and sold, and indeed some informants mentioned the realisation of this as a factor in overcoming their initial resistance to the new form of cultivation.

Much of the land in Soroako before the land alienation had never changed hands, except by inheritance. However, some people had bought land from fellow villagers or from the Christian villagers of nearby Dongi, who fled at the time of the Darul Islam rebellion. Sales were usually negotiated in buffalo. For example, one man told me he had bought land from a Dongi resident for the price of one buffalo at the time of his second marriage. He had given the original plot to his son, to be jointly cultivated with his daughter. Thus the father resolved a domestic conflict by providing the children of his first marriage with a separate allotment.

The fact that rice land became a commodity that could be bought and sold paved the way for wealth differentiation based on unequal land holdings. Under conditions of swidden cultivation, there could be differences in the wealth of households based on differences in labour available both for agriculture and other forms of production. The amount of labour available, however, depended on variable demographic factors and the stage of the developmental cycle of a domestic group. It would not have been easy to establish these differences as inheritable inequalities, before the establishment of private property in land and the availability of traded commodities, which could represent congealed surplus labour.

Indeed, those households with more labour would have been at an advantage in establishing paddy fields in the first instance, in extending the family estate beyond the government allocation. Once land was established as a commodity, the ability to purchase it derived from differential involvement in activities producing wealth through trade with extravillage markets (see below). Table 5.1 gives some idea of the inequalities in land holding, with 13.6% having no paddy fields and 39% having more than the average of 0.93 ha. But it must be remembered that these inequalities were not as pronounced as in the nation as a whole.[3]

Access to Other Factors of Production in Paddy Field Cultivation

Work in the paddy fields involved more complex technology than in the swiddens. The farmers used the transplanting method, with plough and harrow tillage, which was common in Bugis areas (Mattulada 1982, p.93). The establishment of permanent irrigated fields required more labour inputs, as did cultivation. In preparation for planting each year, the ground was ploughed and harrowed, preferably using buffalo to draw the plough and the harrow. Some of the old people told me that, in the beginning of paddy field cultivation, they owned no buffalo and had to prepare the ground with hoes.[4] However, just over half of the households surveyed said they had not owned buffalo. They had obtained the use of someone else's, in return for labour or produce.

> I used to work in X's paddy fields, in return for the use of her buffalo (in my own fields). I didn't own any buffalo, but I would borrow from others, and later pay a 'wage' (*gaji*) in the form of a portion of my harvest.

As with permanent fields, informants usually stated that their parents had owned the buffalo, or that they had obtained one through inheritance from their parents. Those who owned buffalo were at an advantage in expanding their holdings.

Paddy field cultivation contrasted with swidden cultivation not only in that the land was permanently alienated by the producer, but also in that the tools necessary for cultivation, the draught animals and the implements, were more expensive and difficult to come by then the simple equipment of swidden cultivation.

Control of Resources

It seems clear that old people (referred to as *baloki* S.) controlled the productive resources. However, this did not constitute a basis for denial of access to those resources, as custom dictated that children cultivate alongside their parents. Their control of productive resources did however provide an economic base for their customary control of the choice of their children's spouses. The main subject of negotiation for a girl's hand concerned the provisioning of the wedding feast. These days, after the generalised introduction of wage labour, negotiations concern a sum of money, but in the past it concerned a quantity of rice and the provision of the beast(s) (buffalo or cow). Because the old people no longer control these resources, they no longer have as much influence over the choice of their children's spouses (see chap. 8).

However, it does not follow that the control of resources exercised by the elders constituted a form of exploitation analogous to that established by capitalist class relations. For this control did not imply the right to extract surplus labour from others. Those who jointly cultivated shared the fruits of the harvest. As I stated above, access to land was more important than possession, and kin and affinal ties ensured that access.

Inequalities in land holding came to be a fundamental aspect of social relations in the community, serving to differentiate a wealthy elite, whose trade activities and extensive land holdings buttressed each other.

These inequalities probably derived from a consolidation of an emergent tendency to inequality in the system of swidden cultivation, where supply of labour conferred an advantage on particular households. This crystallised into a structure of inequality when labour was invested in land under permanent cultivation, which, under the juridical influence of the colonial state, was regarded as private property.

The economic advantages of land ownership were translated into political power by way of patronage. Wealthy villagers ensured their preeminence by the establishment of a following. In part this consisted of largesse in the distribution of food to the less well-off, either by providing opportunities for them to work in the fields (paid for in a proportion of the harvest) or by meeting requests for food stored in the rice barn.

Relations of Production and the Division of Labour

Agricultural production was the basic form of livelihood in the village. Everyone was a farmer, and all had access to land that they cultivated, either swidden or paddy fields. Productive units were households, or groups of households, with kinship and affinal ties defining the basic forms of cooperation. However, these relations did not define the extent of cooperation in agricultural production.

In this economy where land was abundant, there was a shortage of labour at certain times of the agricultural cycle (in both swidden and paddy fields), especially at planting and harvest, both having to be carried out within a limited period. The cultivation of two crops, one in the paddy fields and one in the mountains where these activities followed sequentially, presumably exacerbated the shortage. At those times, when labour needs could not be met within the cultivating unit, farmers were dependent on labour exchange with others. After planting, the workers participated in a feast provided by the landowner, and there was an expectation of reciprocation of labour. After harvesting, payment was made in the form of a share of the crop. For paddy fields, the harvester was entitled to one-fifth of the number of bundles he or she had cut. For swiddens, payment was one bundle for a day's work, regardless of the amount cut: the stress was more on the expectation that such labour inputs would be reciprocated.

The difference in form of payment can be accounted for by the different relation to land in the two systems. In swidden cultivation, the main factor limiting the amount of land under cultivation was the amount of labour available to the cultivating unit, especially for clearing and weeding. In contrast, a paddy field, once established, could be used year after year, and so was a valuable commodity that could be bought. Since paddy fields also produced higher yields per unit area, they contributed to the amassing of wealth to those with a lot of land. The amount of rice produced did not vary from season to season, depending on the amount of labour within the cultivating unit. Paddy field ownership allowed for the possibility of exploiting the surplus labour of others, the nonowners who helped in cultivation. The payment for such labour was more like a wage than reciprocation between equals.

However, class relations were only incipient. Superstructural factors tended to inhibit the complete transformation of this division of labour. Wealthy farmers were not simply related to the mass of the villagers as landowners to workers. There were also ties of kinship, affinity, and patronage. Through these ties, some of the amassed surplus was distributed to less prosperous kinsmen and clients, in return for the recognition of power and prestige. For example, a member of one of the former large landowning families told me that the few landless families in the past had more paddy than anyone else. When I queried this, she replied,

> Well, they had the yield of the paddy fields without having to do all the work of preparing the ground, weeding and so forth.

While we cannot accept this statement at face value, it points to a situation wherein a social division of labour that had something of the form of incipient class relations was mitigated—on the one hand, by factors of limited technology and, on the other, by culture and ideology—from becoming a fully developed class structure.

The low level of development of the productive forces meant that large landowners were dependent on the labour of others, in agricultural production and in the staging of the rituals that translated wealth into social prestige and political power. Ideologically, this interdependence was expressed through sentiments of kin obligations and labour exchange similar to the ideology C. Geertz has described for Java. There, for example, landowners were seen as having an obligation to provide work opportunities for less prosperous fellow villagers (1963a, pp.97–100).

Division of Labour in Detail (in the Labour Process)

The division of labour in agricultural production was principally according to age and sex. The most strongly held ideas about the sexual division of labour pertained to paddy field cultivation; men prepared the land for planting, ploughing with the aid of buffalo. Planting, weeding, and harvesting are said to have been performed by men and women, though men often stated that women were more able at these tasks. It seems that there may have been a further sexual differentiation of tasks in each of these operations. For example, in 1981, I observed the planting of a newly established paddy field and noted that the women were pulling up the seedlings in the nurseries while the men planted them in the muddy soil. On other occasions, I saw women planting out the seedlings. Perhaps this demonstrates what Hamilton (1981, pp.82–3) calls 'homosociality.' Though there are notions about the kinds of work appropriate to each sex, in the actual performance of a task, the overriding principle is that, whatever the task, work groups should consist of people of the same sex.

There was a parallel division of labour in swidden cultivation. Men cleared the ground by felling trees and firing them. They also built the fences: an important principle was that only men used axes. Planting was done by mixed sex and age groups, usually neighbours from the same cultivation hamlet. Again, there was a sex-based division of tasks. Men wielded the dibble, women and children and young men ran behind, planting the seed rice in the holes. Weeding was done by all members of the cultivating unit. Harvesting again used the cooperative labour of neighbours and kin. The women cut the paddy with the finger knife, the men gathered the bundles and took them from the field.

Children had a number of special tasks, especially in paddy field cultivation. They would, for example, carry the sheaves of seedlings from the nursery and guard the ripening crop from hungry birds. Little boys were entrusted with the care of buffalo.

In agricultural production, though there was a clear separation of male and female tasks, women and men often worked alongside each other. In other productive activities there was a greater separation of men and women. As in most societies, women's activities were those most closely connected to the home. Men by contrast were responsible for those tasks that required periods away from home—hunting in the jungle, collecting jungle produce, trading, or felling the jungle and building new field huts.

In particular, women had primary responsibility for the care of babies. Their other productive activities were organised in order to give preeminence to this task. For example, a woman with a young baby would not work in the fields. Ideally, her domestic responsibilities were taken over by a daughter or other young female relative, in order to allow her singleminded attention to child care. For a women, the designation of tasks appropriate to her sex depended upon her age and the stage of the developmental cycle of her household. Men's work was not so dependent on their age, except for the distinction between men's work and boy's work (such as the care of buffalo). (See Robinson [1983] for further discussion of the sexual division of labour).

However, the division of labour by sex was not immutable. A widow or single woman could perform tasks usually done by men. The Soroakan's readiness to accept such changes under certain conditions was evident in the contemporary situation. For example, felling trees was the activity most clearly labelled as male, in swidden cultivation. One unmarried woman felled the timber for her own swidden and proudly proclaimed her ability to perform any tasks a man could. She was treated with admiration, not scorn, by the other villagers. Older women would dibble, if there were not enough experienced men present. Older men would harvest, using the finger knife, if there were not enough women.

This points to an important fact about the division of labour in that community prior to the advent of capitalist production. Even though agricultural production incorporated a division of labour in detail, on the basis of sex and age, this division of labour did not mean that individuals lacked ability at tasks formally relegated to people in other social categories, nor were they ignorant of how their tasks fitted into the organisation of the whole production process. This contrasts markedly with the division of labour in the capitalist enterprise, where the production process is broken up into a series of separate operations, each specific to a category of worker (see Braverman 1974).

The division of labour within production in peasant agriculture did not serve as the basis for the control of one group over another, as it does in capitalist society. For example, in planting fields, the proprietors adopted supervisory roles, deciding on which varieties of seed to plant, and in what quantity, and criticising the work of the others. However, when reciprocating the labour input in the fields of the others, the supervisor became one of the supervised. Thus, supervision of work was not based on the separation of a group of managers with particular skills. This division of labour, then, neither buttressed the control of one group over another, nor entailed relations of hierarchy. Indeed, it did not have the capacity to develop such relations. Rather, labour exchange fostered the reproduction of cooperative customary relationships.

Production Outside Agriculture

Besides providing land for swidden fields, the jungle provided other forms of sustenance that supplemented rice production. Apart from edible plants (the most important being the sago palm), it also provided the principle source of meat—deer hunted by the men, using dogs to track them down and iron spears to kill them. About one-third of the men I surveyed said that formerly they had regularly hunted deer.

Fish was a more significant source of protein. The lake contained a number of varieties of fin fish and shell fish, many unique (Abendanon 1915-18, pp.1336-45). Women and children fished with hand lines from canoes, and Grubauer reported men fishing with spears (1913, p.82). The fish were obtained mainly for personal consumption, though some were bartered in the village economy. Some people mentioned bartering venison and fish in return for rice, a way in which people with inadequate land holdings (or insufficient male labour, for example) could sustain themselves.

Until the turn of the century, production within the Soroakan economy was for use. All goods needed in daily life were locally manufactured. Women fashioned mats and containers from wild grasses and made decorated pots from local clay. Smithing was men's work; the metal they smelted, and the weapons and tools they fashioned, were also traded in the region. Grubauer commented on the wide variety of beautifully fashioned and decorated domestic implements found in Soroako, though he commented that the production of bark cloth (*fuja*) had declined, as had smithing (1913, p.48). Within the village economy, these goods were not commodities; they were bartered, rather than exchanged as commodities to realise a profit. Trade in commodities began to replace barter, with significant consequences for the social system, when the region became incorporated into mercantile trading networks in the last decades of the nineteenth century.

Trade

In Soroako, the initial penetration of capital was not by force, but rather through the peaceful exchange of commodities, as the markets of mercantaile capitalism extended into the centre of Sulawesi. (See Bradby [1975, pp.138–9] for a generalised discussion of this process.) The link was effected through the activities of Bugis and Chinese traders, their own activities being stimulated by the increased Dutch trade in the archipelago. In the area around lakes Matano and Towuti, they sought dammar resin and rattan.

Rattan vines grew wild in the jungle. Village men would collect the vines in slack agricultural seasons. Over half of the households surveyed said a member had formerly collected rattan. They would spend long periods away on the task. The products were exchanged with traders for goods that originated outside the village, including salt, cloth, and cooking pots.

> We never saw money then. We would get goods from the traders and my brother would bring rattan to them.
> Everything was just noted in their books.

Dammar trees also grew wild. They were tapped every few months, and the resin obtained was exchanged with traders. The traders' control of the account books served as a way of appropriating surplus labour in the profit they realised by the resale of the good in Malili.

I do not know if dammar trees were regarded as owned by individuals when the colonial government formalised property relations in the dammar business, presumably in order to collect taxes on the produce. Trees had to be marked and registered with the colonial government. Regulations controlled the manner of their exploitation, as well as the amount of tax on the product.

With respect to dammar production, the enforcement of a notion of private property went hand in hand with the development of a new kind of production relation. Two-thirds of the households surveyed said that a household member had formerly collected dammar. As with paddy fields, they exploited trees that belonged to parents (and parents-in-law) or that they had inherited. An important difference from paddy fields or buffalo was that only males were named as dammar owners. Perhaps this is related to the fact the fact that their exploitation, which involved expeditions to the jungle, was carried out only by males. As with agricultural production, it was common for men to exploit resources belonging to their fathers-in-law. However, there was an important new element to the relation.

> My father-in-law had a lot of trees and I'd often go with him to tap them or I'd tap them and we'd divide the yield. Often the old man would order X and Y [naming another son-in-law and a relative living in the old man's house] to tap them, and then he would take half the yield.

Many people mentioned this practice of tapping someone else's tree and dividing the yield in half. This was a new kind of economic relation in Sororako, one that clearly allowed the exploitation of the surplus labour of others by means of the private ownership of resources. The new form of relation reworked customary relations, for example, the bride-service of uxorilocally dwelling sons-in-law.

The collection of jungle produce increased with the political annexation of the region by Dutch authority, in 1917, since it was the only means of obtaining cash to pay taxes (see chap. 3).

Dependence on trade goods obtained in exchange for jungle commodities increased as time went on. Early visitors comment on the decline of native forms of production, of bark cloth, iron and iron tools, and so forth. Local production, based on a low level of development of the productive forces, was losing out to the superior products the traders brought, such as cloth and European scrap iron. These commodities competed on the existing internal markets, and the local smiths soon stopped producing (see Bradby 1975, p. 153). Grubauer mentioned that, in 1906, the villagers were producing tobacco and sugar cane (1913, p.77). Perhaps these crops also lost out to competition from outside, with villagers choosing to spend time collecting jungle produce, thus gaining access to imported commodities.

Trade and Social Inequality

The expanded trade to external markets was important in consolidating the position of an emergent village elite. I have already mentioned the presence of a group of large landowners. Among these were three families who were the wealthy traders in the village. Profits from trading could be used to buy more land, or to buy buffalo used in the cultivation of more extensive fields. Wealth also conferred an advantage in the control of labour. The wealthy could take in orphans or children of poorer relatives and care for them in return for their service. This gave an advantage in all areas of production.

One woman provided me with a theory of the basis of wealth in the precompany economy.

> The wealthy ones were the ones with lots of dammar, the ones who were energetic enough to go out into the jungle and find lots of trees.

Clearly, control of labour was an advantage in dammar production, too.

Members of the elite translated their wealth into prestige, through the provision of largesse to a following, especially at the time of festivals (see chap. 8). Their wealth and prestige also accompanied political power. Only important trading families provided the Village Headmen.

Other traders were the sons of the last Makole (the District Chief, under the Dutch) to reside in Soroako, and the missionary teacher. They manifested their wealth in building large Bugis-style houses and staging large festivals in the manner of Bugis aristocrats. They bought furniture for their houses, gold, and consumer goods, which provided benefits of saving labour as well as endowing status (e.g., sewing machines and tin roofs).

To the extent that their appropriation of wealth was translated into forms of political and cultural power, and to the extent that they possessed a distinctive consciousness which was an attribute of that power, this group can be said to constitute a nascent ruling class. However, there were important differences from the forms of inequality found in the contemporary situation.

The mass of the villagers were not alienated from the land that provided the basis of their subsistence. The local elite were not entitled to tribute, as the Makole Matano of the Datu of Luwu had been. Except for the appropriation of surplus labour through ownership of dammar trees, appropriation was carried out through extraeconomic means of coercion, embedded in kinship ties. Also because of the low level of technological development in agriculture, the large landowners needed the labour of the other villagers, and thus the ideology of mutual cooperation served the interests of both the elite and the ordinary villagers.

The most important point is that, even in the context of unequal distribution of paddy field land and some other productive resources, because of the possibilities for swidden cultivation, as well as the wide distribution of owned resources, the direct producers were not as a whole alienated from the means of production. There was an incipient class formation in the village, but it was still a kind of stratification, expressed in cultural terms. The links with mercantile capital and the direct colonial rule exacerbated the tendency to class formation, in that one segment of the population came more directly in control of productive resources, and their relation to other villagers increasingly came to be defined in terms of those economic relations.[5]

In addition, with the increasing incorporation into the world system under colonial rule, the local economy came to be more and more linked to external markets and less and less capable of independently reproducing itself either at the level of production or of social relations. Just as the skills of smelting were lost, the smiths becoming dependent on scrap iron from outside, the position of the elite came to depend on connections to the outside, both for the trade that ensured their wealth and the political power that bolstered their domination.

NOTES TO CHAPTER 5

1. See Kahn and Llobera's critique of this approach (1981).
2. A similar attitude to land use exists among some groups of swidden cultivators in Thailand, especially the Hmong. Evidently land is viewed

by these farmers as a relatively free consumable good over which only temporary use-rights are appropriate. Land claims are not recognised after the fields are fallowed or abandoned (Kunstadter and Chapman 1978, p.11).

3. Many of those listed as receiving compensation for dry fields, but not for paddy fields, were people who had access to irrigated land owned by their parents.

4. It has been observed in other parts of south Sulawesi that new paddy fields are often first cultivated with a hoe, because of roots and stumps. It is only when these rot away after about three years that the plough can be used (Furukawa 1982, p.41).

5. Kate Young describes a similar process, of the increasing capacity for a customary elite to appropriate surplus, in association with the penetration of merchant capital in Oaxaca, Mexico (1978).

Chapter 6

Peasants, Proletarians, and Traders in the Peripheral Capitalist Economy

The establishment of the nickel project has brought fundamental changes in the organisation of production in Soroako. This chapter principally investigates those changes with respect to the work of the indigenous Soroakans, whose productive activities prior to the project's development were discussed in chapter 5.

Changing Occupations

The conditions under which people have been able to make a living have been constantly changing since Inco first began exploration in 1969. In the early days, only a few indigenous Soroakans were employed in the small labour force, and for them wage labour provided additional income in what remained basically a farming economy.

The situation altered dramatically with the land alienation in 1972, in which the Indonesian government appropriated the village's highest yielding and most accessible agricultural land, to provide for the company townsite (see map. 6.1). In a textbook case of capitalist development, the indigenous Soroakans were reduced to dependence on wage labour with the mining project. Without their

133

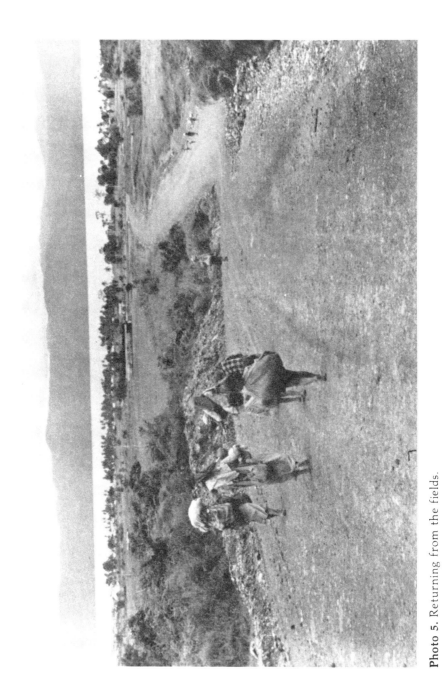

Photo 5. Returning from the fields.

land they could no longer autonomously reproduce themselves as peasant farmers. This action was not in any way precipitated by a need to ensure a supply of labour, as consultants' reports had assured the developers that other parts of the province could provide them with more than enough unskilled labourers. Also, the Soroakans had already shown a willingness to work on the project, and the few hundred indigenous males were insignificant in meeting the total labour needs of the project. The land appropriation, discussed at length in chapter 7, illustrates rather that the interests of the local population were irrelevant to the planning of both the government and the company, except at the level of rhetoric that constantly stressed the benefits to local people.

Wage labour for the company became the mainstay of the village economy. This change was initially well-received by the Soroakans, who had high expectations of good fortune from the project. However, the loss of control of productive resources introduced a high degree of instability in the livelihood of indigenous Soroakan households. Inco's fortunes rise and fall with those of the world economy, and the years since the end of the construction phase, in 1977, have been characterised by periodic retrenchments and instability of employment.

Payment for the land was conceived by the government as a land sale at market prices, rather than as compensation for lost livelihood. This was unfortunate, as immediate payment of a good sum of money would have allowed the opportunity for alternative income-earning pursuits that required capital inputs, including the possibility of buying land elsewhere. This was especially hard on those men who were too old (over 40) for recruitment by Inco.

The construction of the project, begun in 1973, created opportunities for employment (fig. 6.1), the number of jobs in the company and its contractors peaking at 11,000 in 1977. Further, the influx of immigrant workers provided opportunities for the indigenous householders to rent out rooms or house sites and to open shops. However, lack of capital limited their ability to realise these opportunities.

The establishment of the project stimulated the degree of penetration by the capitalist market. The increased circulation of money attracted immigrant traders. Commercial activity provided a source of livelihood for some Soroakans: indeed, for a small elite, it brought greater prosperity than long-term wage labour. Petty trading pro-

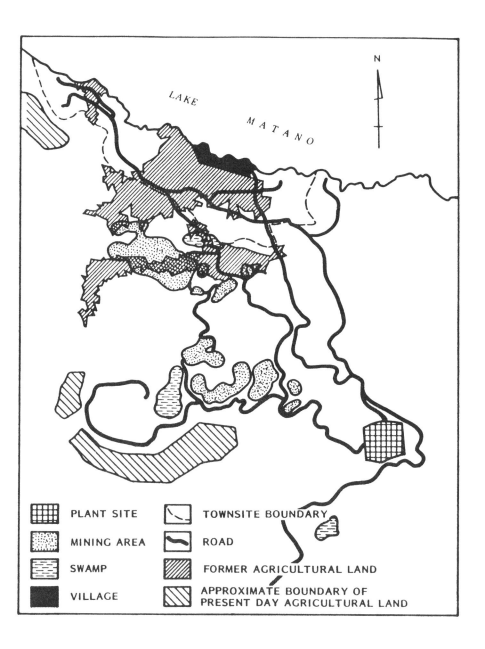

6.1 Soroako and Environs, Showing the Alienated Irrigated Land in Relation
to Current Land Use

vided supplementary income in households where farming remained
the principal source of livelihood, or where wages were low.

Capital penetration has had profound effects even on areas of the
economy not subject to direct proletarianisation, in particular in
agricultural production. What appeared to be a traditional or 'noncapitalist' sector, in fact had experienced enormous changes since the
establishment of the project, most significantly the loss of the paddy
fields. The land still available for farming was further from the village,
not irrigated, and, by the Soroakans' evaluation, harder to cultivate.
Farming could no longer provide a sole livelihood for Soroakan

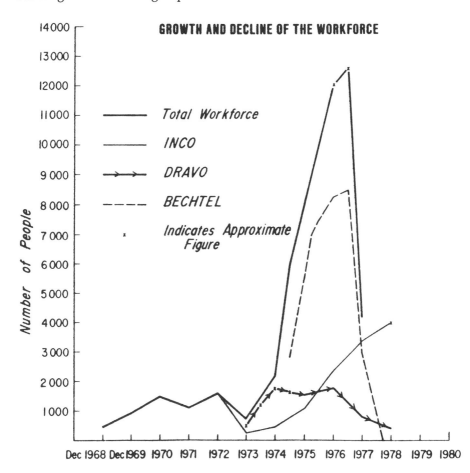

households. The company's domination of land use, and its selective recruitment of labour, have had consequences for the agricultural sector.

The local economy exhibited the heterogeneity characteristic of peripheral capitalist economies, with many sectors of the work force engaged in activities outside formally organised employment, but whose work formed an integral part of the system (Long and Richardson 1978, p.177). This has customarily been referred to as the 'informal sector,' comprising activities like trading, petty commodity production, and provision of services. Marxist critiques, however, argue that conventional approaches do not sufficiently stress the interrelationship between this sector and that organised by the capital-wage labour relation (Long and Richardson 1978, p.177; Davies 1979). With the expansion of capitalism, some precapitalist and noncapitalist activities are dissolved, but others are preserved because they contribute to capital accumulation; for example, in Soroako, informal sector entrepreneurs provided timber at a cheaper rate than the company could provide and cheaper transport services.

The winding down of the construction phase and the retrenchment of about 7,000 workers, beginning in 1977, meant not only that many indigenous Soroakans lost their jobs, but also that the immigrant workers who were paying tenants and customers of the small businesses left the village. The period of my field work (1977–79) coincided with the end of construction, and I witnessed the efforts of Soroakans to adjust their productive activities to the difficult economic circumstances.

The effects of capitalist penetration go beyond production and production relations. These material changes have ramifications for the people's culture, for their daily lived experience, and for their apprehension of that experience. In Soroako, there have been profound changes in the nature of work, under conditions of wage labour. As an increasing number of goods and services become commodified, customary forms of social relations are being affected. Capitalism brings about a separation of work and home, and also new forms of gender relations. The creation of newly felt needs for an ever-expanding range of goods and services available in the capitalist marketplace has been a powerful force for capitalist expansion, as well as changes to capitalist forms of production (McGee 1982).

(T)here is no such thing as economic growth which is not, at the same time, growth or change of a culture. . . . (Thompson 1965, p.97).

Working for the Project

Wage labour was the preferred form of work in contemporary Soroako. The monthly wage provided the most secure source of livelihood, and it gave access to the new consumer commodities and to pastimes for which one needed money. In addition, it guaranteed free medical treatment for the employee and his/her dependents, as well as access to interest-free housing loans. All but a few men (most of them old or ill) had applied to Inco, although many were rejected on grounds of ill health, usually tuberculosis. Table 6.1 (based on a survey of all indigenous Soroakan households, which I conducted in December 1978) shows that wage labour was the largest category of occupation for household heads.

All but one of the indigenous Soroakans employed by Inco in 1978 were in the 'unskilled labour' category, for which the average wage was Rp. 41,000 (US$99) per month. They worked from 7 a.m. to 4 p.m., 5 days a week (a 40-hour week). Overtime had regularly boosted the take-home pay of most employees, until cutbacks in 1978.

Contractor employees consistently worked weeks of 54 hours (6 9-hour days), 14 hours of which were compulsory overtime, which

TABLE 6.1.

PRINCIPAL OCCUPATION OF INDIGENOUS SOROAKAN HOUSEHOLD HEADS, 1978

Occupational Category	% of Total
Full-time, full year waged employment	39.1
Farming	29.3
Self-employed (retail, trade, contractor)	9.3
Government (army, teaching, administration)	3.8
Casual paid work	8.5
Unemployed	7.5
Other	2.5
N = 182	100

provided higher take-home pay than that of Inco employees, despite lower base salaries.

The main divisions within Inco were Exploration, Mining, Process Plant, Administration, and Services (including Town Administration, Roads, Medical Services). There were Soroakans in all these divisions, mainly working as unskilled manual labourers. The most highly paid Soroakans were operators in the Process Plant.

A number of Soroakans had clerical positions with the construction contractors, including one who had worked in the cost engineering section of Bechtel, on a base salary of Rp. 90,000 (US$217) per month. Only two Soroakan men had obtained clerical work with Inco.

Job classifications used by Inco and the contractors were not directly comparable, but it seemed that the Soroakans working for the latter were in more-skilled positions. This was partly a consequence of the concentration of long-term Soroakan employees in Inco's Exploration Division, where most jobs were unskilled. However, the construction companies (unlike Inco) were experienced in the short-term training of unskilled labour with poor formal education, in remote corners of the Third World. Many young Soroakans had certificates testifying to their success in short-term courses run by the contractors in welding, plumbing, blasting, and electrical wiring. Likewise, whereas only one of the Soroakans had attained the status of foreman (and therefore 'skilled worker') with Inco, a number had reached equivalent rank working for contractors. Inco's training programme was more elaborate in conception, but had a lot of trouble getting off the ground. There was no attempt made to recruit talented young Soroakans to the training programme; instead, recruiters brought in young technical school graduates from Tana Toraja and Ujang Pandang.[1]

Thus, especially in Inco, Soroakans were concentrated at the least skilled, lowest paid, most exploited segments of the labour force, and their chances of rising from this position through access to Inco training were limited. As discussed in chapter 2, Inco's work force was predominantly male, especially in the lowest category. Only a few indigenous Soroakan women had ever worked in paid employment, and they worked mainly as domestics in the construction camp, or as housemaids.

Changes in the Organisation of Work

The dominating presence of the mining company and its significance as the major employer has brought profound changes to the work experience in contemporary Soroako. The company owned the mine and the plant; the labourers sold their labour power in return for wages. Inco controlled the conditions and availability of work.

The situation contrasted markedly with the conditions of work in the predominantly agricultural economy. All households had access to land and directly consumed the product of their labour. Work was organised by the cultivators, within their own households and their own community, and was integrated into the ongoing life of the community.

Its rhythms were those of the agricultural cycle, rather than the daily discipline of the industrial enterprise (Thompson 1965, p.60). In the peasant community, periods of intense labour were interspersed with periods of idleness.

For those engaged in wage labour for the mining company, the work place was separate from all other aspects of their lives. Work was under the control of management, ordinary workers having no influence over its organisation. The mass of unskilled labourers understood neither the totality of the labour process nor their place within it. Skills required for different aspects of the production process were not for the most part interchangeable. The division of labour in detail serves as one of the mechanisms of capitalist control within the modern capitalist enterprise (see Braverman 1974). The social relations of the enterprise were in marked contrast to work relations in the past.

Although the company's workers did not complain about boredom in their work, they expressed no joy in the work itself. Status and pay levels were their principal concerns, apart from job security. The contrast between conversations about work in the mine and work in the rice fields was marked. (Farmers would converse with intense interest on the growth of the seedlings, the danger from pests, and so on.) Thus the fundamental antagonism of interest to the wage labour relation was manifested in the alienation from pleasure in work in the capitalist enterprise.

The Soroakans were aware that they had lost their most important agricultural land and that, for most of them, employment with Inco was the only alternative stable livelihood. They found the lack of control over their right to engage in productive work, which arose from the loss of control of productive resources, a difficult aspect of the new situation, one they often complained about.

Among Soroakans, the generally held view was that Inco, having taken their land, had a moral obligation to provide them with work. In a typical statement of this view, one man said:

> I am an indigenous Soroakan (*orang asli Soroako*). The company has taken my land, and I have a right to work.

Soroakans maintained that Inco managers had undertaken to give preference to (*mengistimewakan*) indigenous Soroakans in employment. Such promises were made, for example, at a public meeting in the village mosque, early in 1977. However, the man alleged to have made that promise denied to me that he had done so. A village leader told me that on a number of occasions he had heard managers assuring Indonesian government officials that locals were being favoured in employment.

The personnel office confirmed that such a policy existed, but that it was difficult to implement, because indigenous Soroakans were difficult to identify and also lacked necessary skills. Hency they compromised by giving preference in rehiring to people regarded as 'local hire,' that is, recruited in either Soroako or Malili, regardless of place of origin.

The Soroakans tended to dismiss the argument about their lack of suitable skills as an instance of the company's prevarication. They deemed Inco to be morally responsible to provide them with employment, to fulfill promises given to that effect. Problems in obtaining work underscored their powerlessness in the context of the new developments. 'If only the company would give everyone jobs, life would be good in Soroako,' one man stated.

Conflicting Views of the Organisation

The conflict over the implementation of assurances of preferential treatment indicated the gap between the company's and the villagers' perceptions and values. Inco was willing to accommodate the needs of the local people, insofar as it did not interfere with the primary goals of the organisation.

The life experience of the Soroakans denied them any model from which they could understand the rationality of the company. They (and immigrant workers from similar backgrounds) related to their bosses in terms of a 'patron client model' of human relations not altogether appropriate to the situation of wage labour. They expected protection and guarantees of livelihood in return for their loyal service. Retrenchment was seen as personal betrayal by the boss. Their view of their relations with superiors was reinforced by the behaviour of many of the bosses, who indeed patronised their employees. Many men prospered, gaining promotion and escaping retrenchment because of favoured treatment by a boss (see chap. 8 for an illustration of such patronage). Within the workplace, then, personal relations were important, disguising the impersonal nature of the wage labour relation, which was revealed by the mass retrenchments that have been a feature since 1977.[2]

Retrenched workers felt a strong sense of betrayal. Some of my informants made an explicit connection between the high level of pilfering from the company and the anger of workers, who they said felt 'sick at heart' (*sakit hati*) at their dismissal (see chap. 9). The conflicting expections of villagers and management were well exemplified by incidents at the time of the winding up on Inco's Exploration Division in 1978. Most of the Exploration employees had served the company for many years, some since 1969. The unskilled nature of the work meant most had not acquired skills that were transferable to other divisions. They had worked very closely with their bosses, the exploration geologists in teams out in the jungle, and this heightened the personal nature of their relationship. A commonly held view was that the organisation of work in the Exploration Division had not inculcated in these men the requisite degree of discipline to the organisation of work in the enterprise.

Under Indonesian labour laws, Inco could not readily sack these people and so offered severance pay (normally only paid to retrenched workers) to any who resigned. Managment insisted that no one who still wanted to work would be retrenched. These men were moved to new positions, requiring very low skills. Many took offence at what they saw as a slight to their standing in the company. Both the ex-Exploration Division employees and their fellow villagers commented on the ignominy of their situation. After such long service, they expected better protection by the bosses and more respectful treatment from the company. They had little understanding of the company's concerns about skills required for particular positions.

There were also problems with those workers who accepted severance pay. Many felt the pay to be less than they had negotiated and that they were being cheated. They took the action of refusing to take the money, and the matter was unresolved when I left in 1979.

In the mining town, willingness to work was no guarantee of employment. This was hard felt in a situation where the company's monopolising of land limited other options for earning a living.

Stress—Adaptation to a New Culture of Work

Thompson has written that the transition to industrial capitalism entailed

> a severe restructuring of working habits, new disciplines, new incentives, new human values and a new human nature upon which these incentives could bite effectively (1965, p.57).

For most of the Soroakans, indeed, for most of the unskilled labourers on the project, Inco provided their first experience of wage labour. Staff at company clinics reported high levels of stress, especially among heavy-equipment operators.

The stress was exacerbated by the accompanying uncertainty of continued employment. Soroako abounded in rumours and gossip about the fate of Inco's fortunes, the possibility of retrenchments, or growth of the labour force.

People who had been retrenched would often accept their immediate fate philosophically, saying that a number of years of continous employment had worn them out, so that could do with a rest before seeking further work. Work in the mining company contrasted markedly with the seasonal rhythms of the agricultural year and the autonomy of peasant production.

Proletarianisation was beginning to affect the nature of work in Soroako. The change can be better understood by examining the organisation of work in the agricultural sector.

Farming in Soroako

In the contemporary economy, even those sectors not organised on the capital-wage labour relation were subject to the influence of capitalist penetration. This was especially so with farming, which was the principal source of income for 29.3 percent of the indigenous Soroakan household heads surveyed in December 1978 (table 6.1).

Inco's restrictions on land use were critical means by which the capitalist sector dominated all economic organisation in Soroako. The most important was the appropriation of the paddy fields for the townsite. In addition, mining and associated activities monopolised large tracts of land. Inco simultaneously strip mined seven hills behind the Soroakan plain (see map 6.1). The hills were defoliated, the overburden stored for later reforestation, and the ore-bearing soil trucked to the processing plant. Old paddy fields, in the valleys behind the mine, were used to store the overburden.

The mine monopolised other land that, although not previously cultivated, was of importance to the village economy. As one man said:

> The hills behind the village are being mined now. They were great places for collecting dammar and rattan. Now, if collecting jungle produce is your occupation, you have to go a lot further.

Many of the known stands of rattan have either been destroyed by mining or are in areas that the company has declared out of bounds, because they border on the mine. Similarly, the land in the foothills, formerly used for orchards or for tubers, had become part of the mine's concession.

Inco adopted an active role in ordering the local environment. They banned the keeping of buffalo in fields near the village because, on a number of occasions, the beasts had wandered into the townsite and destroyed gardens. The rule was enforced by the effective sanction of shooting buffaloes found in the townsite. Most of the hunting dogs were shot by company security guards during a rabies scare. Inco also prohibited the cultivation of slopes adjoining the townsite, claiming the fires (for preparing the fields) could get out of hand. They were able to do this because of the low profile of the Indonesian

government in the region and the weakness of the village government (see chap. 7).

Thus the Soroakans could farm only outside the orbit of the company's activities—the land on high mountain slopes behind the mining area (map 6.1), as well as on slopes near several hamlets that were
accessible by boat (not shown on map 6.1).

The fields beyond the mine were accessible on foot, although
there was access for part of the way on the roads leading to the mine.
Leaving on the two-hour journey in the early hours of the morning,
villagers would take a shortcut through their former paddy fields,
which had become the golf course. (The fruit trees they had planted
remained, forming part of the hazards of the course; the fruit was no
longer being harvested.)

The mountain slopes were suited to cultivation of dry field rice
only. For those households principally dependent on farming, the
swiddens that had formerly accounted for the lesser part of the annual harvest were now the mainstay. The hillsides also had to be
planted in tubers, vegetables, and fruit, which were formerly grown
in lowland fields since alienated by the company.

Scarcity had invested farmland with a value it previously lacked,
especially in areas close to the village or within easy access. In earlier
times, swiddens were salable commodities only in cases where the
owner had established permanent crops, like fruit trees or cloves. An
exception concerned farming hamlets that had formerly been the site
of Christian communities abandoned during the Darul Islam
rebellion. The former inhabitants of one such village, who had
relocated north of Matano, attempted to claim reimbursement for
their abandoned land. These claims were not acknowledged. The
claimants were attempting to follow the lead of Soroakans who were
asserting customary rights in house land in the village on the basis of
having cultivated the land in the past (chap. 7).

The dominant rhythm of life in the mining town was given by the
cycle of pay days, the last Friday of each month. On pay day, not only
employees but also landlords, moneylenders, shopkeepers, and
dependants were paid. (These people talked about being paid in the
same terms [*terima*] as employees.) Farmers, who would spend
days, even weeks at times, away at the farming hamlets, came down
to the village for pay day to receive rent, money owed for vegetables,

or casual work for other villagers. For a few days, the market was very lively, swelled by itinerant vendors for Palopo.

However, the old rhythms of the agricultural year remained the dominant pattern in the lives of farmers. The agricultural year began in the dry season, in September or October, when the men cleared the new plots. Fields were cultivated for two to three years (in one case, four), apparently a little longer than had been the norm in the past. Women helped with the clearing of regrowth from the previous year's fields, weeding, or if there was imperata grass, hoeing.

In November, the cleared fields were fired. From the village, brown patches appeared amidst the green. At this time, there was much concern about the weather: too short a dry season meant that the timber would not be dry enough to burn well. The farmers recognised the importance of the ash as fertiliser (*pupuk*) for the soil. But they were also anxious that the wet season begin when they were ready for planting in late December.

The newly fired fields were immediately planted with corn, which matured in time to be eaten during weeding, as well as with green vegetables. The men also built fences to protect the fields from pigs. For many, the latest aspiration was to buy barbed wire, too expensive for most but a commodity that would save much effort in fence building. Those households whose principal livelihood derived from farming were the least able to afford such a luxury.

Each field was planted in a single morning, using a large labour force. Each hamlet organised a timetable, to maximise labour exchange among them. Because the labour inputs of workers was essential, Sunday was the preferred day. The extra labour was invited (*dipanggil*) from among friends and neighbours. They were woken before dawn on the appointed day, and the party would leave the village before it was light. It took about two hours, either by boat or on foot to reach the hamlets. The aim was to have the task finished before the hot part of the day. Occasionally a sympathetic company supervisor lent a vehicle to transport some of the helpers, and young motorcyclists were also pressed into service.

Farmers were always anxious that too few people would turn up. I once saw someone who had finished planting quickly send his forty helpers to a nearby field where there was insufficient labour.

Planting was a jolly occasion, in marked contrast to the work atmosphere in the mining company. The majority of helpers were usually young men and women who engaged in flirting and joking. The Imam said to me:

> Planting paddy doesn't feel like hard work, because we chat and joke. Before I was married, I was often invited because I was such a good story teller.

Planting was still done with wooden dibbles. However, the paddy planters were more likely to dispense the seed from plastic margarine containers salvaged from the townsite rubbish than the woven baskets of former times.

Helpers ate a snack before beginning and halfway through the task, and all joined in a feast on completion. The feast always included a chicken, which was slaughtered prior to planting, the seed rice sprinkled with its blood. However, the Darul Islam period has made Soroakans self-conscious about such rituals, which some farmers denied still took place. The feast was considered as part of the payment to those who helped, thought the hosts were also expected to reciprocate with labour. They referred to this as a debt (*hutang*). Noncultivators could make claims on the farmer's produce, especially vegetables, in return for their labour.

Farmers claimed that the number of varieties of rice has declined, although most still planted six to eight varieties. Many were for special use, for example, for rice flour (used in cakes) or for fermenting. Planting lasted through January, ending in February, when the remaining small tracts of paddy field were also seeded.

Weeding began about a month later. The work included thinning out seedlings in places where they had been too densely sown. This practice is unusual in swidden cultivation and represents the transfer of a paddy field technique to shifting cultivation. The fields were weeded a second time after a further month's interval. Although some households with a member in paid employment would engage casual labour at this time, weeding was generally carried out with family labour. Indeed, the amount of labour at a households' disposal for weeding was crucial in deciding the size of the plot to be cultivated. As mentioned in chapter 5, the amount of weed regrowth was the critical factor in the traditional economy, determining whether fields would be cultivated again or left fallow. These days, other factors (discussed below) are also taken into account.

Both men and women used the customary weeding hook, manufactured by local smiths. However, at the time of my field work the predominance of women in cultivation meant that this was principally a female task.

By the time of weeding, the corn was ripe, and farmers would invite people to the fields to eat fresh roasted young corn. The Soroakans ate corn as a snack and never regarded it as an alternative carbohydrate staple to rice.

After the weeding, farmers resumed tasks they had set aside during the early phase of rice cultivation. Men began planting bananas and cassava, often in fallow rice fields. Women resumed fishing, using handlines, and some men collected rattan, if the price was high enough. They again had time to sell vegetables in the village.

This was the pattern of activity for farmers through April and May, as the rice grew and ripened. Conversation was full of reference to the paddy; its height, whether the fruit had formed, and so on.

As the rice grew, the vegetables died off. Farmers began preparing for the harvest. Men manufactured new finger knives, using razor blades, not locally smithed metal as in the past. They also collected bark for making twine to tie the bundles of paddy. Women wove wide brimmed hats to wear in the fields, while men constructed frames for stooking (and displaying) the harvested bundles of rice.

Harvesting began in late May. As with planting, each hamlet arranged a timetable. It was mostly women who harvested. I commented on this to a young man who accompanied me to the harvest in one field, where he merely sat and ate snacks while, out in the fields, a gang of women worked. He said:

> Indeed that is the way it always is here. The women cut the rice and the men help, carrying the bundles, and so on.

The women worked in groups of four or five, ranging over the mountain side. Harvesters received one bundle of rice for a day's work, regardless of how much they had cut.

In 1978, the average yield was 131 bundles (*ikat*), 327 litres, the range being 40 to 500. In most cases this was not enough for the annual rice needs of the cultivators. Only one family achieved this goal, harvesting 500 bundles. They used exclusively family labour, in order not to be required to share with anyone. Their individualistic behaviour drew comment but not criticism from others.

In 1977, the farmers did not perform a harvest festival in the village. The Imam said:

> We don't have a harvest festival in Soroako anymore. The yields from the swiddens are too low. It's not worth it.

There were, however small festivities in the cultivation hamlets. In 1978, a village harvest festival was held, involving a communal prayer and feast (attended by men) in the village mosque. The (newly reappointed) indigenous village headman told me that he had organised it at the request of the cultivators. The disarray in village government prior to 1978 (chap. 7) was probably significant in the lack of a harvest festival. Perhaps also significant in the reinstatement of the festival was the return of many of the retrenched workers to farming.

Low Productivity in Agriculture

In all except the one instance mentioned above, farming households could not meet even their rice needs from swidden production. This was puzzling for those households where this was the principal ecnomic activity. If the village economy had been based on swidden cultivation in the past, if the population of neighbouring Nuha subsisted by swiddening, why did Soroakan households fail to do so? The shortfall in rice was in absolute terms, not relative to new needs and expectations.

Some villagers answered my queries about this in terms of shortage of good land.

> Before our forebears established paddy fields, there were fewer people in the village, and we cultivated the plain. The soil there is more fertile than in the present-day farms.

Others referred to labour shortages.

> Now, all the young strong men work for Inco, so the old people can't cultivate as much land.

Also, the dependence on the jungle to supplement rice production was greater in the past (chap. 5). For example, they probably ate more sago then. And before the decline in local manufacturing, which accompanied the penetration of mercantile trade, metal produced by Soroakan smiths was probably traded for food as well as other commodities (chap. 3).

However, a critical factor is the labour available for farming, which is affected by the labour demands of the mining company. Inco differentially recruited from among the population, taking principally males in the 15 to 40 age group. They did not employ men over 40 and preferred the younger ones. Table 6.2 shows that most of the male farmers (men for whom farming was the principal occupation) were over 35. These men were too old for recruitment by Inco. The table also shows the relative youth of the wage labourers.

Table 6.2 also shows that there were twice as many female as male farmers. In many households, female farming supplemented the male wage. The situation was similar to that described in many capitalist situations, where wage labour is primarily available to men (Deere 1979). Because there are so few jobs for women in the mining project, farming was the only real alternative for female-headed households.

TABLE 6.2

INDIGENOUS SOROAKAN MALE WAGE LABOURERS, MALE FARMERS
AND FEMALE FARMERS BY AGE, 1978

Age in Years	Males in Wage Labour		Male Farmers		Female Farmers	
	Relative frequency	Cumulative frequency	Relative frequency	Cumulative frequency	Relative frequency	Cumulative frequency
10–14	0	0	0	0	4	4
15–19	6	6	5	5	12	16
20–24	24	30	5	10	10	26
25–29	32	62	8	18	9	35
30–34	20	82	14	32	18	53
35–39	16	98	13	45	16	69
40–44	1	99	14	59	11	80
45–49	0	99	8	67	12	92
50–54	1	100	20	87	4	96
55–59	0	100	5	92	2	98
60 +	0	100	8	100	2	100
Total	100 N = 90		100 N = 54		100 N = 101	

SOURCE: Census by P. T. Inco Medical Services, 1978.

Male labour was important in the swiddens, especially in the early stages of opening up the fields. Men cleared the jungle and built the fences. Young males contributed little to agriculture at that stage, their labour being monopolised by the mining company. This meant a reduction in the amount of land farming households could clear.

Table 6.2 also shows that there were fewer males than females in the under 20 age group whose principal occupation was farming. The Soroakans had realised that the future did not lie with farming. Their children's future was dependent on their ability to earn a wage. Hence all families who could scrape together the means to do so, sent their sons away to high school. Because they could not attend the Inco High School, they had to leave the village to continue their education. Consequently, those male household members who were not in paid employment were likely to be away at school.[3]

The changes in the kind of labour available for farming were having crucial consquences for patterns of land use. I noticed a tendency to cultivate fields continuously for longer periods than in the past. They were cultivating in the farming hamlets closest to the village only, and this meant that they did not have as much land available.

From the hamlets, former fields were evident in the distant hills. I asked why they were no longer cultivated. One man replied:

> Those areas never seemed to be far away before. Now it just seems too far to walk.

His comment perhaps in part reflected changed perceptions of distance in a community where cars, buses, and motorcycles had become commonplace, even though the lack of roads meant fields could be reached mainly on foot. But it also related to the changes in the availability of labour. Farmers were dependent on the cooperation of other villagers during planting and harvesting. In particular, they relied on young workers who would contribute a day's work on their day off from the company. Farmers were always anxious that too few people would congregate to complete planting or harvesting in the required time. Fields had to be at a convenient travelling distance for volunteers to come and go in a day.

Moreover, farmers had other sources of income, which depended on proximity to the village, e.g., selling vegetables and firewood. It would have been difficult to participate in the cash economy and thereby have access to the new consumer commodities, if their fields were too far away.

The techniques of agricultural production were not much affected by changes in Soroako, except, for example, in regard to such materials as barbed wire. However, the organisation of production with respect to land and labour had been significantly transformed since the establishment of the project.

Small Business

An important consequence of the development of the project was the increased penetration of Soroako by the capitalist market. Goods and services once provided through the socioeconomic mechanisms of the peasant economy have increasingly been replaced by commodified transactions. For example, house construction, once done by the householders with aid from neighbours, was in contemporary Soroako more commonly done by building contractors, using modern, factory-made materials such as hammers, nails, and tin roofing.

Food, rather than being produced by the consumers as in the peasant economy, was bought with the wage. Table 6.3 shows the sources of food for twenty households surveyed in 1978.

The fact that no households were self-sufficient in fruit production reflects the fact that fruit trees were part of the estate that was alienated for the project.

This change in the nature of the village economy opened the way for the establishment of shops to provide the food and consumer

TABLE 6.3.
SOURCES OF FOOD OF SOROAKAN HOUSEHOLDS, 1978
(% of households)

| | Type of Food | | | |
| | Rice | Fish | Vegetables | Fruit |
Source of Food	(staple)	(main protein)		
All bought	57	52	52	67
All produced by household	5	10	14	0
Some self-produced, some bought	38	38	33	33
N=20 Total	100	100	100	100

goods needed by the swelling population of the mining town. In 1978, retail or trade was the principal source of income for 9.3% of Soroakan household helds (table 6.1). In the same year, I conducted a survey of all 146 small businesses. There had been an even greater number at the height of the construction phase. The survey did not include the vegetable market, comprising about twenty small stalls. The largest single category comprised retailers of food items including rice, kerosene, tea, coffee, sugar, and dried fish (table 6.4).

Fruit, vegetables, and other foodstuffs were obtained at the vegetable market (see map 2.3), although some of the small shops also sold them. A few shops carried a range of consumer commodities, such as cassettes, torches, fabric, clothes, and kerosene lamps. However, most of these items were sold in the main market (map 2.3). Of the 39 market stalls, 80% sold textiles and clothing, the rest hardware.

Almost 80% of business owners were immigrants, most of them natives of South Sulawesi.[4] Almost all had come to Soroako with the intention of establishing a business. The small number of Soroakan business owners, by contrast, tended to be former workers. Retrenched immigrant workers tended to return to their home villages. Soroakans had nowhere else to go. Retrenched Soroakan workers used severance pay as capital to open a business. Forty-five percent of Soroakan owners had been in business for less than a year, and 80% for less than three years. Unfortunately, these late-comers missed the boat, and big profits having been made by the (mainly immigrant) traders in the boom years. (By 1977–78, many businesses were closing and the remainder reported declining profits since the end of construction.)

Soroakan-owned businesses mainly sold food and 85% of them were located in Old Village. However, the majority (80%) of all business enterprises were in New Village, located in either the market or the nearby commercial centre (map 2.3). A few small shops were scattered throughout the village, usually built under the owners' houses. (They were akin to the corner shop in Australia.)

Most businesses were small concerns using family labour and did not create jobs for other people. On average, they involved two people who were usually related: husband and wife, parent and child, or aunt/uncle and niece/nephew. Only 13% of all business enterprises employed people for wages. These included bars, restaurants, tailors, and a couple of large stores, none of which had Soroakan proprietors.

TABLE 6.4.
COMMERCIAL ENTERPRISES IN SOROAKO, 1978

Types of Business	Absolute Frequency	Relative Frequency %
Kiosk (small food stall)	25	17.2
Small shop selling food only	30	20.0
Small mixed business (food + luxury goods)	7	4.8
Large mixed business (food + luxury goods)	5	3.4
Restaurant and other prepared food sellers	17	11.7
Tailor	16	11.0
Other services (repairs, hairdressing, etc.)	9	5.6
Small manufacturer	2	1.4
Textiles—market stall	32	21.4
Hardware—market stall	3	2.8
N = 146	146	100

A few large nonretail enterprises that did generate employment were not included in the survey. In particular, one indigenous Soroakan and his brother were building contractors, constructing low-cost housing for Inco employees in Wawandula. Two other Soroakans were suppliers of sawn timber, who employed gangs of sawyers.

Debtor-Creditor Relations

All retailers operated on credit. The small shops obtained goods from larger local businesses, accounts being settled after pay day. Other obtained goods from traders in Wawandula or Malili, or even Palopo. Larger retailers had suppliers in Palopo or even Ujung Pandang.

Customers also depended on credit. Purchases of the necessities of everyday life, such as rice, kerosene, salt, sugar, and coffee were entered in a book, and all or part of the debt was settled on pay day (in the case of workers) or whenever they could obtain cash income (in the case of the irregularly employed). Dependence on credit is a common coping strategy for the urban poor of the Third World (McGee 1979, p.55). Interest, forbidden by Islam, was not formally charged but many stores had a dual price system: one for cash sales and another for credit. By giving credit, stores were assured of custom, as the bulk of a household's purchases would come from the creditor store. The majority of households had a constant debt incurred for food and other routinely purchased items. In a survey of a 25 percent systematic sample of indigenous Soroakan households in December 1977, two-thirds said they had a standing debt of which they paid only a part each month. Credit was important for farmers and the semiemployed, and for the employed who were on low wages, paid only monthly. The cycle of debt began, especially for immigrants, in the period while they waited a month for their first pay packet. (Indeed, some retrenched workers fled Soroako, leaving large debts behind them.) Even in households where the wage was sufficient to purchase food needs, the newly felt needs created a call on wages, ensuring there was never enough to go around.

The very small stores, especially those scattered in the residential sections, served as a way of circulating money among kin. People in receipt of wages would shop at the store of a kinsperson, although prices were often higher than at larger stores, thus ensuring nonemployed relations some custom. Indeed, the small amounts of capital needed for such enterprises, about Rp. 50,000 (US$120) were often supplied by an employed kinsman. For example, I once observed two sisters settling accounts, one of them the wife of a foreman with the plant maintenance contractor. His job status entitled her to shop in the company store, where she would buy low-cost items, which her sister would resell. The cost of these items would be deducted from the bill that the worker's family had accumulated (for items like cigarettes and kerosene). Many households had both a small shop and a number of tenants, who were a captive market for the shop.

The monetisation of the economy allowed the creation of a large retail sector, and the opportunities thus provided allowed some people to become wealthy, relative to fellow villagers. However, on the whole, retail provided a survival strategy for households running small family businesses. Most Soroakan-owned businesses made very small profits and retail was only one of several income-earning activities in the household (table 6.5). Those without a household member in paid employment lived in hope that the company would again increase its work force, so the family could obtain its income from wages.

The small scale of most of these businesses, their dependence on family labour, and the often personalised ties to customers gave them a character typical of the 'informal sector' in the capitalist periphery. However, they did not operate in a manner independent from the capitalist enterprise: debts were settled on pay day, and the size of the consumer market was dependent on the rise and fall of the company labour force. The consumer needs to which they catered were a product of the specific mode of operation of the mining company and the character of capitalist expansion in general. Because village residents could no longer be self-sufficient in food, they were dependent on retailers to supply their needs, even in the case of Soroakan natives who still engaged in agricultural production (table 6.3). Newly felt needs for consumer commodities arose from emulation of the lifestyle of the higher-status townsite residents. The expansion of the capitalist market into Soroako, bringing an abundance of consumer items, and the more generalised monetisation of the economy that enabled their purchase, were as much part of the process of capitalist penetration as the creation of new forms of production relations

TABLE 6.5.
SOURCES OF INCOME OF INDIGENOUS SOROAKAN HOUSEHOLDS, 1978

Income Source	Relative Frequency %
Wages	21
Wages/agriculture	18
Wages/agriculture/rent	3
Wages/rent	9
Wages/trade	2
Wages/trade/rent	1
Agriculture	18
Agriculture/rent	9
Agriculture/rent/other	2
Agriculture/rent/trade	3
Rent	2
Rent/trade	2
Rent/other	1
Trade	4
Other	2
No apparent source of income	3
	100

N = 182

(McGee 1982). The desire for access to new consumer commodities was a determinant of their positive response to the project, as well as a factor attracting immigrant workers to Soroakao.

The Economics of Survival

In very few households could a single source of livelihood provide for all the members' needs. They adopted the coping mechanism commonly formed among the poor of the Third World: as many household members as possible sought work, in a variety of income-earning activities, in both the formal and informal sectors. Dependence on credit was also part of this common strategy (McGee 1979, pp. 52–53).

In the survey of household income conducted in 1978, I attempted to discover the productive activities outside the home, of all household members. The activities adopted for survival are so many and so diverse that table 6.5 does not begin to capture them all. But it does show how few households were dependent on a single source of income.

The table shows that, in 1978, wages constituted the sole source of income in only 21% of households, usually those of young, relatively highly paid workers with small, young families. In such cases, their wages were sufficient for their monthly needs, and the wife was engaged in full-time domestic labour, including child care. This followed the pattern provided by the urban elite in the company townsite. (The wives engaged in occasional petty trading, for example, selling fabric or clothing, such intermittent activities not being reported in the survey.)

In most households with a wage earner, women's productive activities supplemented their husband's wage: women farmed, fished, sold goods, and took in boarders. Other household members, e.g., children and the elderly, contributed to household income by helping in the fields, fishing, or selling vegetables.

The wage-earner was in many households an unmarried son, younger brother or brother-in-law of the household head. Whereas married men customarily gave the pay packet to the wives, unmarried men retained more control over their earnings, many of them buying motorcycles and other luxury goods for personal use.

In about eight Soroakan households, unmarried daughters worked as housemaids in the townsite. On the whole, Soroakans were
reluctant to allow their daughters to be exposed to the assumed
potential moral dangers of domestic service, but in very poor
households, for example, those of widows, pragmatic considerations
held sway over moral concerns.

A large proportion of household heads had either no employment (7.5%) or some form of casual (and therefore intermittent)
employment at the time of the survey (8.5%) (table 6.1). For those
who could not obtain paid work, the main avenues for earning a
livelihood were farming and petty trading. A small number of men
were local government officials or teachers (3.8%). All of these men
and their families supplemented their meagre remuneration with
farming and/or petty trading.

In all cases, except the small number of successful traders, adult
males sought paid work with the company or one of the contractors,
the other forms of income earning being regarded as a stopgap.

Those households without a member in full-time, year-round
employment were the most dependent on a variety of income-
earning strategies.

Rent was an important source of supplementary income,
especially for those households without a member in paid employment. In 1978, 62% of Soroakan households reported they had at
some time obtained income from rent. For many, their house was
their only asset capable of generating cash income; rent added an
average of Rp. 3,000 per month to household incomes, though rents
could be as high as Rp. 20,000 (US$48) per month.

Apart from all these activities, there were other ways of earning
income, most of them irregular and poorly paid. Men could collect
jungle produce, but many of the customarily exploited stands of rattan close to the village were lost to the mine. The loss of draft animals
limited the potential collection areas to those accessible by boat. In addition, if market prices were low, its collection was not worthwhile.
One village resident commented, in late 1977:

> Now those without a job collect rattan or saw timber, but rat-
> tan has dropped in price, so not many want to do that.

Transport of the rattan to Malili was arranged by traders, who
were active in Soroako only when the market was buoyant. Other-

wise, marketing problems were too great for the small producer. The revaluation of the rupiah in November 1978 led to an increase in the price of rattan and an upsurge of activity by traders.

The Soroakans no longer exploited dammar. The trees had been felled by a Japanese logging company in the early 1970s. In a rehearsal for the later land alienation, the villagers were forced to accept a price of Rp. 1,000 (US$2.50) per tree, a paltry sum compared with the potential lost.

A number of local contractors sold sawn timber to Inco and to other village residents for house construction. They used contract labour, often men from other parts of Sulawesi who brought their own saws. The sawyers lived in camps on the edge of the jungle and were provided with food, the cost of which was deducted from their wages, which were paid at piece-work rates. Only a few Soroakans were employed as sawyers.

There was occasional daily work available to farmers and others without full-time, year-round paid work, for example, in another household's rice fields, or building houses and digging wells or toilet pits. Inco and the other contractors employed some casual labour. The daily rate for such work ranged from Rp. 500 to Rp. 1,000 (US$1.20 to $2.40). Women received less than men. These rates compared favourably with payment for casual work in other parts of Indonesia (Borkent et al. 1981).

Inco's divestment policy, by means of which the company intended to relinquish many service functions to local contractors, created more of this lower-paid work, while bringing about a decline in the number of full-time, year-round jobs that enjoyed greater stability, higher pay, and more privileges. The limited work opportunities for retrenched workers have already been discussed.

Farmers and the irregularly employed were especially dependent for their survival on aid from other villagers. In particular, poor families benefited from being clients of wealthier patrons. For example, in the house where I lived, children would often deferentially present unsolicited gifts of vegetables to the women of the house and receive in return gifts of sugar, salt, or coffee from the small shop downstairs. The poorer members of a religious sect (*Jemma'a*) similarly depended on the patronage of wealthier, shop-owning members. People in full-time, year-round employment would help their kin who did not have a regular source of cash income. For example, one of my neighbours, an old man with one child, an unmarried daughter, received rice and occasionally money from his employed nephews. They had all contributed to buy an engine for his boat, so he could more easily travel to his fields. It was common for people to give poorer relations salt, sugar, or rice.

However, these forms of mutual support, which derived from the mode of organisation of the peasant community, were under attack in the monetised economy. Credit from a small shop (often owned by a kinsperson) had become the more usual method of survival for farmers and semiemployed as well as low-paid workers. When I asked farmers how they survived when rice or money ran out, they would reply in such terms as:

> We go and get rice from one of the shops and put it on the books. Then we endeavour to earn some money to pay off the debt.

The fatalistic acceptance of these conditions of life were expressed in religious terms, in the common aphorism: 'We human beings can only strive. It is God who determines the outcome' (*Kita manusia hanya usaha. Tuhan yang menentukan semua*).

For those families who had neither a member in waged employment nor income from large-scale trade, it was difficult to make a living. Survivial depended on all household members engaging in various forms of work. When I returned to Soroako in 1980, the wealth difference between farmers and those who had remained in paid work was more apparent. The former category seemed to have stood still, their style of life remaining as it had been almost two years earlier. The latter category were markedly more affluent than previously, with comparatively luxuriously appointed houses, furnishings, television sets, and, in one case, a motor car. However, the instability of employment and constant retrenchments meant more people were falling into the less privileged category while the elite consolidated its position. There was considerable overlap between the membership of the new elite and the traditional elite, whose wealth had been based on ownership of land. Many of these people still owned land in the village, which they rented to immigrants. Among them were the established traders, who continued in this role after the project, although in this regard they were eclipsed by wealthier immigrant traders. However, in the contemporary economy, the differences between the affluence of this group and the mass of the villagers was increasing. The exception was the small number of households which had a relatively well-paid project employee. Many of the traditional elite also fell into this category. The increased differentiation among Soroakans was consistent with the high degree of inequality within the mining town as a whole (chap. 2).

For some poverty was absolute. They had difficulty in obtaining sufficient food, or providing for other basic needs. Government officials in January 1981, were aware of fifty-three children of 12 years of age and younger, who were not attending primary school because their parents could not afford the small monthly fee entailed (Rp.200). All of these children were from families whose income was irregular or came from farming. Poverty for the majority of the poor was relative; they were managing to survive at a simple standard of living. Some could barely afford a pressure lamp, while the relatively affluent had television. Their houses were still made of jungle materials, while fellow villagers installed tin roofs and concrete floors. They could keep their children at primary school, but their high school education, commonplace for others, remained a dream.

Retrenchment

During the construction phase, almost all Soroakan householders had income from wages. In December 1978 when I surveyed all indigneous Soroakan households, there were eighty-four indigenous Soroakans still in paid employment and seventy-two former workers who had been retrenched from Inco or one of the construction companies. Fourteen percent of households contained at least one member described as 'unemployed'—without paid employment at the time of the survey, but seeking work. Sixty-six percent of the unemployed former workers were household heads, customarily the principal income earners.

The majority of former workers still had not found alternative stable sources of income (table 6.6). Some had used retrenchment payments to establish small shops or businesses. One-quarter had returned to farming. However, if a man was retrenched after the planting season, he could not cultivate rice until the following year. Many in the unemployed category would probably have planted fields in the following rice season. One such retrenched worker had established a banana plantation, hoping to sell the fruit in future, but

TABLE 6.6.
CURRENT OCCUPATION OF FORMER WORKERS (1978)

	Absolute Frequency	Relative Frequency (%)
Self-employed	11	15
Casual work	16	22
Farming	18	25
Unemployed	22	30
Unremunerated public service (village government, religious official)	6	8
N =	72	100

he had no immediate source of income. When I questioned him about this he replied with the common aphorism already quoted: 'We human beings can only strive (*usaha*). God determines the rewards for our efforts.'

Some of the former workers had managed to find casual work with Inco or a local contractor. Their rates of pay were lower than those of permanent employees and the work was intermittent and unreliable. The largest of the local contractors, had at the time of the survey failed to pay its employee for several months.

Table 6.7 shows changes in the principal sources of household income from December 1977 to December 1978, the period coinciding with the end of the construction phase. There was a drop of 12% in households with a member in paid employment and a drop of over 8% in householders receiving income from rent, as retrenched immigrant workers returned home and others moved to Wawandula

TABLE 6.7.
CHANGES IN SOURCES OF INCOME OF INDIGENOUS
SOROAKAN HOUSEHOLDS, 1977–78

Source of Income	% of households	
	1977	1978
Wages	66.2	54.0
Farming	50.9	56.3
Retail	15.1	17.2
Rent	43.4	34.9

(chap. 7). However, the percentage of increase in the alternative sources of livelihood—farming and retail—were not so great. Neither provided the same surety of income as the wage.

By 1978, many more Soroakan households were endeavouring to survive by self-employment, using retrenchment payments as capital to open small stores. The survey of all small businesses in Soroako in 1979 found that the majority of Soroakan-owned enterprises were established after 1977. However, the decline in village population meant a simultaneous shrinking of business opportunities. The Soroakans were opening businesses just when many of the immigrants, who had benefited from the massive numbers of people in the construction phase, were closing up shop and moving on.

Other retrenched workers used severance payments to buy motors for boats that facilitated access to fields and enabled income earning through provision of transport services, collecting firewood, and bringing agricultural products to market. A few had bought large fishing nets.

Separation of Work and Home

Capitalist penetration has brought significant changes to the relations between men and women in Soroako. In the peasant economy, the household was a basic unit of production: husbands, wives, and other household members worked side by side in agricultural production. In those households where the male head was in paid employment, women stayed at home, performing domestic labour or engaged in some other income-earning activity, usually farming or retail, relatively independent of their husbands.

This separation of work and home meant that the husband's work life was a mystery to his wife. I would often ask women where their husbands worked. Typically, they would reply after some thought with a creolised label for the division of the company— *werhaus* or *proses*, for example. None could describe what their husbands did at work. None had ever visited the work place.

Men also identified their place of work with the same creolised terms. In gatherings of neighbours and kin, men rarely discussed the daily routines of their work in the company. Any work-related conversation was more likely to be gossip about company politics, rumours about retrenchments, the state of the world nickel market, promotions at high levels. All these factors affected their job security, the central concern.

Much has been written on the segregation of male and female worlds in peasant societies, especially those that practise Islam.[5] Certainly, this kind of segregation existed in Soroako: many events were attended by men or women exclusively, or the different sex participants were segregated. These patterns apparently intensified under Darul Islam.

However, this segregation of certain aspects of ritual and social life is not of the same order as that which has arisen from the men spending most of their days in a foreign arena outside the village. It contrasts with the conditions of agricultural production, where men and women worked together and understood each other's tasks (chap. 5). New forms of the social division of labour articulated with the sexual division of labour, segregating men and women into different worlds.

There were few jobs for women in the mining company. This was a consequence of their employment policy: women were only hired in those areas customarily the province of female labour under capitalism. Women were domestics, secretaries, teachers, and nurses (see table, note 1, p. 54.) Company policy coalesced with the values of the indigenous Soroakans, which held it to be inappropriate for women to work outside the village and its immediate environs (Robinson 1983).

In the agricultural economy, women who had young children did not participate in agricultural production. However, the exclusion from social production was but a stage in their lives. Yet, in those households primarily dependent on the wage, there was a tendency for this exclusion to become a permanent condition of women's lives. The values of the urban elite were encouraging ideological changes that supported the emerging sexual division of labour (Robinson [1983] gives a more detailed discussion of these changes).

Consumerism

In spite of the fact that the wages Inco paid to unskilled workers were higher than the average wages in Indonesia, although in line with the mining sector (Borkent et al. 1981), unskilled workers constantly complained that the wage was not enough, or that it was 'only enough to eat (*cukup untuk makan saja*).' This reflected the high cost of living in Soroako, in comparison with other parts of Indonesia. Calculations by Inco officers that were used to suport a request for a wage rise for unskilled workers showed the cost of living for an average family to be higher than in Jakarta (Dagg 1978). I overheard a visitor from Palopo complain to a fish vendor at the price of his goods. He replied, 'But this is Soroako. Things are different here (*pengaturan lain*). There's more money here.' In the townsite, life was easier: salaries were higher, but rents were cheaper, as was food from the company store.

But apart from the objectively higher cost of living, residents of the mining town were developing new aspirations that the wage was never sufficient to meet. There was an ever increasing quantity and variety of goods available in the village. The increased monetisation of the economy, and the ready availability of credit, enabled people to exercise a choice to obtain those goods, even if it meant a degree of hardship in meeting other needs, or reneging on responsibilities to less affluent kin. Such goods as sewing machines, furniture, and gold jewelry that had previously been owned by only the wealthy elite among the indigneous Soroakans were available to the majority. I often heard people express the view that, although they clearly enjoyed the new consumerism, there was 'too much thinking to be done' or 'too many choices' to be made in the modern market place.

Table 6.8 records the proportion of indigenous Soroakan households, from a 25 percent systematic sample, that own the most popular of the new consumer items.

TABLE 6.8.
OWNERSHIP OF CERTAIN CONSUMER ITEMS
BY INDIGENOUS SOROAKAN HOUSEHOLDS, 1977

Item	% of Households
Pressure lamp(s)	86.8
Watch(es)	79.2
Sewing machine	68.2
Radio/cassette player	52.8
Kerosene burning stove	26.4
Motor for boat	24.5
Bicycle	16.7
Motorcycle	13.2

N = 53

There was pragmatism in their choices. Pressure lamps and sewing machines were among the most popular items. Watches were an important status symbol, although villagers like to stress their value in helping them observe properly the five daily prayers required by Islam. Interestingly, Thompson notes that, in England, there was a general diffusion of watches and clocks at a time when the Industrial Revolution was demanding greater synchronization of time. When a group of workers improved their lifestyle, their acquisition of time pieces was one of the first things noted (1967, pp.69–70). Gold (not recorded in the table) was almost universally owned and regarded as a form of savings. Women would sell their gold jewelery, for example, to help pay for house renovations.

New styles of clothing were an important aspect of the changes in daily life. Cloth, the main item sold in the market, was made up on the ubiquitous home sewing machine or by one of the many tailors in the village (see table 6.4). A village official said to me:

> It's funny, we used to be content with just two sets of
> clothes. Now we seem to need at least eight!

When I first arrived, in 1977, Soroakan women always dressed in traditional sarongs and blouses, even at meetings of women's organisations. During the time of my stay, Western-style dress became the norm at such gatherings. I was commissioned by many of the women as a seamstress; as a foreigner I was deemed an expert on the new styles. The woman I lived with (one of the most innovative) was always asking my advice on dress, for example, if a particular outfit matched, saying, 'I've only just begun to wear these sorts of clothes. I'm still learning.'

The women's savings association (*arisan*) provided a means by which women could meet their desires for consumer goods. These groups were set up by the elite Indonesian women in the townsite, under the auspices of the Inco Women's Association (*Ikatan Keluarga Inco*, or IKI) (see chap. 10). Each member of a group contributed a fixed sum of money to a common fund monthly, and all contributors drew lots to determine the month's winner, who received all of the pooled funds. Each group member had one chance to win, until all had a turn. The women used the money, which came from their husbands' wages, to purchase furniture and sewing machines, or building materials for house renovations.

House renovation was the most public manner of displaying wealth. Improvements included iron roofing, glazed windows, wooden floors throughout, larger and more substantial kitchens, extensions, cement floors downstairs, and indoor bathrooms and toilets. Of the houses I surveyed in December 1977, 50% had iron roofing, 80% wooden (not *atap*) walls, and 33% glazed windows. By 1980, many more Soroakans had very substantial houses with these innovative features. However, the contrast between those of long-term employees and the unrenovated houses of the farmers and semiemployed was a dramatic manifestation of the growing gap between the relatively rich and the poor. Consumption aspects of lifestyle were the concrete manifestations of inequality. Benefits were not equally spread, whether it be consumer goods for pleasure, like television, or such labour-saving commodities as motors for boats, sewing machines, or chain saws.

The desire for new consumer items, and the lifestyle they supported—the model being given by the Indonesian elite in the townsite—put pressure on the wage, hence the common view that it was never adequate.

However, the monetisation of the economy, coupled with new consumer desires, also put pressure on the customary forms of social relations, of mutual support and reciprocity.

In the peasant economy, savings/wealth were held as a store of rice. A common claim was that in the past the rice barn was never empty. A request for food from a fellow villager was met from this replenishable store, produced in an agricultural sector over which they had control. Even the effects of natural disasters were mitigated by the spread of risk by cultivating wet and dry rice, in different locations.

In the mining town, income was in the form of money, even, to an extent, for farmers and the semiemployed. Money is more universally exchangeable than rice, against a variety of needs, such as clothes, new houses, and furnishings, or for an elaborate ritual.

In the peasant economy, the older generation controlled economic resources, but did not have the right to withhold them from their dependent children. Now it is their children who earn the money: the parents are not regarded as having an automatic 'call' on the child's wage, or the goods it buys. Married men would hand over their pay packet to their wives. Few unmarried men would do the same with their mothers. It was their right to use the income for personal expenditure, on clothes, on motorcycles, or building their own house, providing only some support for the household. An old man commented that, once his sons married and left home he could hope for money from them, but he could not expect it.

In spite of the fact that the wage supported a more materially elaborate lifestyle than had been the norm in the peasant economy, the wage was insufficient to meet new felt needs, defined more in terms of the lifestyle of the elite in the townsite than their own former lifestyle. Even the best-paid Inco employees in the village always fell short of cash; indeed, most were always in debt. A request for help from a kinsperson would not, or could not, always be met. And farmers and the semiemployed required cash payment to perform services for the more privileged wage earners, which in the past would have been reciprocated by labour exchange, for example, helping with cultivation or house construction.

Of course, there was a constant state of flux between social relations determined by the ideology of the peasant community and those of capitalism. It was still common for wage earners to give small cash payments to poorer kin, or for kin to make contributions to a ritual feast, for example. But clearly, in many situations the power of capitalist rationality prevailed. These changes in social relations were tragically illustrated when a deserted wife, who lived with her old mother and mother's brother, died of starvation. In the shock that followed, the explanation offered by a number of villagers stressed the breakdown of systems of mutual support and obligation.

Marx made the following comment on the development of capitalism:

> The dissolution of all products and activities into exchange values presupposes the dissolution of all fixed personal [historic] relations of dependence in production, as well as the all-sided dependence of the producers on one another (1973, p.156).

Indeed, money serves as a dissolver of personal relations, substituting those of the marketplace.

Resistance to New Values

In an important area the Soroakans were not bowing to the pressure of consumerism: their diet. It has been commonly found, with a shift from subsistence production to wage labour, that people who buy rather than produce their own food tend to consume less nutritious processed food, with negative consequences for their health. Corporate advertising promotes bread to people who have customarily eaten whole grains and infant formula to women who have always breast-fed. Advertising creates desires for processed foods that reap profits for corporate food producers.

All Soroakan households showed some dependence on purchased food. However, in a survey of expenditures on food, I found that they tended to purchase the same foods they would customarily have produced: rice, leafy green vegetables, and fish. Processed foods were not readily available in the village, although some shops sold canned food or biscuits. The company store, however, sold all manner of processed food, including frozen TV dinners. The villagers had limited access to these goods, but, except for Coca-Cola and fat frozen chickens, they had little interest in them.

All households purchased tea, coffee, and sugar, and most bought canned, sweetened condensed milk. The most potentially harmful change in diet was the increased consumption of sugar and sweetened condensed milk. As household income rose, more was spent on these items.

Conclusion

The development of the nickel project has had profound effects on the organisation of production in Soroako. The loss of the villagers' irrigated land set in motion a process of proletarianisation: divorced from the principal means of production, they had no option but to seek work in the mining project. However, this work has been intermittent and unstable for many. The security of the peasant economy has not been matched.

For a substantial and increasing minority of indigenous Soroakans, land remains the principal means of production. However, the poor quality of that land, as compared to the land they have lost, and the constraints exercised by the dominating presence of the company, have made it difficult to make a living from the land.

The earlier penetration of the capitalist market began a process of change that the development of the project has consolidated. In particular, the desire for, and dependence on, consumer commodities established in that earlier period ensured that the villagers welcomed the project. That earlier period also set in motion changes in social relations among villagers. The group whose political ascendance was tied to their control of productive resources has become the core of a new elite in the village.

Accompanying the changes in production have been changes in everyday behaviour. The Soroakans are becoming accustomed to new patterns of work and new expectations in their relations with others, and they are accommodating to new ways of interpreting their experience, especially through contact with the Indonesian urban elite in the mining town.

However, we have already seen that these changes, though generally welcomed, have not always proceeded smoothly. Although the Soroakans have accommodated to new ideological forms (like changes in gender relations) that facilitate capitalist production, they are by no means completely hegemonised. They have responded to the contradictory nature of of capitalist development, notably its tendency in the periphery to bring affluence to the few and poverty to the masses. In the next chapter I will examine a number of instances of conflict, in which the Soroakans have attempted to influence the course of events in their region, particularly their struggles over land rights.

Postscript—the 1982 Industrial Action

Inco has continued to cut production and retrench workers, in response to the continued slump in the world nickel market. In October 1982, the company resolved to retrench 427 workers, all of 'unskilled' or 'skilled' status. The amount of severance pay was negotiated with the union, the Organisation of Mining and Oil Industry Workers (*Sarekat Buruh Minyak Gas Bumi dan Pertembangan*) (*Kompas* 1982a).

At the same time, the company undertook other cost-cutting measures, including limiting development of the project's environs and cutting back on expenditures in the community relations category (presumably items like community health) (*Pelita* 1982). They had reduced the expatriate workforce by 30 percent in the previous year (*Kompas* 1982b).

The South Sulawesi Government announced it was prepared to find alternative employment for the retrenched workers; unskilled labourers would be taken on in an oil palm project, to be established by the Government, or given irrigated rice land elsewhere in Luwu. Technical staff would be taken in to the Public Works Department (*Terbit* 1982).

However, in early November, 200 of the retrenched workers who had refused to accept severance pay occupied the company offices and the process plant, demanding to keep their jobs. The Executive Council of South Sulawesi (comprising the governor and the top military and police officials) flew to Soroako to resolve the matter (*Kompas* 1982c). They were reported to have approached the occupying workers in a 'father-to-son' manner. Subsequently, the workers left the work place in an orderly fashion. The Government officials attributed the action to a 'misconception' between workers and the company and also blamed the intervention of a lawyer retained by some to act on their behalf. The protestors gave written undertakings not to repeat their action, and the Executive Council threatened to take firm action against anyone who broke the agreement (*Pedoman Rakyat* 1981).

Apart from not wanting to lose their jobs, the workers had a grievance about their houses (*Pedoman Rakyat* 1982). Many had bought houses with company loans, and all had used much of their earnings to build houses. In the current economic climate, they could never sell them. Thus, unskilled workers were more disadvantaged than skilled workers and managers, who had cheap, rented company accommodation for the duration of their employment. After the Government's intervention, the company agreed to buy the houses (*Pedoman Rakyat* 1982).

Another source of grievance for the workers was their feeling pressured by the union, and they were angry that there were no union organisers among those retrenched (*Merdeka* 1972). Indeed, the union could not claim to represent workers' interests, since its officials were drawn from the ranks of company management.

NOTES TO CHAPTER 6

1. Many Soroakan youths were receiving secondary education in other parts of the province. Many hoped for employment with Inco. Meanwhile, the company recruited secondary school graduates from other places, and the personnel managers worried about how to keep the skill-

ed workers from seeking alternative employment closer to their natal villages.

2.   Hofstede (1982) discusses the contrasting orientations in the work place of Indonesian and expatriate personnel.

3.   The boys went to Malili, Palopo, or Ujung Pandang, where they lived with a kinsman or worked as a servant in a household that supported them. Some lived with groups of students, obtaining food each month from their parents. Only the relatively well-off could support a son away at high school.

4.   In particular, business owners tended to originate from Bugis areas of South Sulawesi. The Bugis are well known for their involvement in commerce and for spontaneous mirgration in pursuit of trade. Only 8% of businesses were owned by people originating from Tana Toraja, despite the fact that people from that area comprised almost half the number of unskilled labourers for the project.

5.   See for example Friedl (1967), Reiter (1975) and Rogers (1975).

Photo 6. Workers at the nickel plant.

Chapter 7

Domination and Conflict: The Company, The Village, and The State

The alienation of the irrigated rice land, the principal means of production in the preproject economy, gave rise to a protracted conflict that involved the mining company, the villagers, and the Indonesian Government. There were further conflicts over land rights when the local representatives of the government implemented a plan to redevelop Soroako Village. The company's appropriation of the land surrounding the village put pressure on the remaining estate. Housing land became scarce. Disputes among indigenous Soroakans over land were one aspect of the emerging kind of social relations based on private ownership of resources.

In addition, the dominating presence of the mining company, and the environmental degradation through such problems as soil erosion and water pollution that accompanied its activities, brought it into conflict with the villagers. These disputes, all instances of class conflict, which arose in the context of capitalist penetration, are the subject of this chapter.

In all the events to be discussed, the principal protagonists were the village population, the mining company, and the representatives of the Indonesian Government. But to understand the course of these disputes, we must look beyond the actions of these main actors. They must be interpreted in the context of the role of the political level in integrating local communities, regions, and nations into the economic structures of the world system.

Dependency theorists have stressed the important role of the indigenous elites of Third World societies in establishing conditions whereby the international bourgeoisie can effect economic exploitation in the periphery (See Mortimer [1973] for an application of this model to Indonesia). In his characterisation of the postcolonial state, Alavi argues that colonial rulers generally established a strong state apparatus to facilitate colonial exploitation and subdue indigenous classes that had competing interests, such as the landowners and national bourgeoisie. Postcolonial nations inherited the strong state apparatus and its rule of law, which provided conditions for the operation of foreign capital. This strong bureaucratic organisation has commonly come under the control of a military-bureaucratic oligarchy, who maintain their position by mediating between the competing factions within the propertied class—principally the foreign bourgeoisie, the national bourgeoisie, and the traditional landowners (1979). At the same time, the state acts on behalf of all factions of the ruling class, preserving the

> social order in which their interests are embedded, namely the institution of private property and the capitalist mode as the dominant mode of production (Alvai 1979, p.42).

Robison has provided a similar analysis of the Indonesian military-bureaucratic elite, but he argues further that they pursue policies that favour the interests of foreign and national Chinese business interests, to the detriment of the national indigenous bourgeoisie (1978, p.3.) The Foreign Investment Law of 1967 exemplified this pattern, providing a legal framework that facilitated foreign investment to the detriment of indigneous businessmen (Robison 1978, p.37).

With respect to the Soroako nickel project, the Indonesian Government has favoured the interests of the foreign corporation over those of the citizens resident in the area. For example, the Contract of Work committed the government to acquire compulsorily any land deemed necessary for the project, and government officials have directly intervened on the company's behalf in instances of conflict, whether it be industrial conflict (see postscript to chap. 6) or conflict over the compensation paid for alienated land. In Indonesia generally, peasants are powerless to protest the resumption of land for capital-intensive projects (Lubis and Abdullah 1981, p. 22), and workers are powerless to withhold their labour in order to secure better wages and working conditions (see Borkent et al. 1981).

Except for these dramatic interventions, the government kept a low profile in the project area. The mining company had to develop the transport and communication infrastructure for the project and to provide medical, educational, and other services to employees. Provincial and Regency level officials rarely intervened in the area (one can imagine them hoping that the company's efforts would relieve them of responsibility for the region, to deploy their scarce funds elsewhere). District and village levels of government were weak and lacking in resources. The company's Contract of Work did endow it with the responsibility for the well-being of its work force, but no authority enforced this aspect of the Contract.

Company officials constantly stressed that they did not wish to become the alternative government of the region. But Inco did adopt an active role in ordering the environment to suit its needs; for example, its security guards searched everyone leaving the project area, and its Town Administration prevented farmers from cultivating land that, although still part of the public domain, bordered the townsite. In meetings between local government and company representatives, company officials took the chair. There was much confusion in the minds of the population, shared by some local government officials, about the respective roles and responsibilities of the government and the company. Inco's preempting of aspects of state ideology contributed to the confusion (see chap. 4).

The weakness of local government (i.e., at the village and district levels) meant it was difficult for the ordinary people to seek redress for legitimate grievances. The venality of local government officials contributed to the problem, as did the disarray in village government during the construction phase of the project.

In Soroako, village government officials had always been chosen from among a number of influential families, chiefly the members of the Tosalili *fam*, and the descendants of the Makole Matano (see chap. 3). In 1973, the Village Headman, a Tosalili, resigned to take up more lucrative employment with Bechtel. He had overseen the beginnings of an orderly growth of the village.

Anticipating the massive expansion of Soroako, the Regency government appointed a career civil servant to replace him. The appointment was a disaster: his administration lost all control of the physical expansion of the village, even of registration of the burgeon-ing population. It could not cope with the problems of the new urban environment, ranging from prostitution to garbage collection.

In mid-1977, the new Headman was transferred and replaced by a District government official, regarded as temporary until the Regent found a permanent replacement. This man oversaw the implementa-tion of the redevelopment plan, described below. He was not as in-competent as his predecessor, but his authoritarian manner and his venality made him unpopular. Further, he did not overcome the disarray of village administration.

After intense lobbying by village leaders, in mid-1978 the former indigenous Soroakan Headman (since retrenched from Bechtel) was reappointed. He managed to reestablish order in village administra-tion, reflected in his government's greater control of daily events. However, he was powerless to change the fundamental structure of political relations, which meant that the village population had very little impact on the decisions affecting their lives, and no power to con-front the company.

CONFLICTS OVER LAND

Land Alienation

Conflict concerning land arose soon after Inco began operations in the Soroako area. Road construction and early mining excavation led to the destruction of some irrigation channels. The farmers com-plained of crop failure, in some cases from lack of water, and in others, because the water was fouled with silt. They asked for com-pensation from Inco, but said they never received any. Inco officials give conflicting accounts of these events. One manager told me that they had consulted an agricultural expert, who declared the crop failure was not related to construction and mining. He urged me to request the report from a member of his staff. The second company employee insisted that the company had paid some compensation in 1971, he said he did not know the whereabouts of the expert's report.

This affair was only a hint of impending events. In the early 1970s, the indigenous Soroakans heard rumours that they would lose their paddy fields to the project. Such rumours usually preceeded major Inco initiatives, and indeed, on 29 September 1972, the Village

Headman announced that they were required to sell their land to the company.

The appropriation of the land, to be carried out by the government at Inco's request, was in accord with the terms of the Contract of Work. At that stage, the Soroakans said they were quite happy with the situation. They had no objection to selling their land, at a suitable price, and assumed they would negotiate with Inco for adequate recompense. They had no attachment to a way of life based on subsistence cultivation per se and they were willing to accept the changes in their lifestyle brought by the project.

A number of decrees issued by the Governor of South Sulawesi and the Regent (*Bupati*) of Luwu outlined the manner in which compensation was to be determined.[1] The land was to be measured in the presence of the landowner, representatives of village elders, a member of the (village) Compensation Committee, and a representative of Inco. A Committee for the Evaluation of Land Compensation (*Panitia Penaksir Harga Ganti Rugi*), comprising representatives of both Regency and Provincial Governments, was to oversee the process.

The District Chief (*Camat*) urged the Soroakans to form a committee to represent their interests in the negotiations with Inco. The Village Headman called a meeting of village leaders (*pemuka rakyat*), who nominated a five-member Compensation Committee (*Panitia Ganti Rugi*), all of whom were members of the traditional elite.

Inco engineers carried out the land survey in the presence of these witnesses. The accuracy of this survey has never been questioned, except in relation to the classification of some of the land. In particular, some land already affected by road construction was listed as dry fields, hence liable for a lower rate of compensation. The Soroakans claimed that such land should be paid for at the rate established for wet rice fields.

Negotiations over the amount to be paid took place in Palopo (the Regency capital), in May 1974. The members of the village Compensation Committee went to Palopo for the meeting, but their expectation that they would be party to the negotiations was soon dashed. They were neither called into the meeting, which took place between representatives of Inco and the Regency, nor were they notified of the outcome of the negotiations before returning to Soroako.

An expatriate manager who represented Inco at the negotiations gave me the following account of the meeting. He and an Indonesian employee went to Palopo with a bargaining position of US$80,000 for the land. This amount had been calculated from the price paid for land already appropriated at Lampea, near Malili. The government asked for an amount equivalent to US$120,000, calculated on the basis of land prices then current in south Sulawesi. (The price was determined in relation to the class of land, and it was considered there were no first-class paddy fields in Soroako.)

Inco's representatives expected the government to ask more; they had anticipated a tougher battle. Nevertheless, they negotiated for the lower price. The government replied that it could not agree because the price was based on established land prices. To break the deadlock, a smaller committee was formed, and a compromise of US$100,000 was reached. When the decision was announced to the Regent, he said, 'Make it a little more.' They negotiated again, but the figure remained US$100,000. I asked if, during negotiations, any consideration was given to compensation for lost livelihood. He replied that it had been seen only as a land sale.

The Indonesian who accompanied the above-mentioned manager to Palopo gave a different version of events:

> The government has a standard price for land in each
> classification: dry land, grazing land, and so on. The price per
> square metre was set by the People's Assembly [DPRD] in
> Palopo. They made a decision about the price and the Regent
> issued a decree. Inco didn't negotiate the price with anyone.
> On the basis of our Contract of Work, if we need land, we
> first ask the government and they arrange it. We just wait for
> the decision.

The Inco representative said the government was concerned that, if the mining company paid above market prices, it would have a bad effect on land prices in other parts of Luwu Regency. Thus, they assumed a stance of inhibiting the market in land, to the benefit of capital. Forced sales of land at cheap prices for large-scale development projects have been a feature of the Indonesian Government's development strategy since 1967 (Lubis and Abdullah 1981, pp.21–22).

The Soroakans were not happy to hear the report of the committee members, returned from Palopo. One man commented:

> We never thought that we wouldn't get to talk to Inco; we at
> least thought the Compensation Committee would negotiate
> with them. We didn't have a dialogue.

The indigenous Soroakans first heard the result of negotiations a few months later. They were all called to the mosque by district government officials, who had been instructed to distribute the money Inco had already paid the government.

The Regent's decree of 29 May 1974,[2] listed the total amount due to each individual. The villagers were told neither the basic price per unit for land or per unit for crops, nor the constituent figures for the different types of land and crop of each individual. They were amazed and suspicious. In their view, there were inexplicable discrepancies. Some holders of large estates received less than others who they knew held very small amounts of land. The suspicion that they would be cheated was confirmed. Also, they were disappointed at the small amount of money they were to receive.

They did not make the judgment in terms of comparative land prices, but rather in terms of what they could do with the money. For most it was not enough to establish an alternative source of livelihood, for example, building a house to rent, or opening a small business. They had hoped to fare better from the project.

After the meeting, they were called in one by one to receive the money, and most refused to take it. There was a spontaneous move to present a united front against what was seen as an attempt to cheat them. In the following year, the District Chief made repeated efforts to force them to take the money, with police and army in attendance.

The Soroakan resistance derived from their suspicions with respect to the calculation of the final price, the obvious mistakes on the list, and the inadequate amount of money being offered. In the meantime, the Regent instructed the district government to investigate and rectify any errors in the original list. A revised version was issued in 1975.[3]

Some landholders bowed to the pressure of being called individually to confront the Dictrict Chief, flanked by army and police, and took the money. Most continued to resist. People told the story of an old man who knelt before them, bared his throat, and drew his hand across it, saying 'Better you kill me than take my land, for what other livelihood do I have?' The District Chief asked him, 'Would you rather go to gaol than take the money?' He answered, 'Yes, I'd rather go to gaol.' When others related this encounter, they said he had brought tears to the eyes of the officials. After this event, they made no further attempts to force the landholders to take the money.

The government tried another strategy. They decided that the resistance derived from undue influence by village leaders, and so the members of the village Compensation Committee were called to Palopo, where they were detained (*ditahan*) for four days. Meanwhile, a final attempt was made to force them to accept the money, assuming that without leaders the resistance would collapse. On the whole the resistance continued. Some of the committee members, however, were forced to take the money. One of them in particular was broken and dispirited by these events. In 1978 he told me:

> For three years I haven't made any money. Before that I was really conscientious in making money—but because of the land business I just didn't care. I just spent it. First I made an *empang* (fish pond), and then I thought but this is still being developed. So then I thought I'll build that big house, then all I have to do is sit and receive the money. At the end of the month I'll just go and collect it. But I still wasn't satisfied. So now I'm establishing a clove farm. It's only in the last three months that I have actively begun to make money again [i.e., through trading in rattan, and selling sawn timber].

In June 1975, Inco received a complaint from the Soroakans that they had not received the money. When they found it was a consequence of the villagers' refusal to accept it, they declared it was the government's problem, not theirs. At that stage Inco estimated that about 10 percent of the landholders had accepted the money. According to one of the Soroakans, this comprised the 'old and weak.' (By late 1978, about 25 percent had received the money.)

The Soroakans felt there was no point in further representations to the government. The village Compensation Committee sought the aid of two indigenous Soroakan men—both of them also descendants of Tosalili, and close kinsmen of the committee members—who had become high-ranking civil servants, in Jakarta and Ujung Pandang, respectively.

Following their advice, some of the landholders authorized a lawyer to act on their behalf in renegotiating the land compensation. He would receive 20 percent of any additional money obtained. The lawyer made representations to the Governor of the Province, the matter having been dealt with at Regency level up to that time.

The Governor proved sympathetic and issued a decree, in January 1977, ordering an increase in the amount to be paid.[4] The decree stated that, although the price for the land had been fair in 1972, the matter had dragged on for so long that the value had been eroded, in part as a consequence of the soaring cost of living and price of land in Soroako. He urged that the matter not be allowed to drag on endlessly. Inco was ordered to pay what amounted to a doubling of the amount of compensation paid for land. The amount paid in compensation for crops was not affected.

Inco management were adamant that they not be seen to be giving in to pressure, so the original payment was termed *ganti rugi* (compensation) while the additional payment was termed *kompensasi* (compensation), even though it was identical to the amount of *ganti rugi* paid for the land. The two payments were to be made simultaneously.

Inco paid an additional US$80,000 (Rp.33,363,000) to be the Provincial Government on 29 November 1977, the original sum still being held by the Regency Government in Palopo. A letter of agreement between the company and the Provincial Government stated that the money was given in recognition of their readiness to surrender the land required to Inco and to 'help increase their prosperity and further their development' (my translation).[5] The letter stressed that the payment should not be seen as an increase in the price paid for the land, although this, of course, was how the Soroakan people interpreted it.

The January 1977 decree also ordered the Committee for the Relinquishing of Land (*Panitia Pembebasan Tanah*), which included a Provincial Government representative, to make another inventory, in order to eradicate remaining errors. Inco, rather than the district government, was directed to make the payment, with the latter supervising. The Soroakans interpreted this to mean that the company had to pay them directly.

Inco regarded this as the final word on the land problem. At the same time, the Provincial Government undertook to arrange as soon as possible the legal documentation for the land being used by Inco. From the company's point of view, any further difficulties would be for the government to resolve.

However, the lawyer representing the Soroakans was not satisfied. He was still preparing his case and felt that the Governor had been too hasty in issuing the decree. After further negotiation, the government agreed in addition to give the people land in the vicinity of Soroako. Landholders would receive 50 percent of the amount they had lost, with the proviso that no individual could receive more than 2 hectares, the limit set by national Land Reform legislation. The government again promised to rectify errors in the list of landholders. They resolved to settle the matter within six months, and the lawyer undertook on behalf of his clients to relinquish all rights to the land once all of the money was paid.

The people still did not receive the money, although Inco had made the second payment (*kompensasi*) to the government. A team was sent by the Governor, in September and October 1978, to correct remaining errors. They worked with village officials to check the list against the original map. Village leaders said that their lawyer would not finalise the case until he was satisfied that all errors on the list of landholders were rectified.

By January 1981, the landowners had still not received the money. The lawyer (who represented fifty-six of them) had received some money from the Provincial Government, the portion of the second payment due his clients. In August 1980 he had written to the Governor, asking him to intercede again. He said that the main obstacle to finalising the matter was the Regency Government. They were 'evading the law' by keeping the money, which should have been handed over to the Governor, to give to the people or their representative. He also claimed that there was still a short-fall in the money paid over by Inco, as a consequence of the errors discovered by the investigating team in 1978.[6] He was waiting until he had retrieved all the money due his clients before passing it on to them. A company representative informed me, in 1981, that Inco considered the matter final, and would pay no more. I don't know if the government had approached them to pay the necessary amount to meet the short-fall, which arose from the clerical errors on the list of owners, discovered by the investigating team the Governor sent in 1978.

The recovery of money paid to the Regency presented a problem. When the former Regent left his post in 1979, there were rumours that his successor refused to take up office until financial irregularities were rectified. The Regent had tried to manage the meagre finances of his vast region by circulating funds intended for one purpose in another area. It seems probable that some of the compensation money may have been dissipated in this fashion, and if so, the chances of recovering it seemed slender.

Some money had been paid to people other than the rightful recipients. In the initial stages of the conflict, Regency officials were more concerned to get rid of the troublesome money than to establish the legitimacy of the claimants' rights. By 1980, many of these wrong payments had been rectified. Moral pressure was put on miscreants by other villagers, so that most was paid back to the rightful owners. However, in the lawyer's letter quoted above, he claimed this was still occurring.

The compensation dispute had dragged on for so long, people were resigned to the probability that no more money (other than that already paid to the lawyer) would be received. However, they also felt bitter. One man said:

> We've suffered a loss (*rugi*) for quite a few years; we haven't worked the land, and we haven't received our money.

If the money is eventually received, it will be of such diminished value that the people will not be able to use it to improve their livelihood.

As one person commented:

> Some people would like to buy rice land in another area, to make up for what they've lost, but the money won't be enough for that.

By January 1981, the only people who had benefited were the 25 percent who had accepted the money in defiance of the stand taken by the rest of the community and who used it towards establishing alternative sources of livelihood during the construction phase, opening small stores, enlarging their houses, renting space to tenants, and so on.

According to a member of the Compensation Committee:

> I haven't yet received my money. I refused to take it, because the price didn't suit. I didn't want to give up my land, but I had no choice. Now I have no livelihood. I haven't got anything, as I am too old to work for Inco. But if I still had my paddy fields, that would be my work. Because the price was too low, we reported it to (a relative in Jakarta). If the price is too low, better they just take the land, because what

can we do with so little money? If the price had been fair, we would have bought houses to rent, and so on.

The failure to provide compensation for lost livelihood was consistent with the government's development strategy. It was assumed that investment-led growth would lead to development, which would benefit all the people. The concern with growth, rather than equity, leads to a failure to consider attendant negative consequences of growth, and thus a failure to take action to mitigate potential problems.

It is impossible not to make a comparison with the situation at the Bougainville Copper Mine, Papua New Guinea, where the local people were compensated not only for cultivated land and crops, but also for uncultivated land over which they had customary rights, for loss of fish and clean water due to mining pollution, as well as hardship caused by relocation and adjustment to a new and alien way of life. The Bougainvilleans also negotiated the payment of a share of the royalties accruing from the project (Bedford and Mamak 1977).

There have been similar problems with the agreement to provide alternative land. The government designated land near Wawandula, which was suitable for paddy fields. In late 1980, the Soroakan Village Government organised collective labour (*gotong royong*) in order to dig irrigation channels to the designated land. However, by the beginning of the planting season, December, this had still not received proper documentation of ownership and they did not proceed with planting. It was rumoured that the legal procedures were held up because other people claimed ownership of the land. By 1980, work opportunities with Inco were limited, so the need for agricultural land was pressing. Some people had begun cultivating paddy fields at Seluro, a former dry field site. This was made possible through the loan of a tractor by a doctor in the townsite, which enabled the farmers to clear the dense growth of imperata grass.

People constantly complained about the poor treatment they had received in the land compensation. In a typical conversation a man complained bitterly to me about the manner in which the land was appropriated. He did not question the company's need for the land, but he was bitter at the small amount of money offered, and that it had not yet been paid. 'The government said the land was worthless. In fact it was good land.' They had wanted Rp.100 per square metre for irrigated land, but the government established a price of Rp.15 per metre for the best land. As he saw it, the government, not the company, had let them down.

The Soroakans had limited avenues for ensuring recognition of their rights, or even of putting their point of view to the relevant authorities. The government has taken the role of facilitating the development of the mining project, which has meant favouring the interests of the foreign corporation against those of its own citizens. They recognised the role of the Indonesian Government, in particular the Regency level officials, in facilitating their dispossession. A member of the village Compensation Committee said to me:

> Where can we turn? We go to the company, and they say it's the government's problem. But what help is the government? It was they who established the low price in the first place.

The villagers had few avenues for articulating grievances. Their own legitimate representatives (the village leaders in their capacity as members of the Compensation Committee) were detained by the Provincial Government at the first sign of resistance. One man commented to me that they were frightened to take the protest too far, lest they be labelled Communists. The repressive nature of the state well served the interests of capital.

The Soroakans were fortunate in having connections with more sophisticated people in the city, who introduced them to the idea of engaging a lawyer to fight the compensation case, through the agency of the Legal Aid Institute lawyer. This did achieve some limited gains for them. Any receipt of money by people not represented by the lawyer seems particularly unlikely, however.

Many Soroakans commented that Inco and the government were fortunate that they were such a compliant people. At a meeting with Inco representatives, a village leader commented, 'If this were a Bugis area, people would have drawn swords (*parang*) by now.' Another woman commented that Torajans also would have taken violent action if they had been so provoked. She said the Soroakans were strong in their religious faith and concerned for the consequences of their actions in the afterlife. Whether these stereotypes of other people were true or not, it is clear that they saw their own response to the encroachment on their rights as moderate.

Their response to the land alienation can be seen as an attempt to fight a form of class opression, the alienation of the basic resource necessary for agriculture. The process of alienation had relegated them to the industrial reserve army for capital. The dispute indicates their difficulties in gaining recognition of their interests versus those of the company: even when decisions favouring the Soroakans were taken by the government, there was apparently little will to implement them.

The amount of money Inco paid out in land compensation was minute in comparison to the amount spent to establish the project: it was only slightly more than the rumoured cost of one B house. It is interesting to speculate how differently the indigenous Soroakans would have fared if the compensation had been more, and paid swiftly, or indeed, if Inco had left the agricultural land intact, building the townsite on the Wawandula plain.

Redevelopment of the Village

The bitterest disputes during my field work arose in connection with the plan to reorganise Soroako village. The implementation of this scheme highlighted the confusion of government authority and company power in Soroako, and it precipitated many conflicts in the community.

By 1975 it was clear that some action was necessary to recitify the negative aspects of the development of Soroako village. The overcrowding from the thousands of immigrants who had poured in had created a hazardous environment. Along with the water problems already discussed, the overcrowding in substandard dwellings produced both a health risk and high fire danger. The rapid increase in population had so overloaded the resources of the village government that it was no longer effective. Early immigrants had settled in areas designated by the Village Headman, but the subsequent flood of people settled whereever they liked.

Anticipating that the problem would worsen in 1975 and 1976, when construction would be at its peak and Inco was simultaneously recruiting its operational workforce, Inco requested that the Provincial Government rectify the situation. In June 1975, the Province sent in a team to oversee the development of another population centre in the area, principally to house immigrants, and to redevelop Soroako for the benefit of the indigenous inhabitants. Wawandula was the obvious choice, because of its proximity to the plant site: it was situated on a vast plain, but had a very small indigenous population. The District capital, Wasuponda, was also subject to a redevelopment plan.

The plan for Soroako divided the village into uniform-sized house lots (15 by 20 metres) along wide streets built on a grid system. The lots were to be allocated to indigenous Soroakans only, except for a few set aside for commercial ventures. Even the existing permanent dwellings in Old Village were to be reordered in accord with the plan. Immigrants were to be encouraged to leave their makeshift dwellings and move to one of the new centres, where land was to be allocated free of charge. Company employees were eligible for interest-free loans from Inco to build permanent dwellings. However, only indigenous Soroakans were eligible for loans to build in Soroako Village.

The Town Planner sent by the Provincial Government told me that Soroako had been chosen by the Governor for development as a 'model village' because of Inco's presence: it was unacceptable to have the modern town and the untidy village side by side. He did not mention the company's crucial role in urging the government to take action, though Inco officials were quite explicit about this. The company managers held the view that the company should not become the alternative government in the region, thus they were keen for government participation in the matter. At the time, the company was prepared to provide personnel and funding to implement the plans.

The Town Planner came to Soroako in April 1976. He saw his first task as relocating the immigrants and therefore began with planning and surveying the new population centres. From April until June he surveyed the three villages, locating roads and the distribution of housing lots. The number of lots in Soroako was arrived at by dividing the available land by the area of one lot. House sites in Wawandula were much bigger.

The Planner explained his philosophy of planning to me. After surveying, it was necessary to construct the roads and move the houses into line. The roads had to be established first, because he had seen many houses in Ujung Pandang cut in half by road widening. The construction of roads had to be done with an eye to the future. The roads in Soroako were narrower than in Wawandula, because it was a smaller area. However, he thought it necessary to widen the roads in Soroako in spite of the problems this created in moving existing houses. The roads were to widened enough to take two lanes of traffic, in spite of the small number of vehicles using them. He said that, only after the restructuring of the physical layout of Soroako, would he carry out the final stage of his plan, 'the social part,' the development of facilities such as markets and schools. It is significant that he gave social questions the lowest priority. As we shall see, the problems in the implementation of the very necessary plan to clean up the village derived from this ignoring of the social and political problems.

Construction of roads began in Soroako in early 1977. When I spoke to the Planner in November 1977, he considered this task was well under way, so he was preparing to move houses to their new locations. However, in the course of road construction, many houses had already been moved. Inco provided the labour and heavy equipment to build the roads, which were initially graded but not gravelled. The widened roads were dusty in the dry season, and they turned into quagmires with the rain. One of the arguments for increasing the number of roads was to improve access for emergency services. During the wet season, I often saw an ambulance stopped on the road, not able to reach the house of the patient. The medical staff had to complete their journey on foot, walking through ankle-deep mud.

The Town Planner prepared a list of indigenous Soroakans who were eligible for house sites. He would admit this as a temporary list only, because, by November 1977, problems had arisen in implementing the plan, particularly in allocating house lots. The main problem was getting rid of the excess population, this being the principal reason for the plan. In August 1976, the Planner had ordered the immigrants to move, under threat of having their houses demolished. This threat was repeated in December 1976, and again in April 1977. Only a few people moved, in spite of government threats and company inducements in the form of interest-free housing loans and the provision of a truck for the move. People were reluctant to move to the new towns, which were further away from the work place and had fewer such facilities as markets.

In August 1977, the district government, aided by Inco, took decisive action. A letter was sent to the occupants of all illegal dwellings giving them an ultimatum to move. They took it no more seriously than the previous threats. However, this time things were different. The government sent in company bulldozers to demolish several areas of substandard dwellings. This sent a shock wave through the village. Householders returned from work to find their homes had been razed. Stories abounded of distressed people who had fled their homes clutching their few possessions, and of the bold few who angrily confronted the bulldozers brandishing knives. This decisive action convinced many immigrants that the government finally meant business, and many moved to the new centres. The government and the company had acted in concert to put the plan into effect. The use of company machines and personnel added to the confusion in people's minds concerning who had ultimate authority in the area—the government or the company.

Disputes about Land

The exodus of the immigrants created a stock of house lots that were supposed to be reallocated to those indigenous Soroakans whose names were on the Planner's list. It soon became apparent that this would not take place. Immigrants began building on the land. Some of these people were apparently taking the law into their own hands, but others had the tacit approval of village and district government officials.

The District Chief had been keen to impress on me that it was necessary to allocate some of the lots to non-Soroakans, for commercial use. He said one of these lots would be used for a store, which would bring goods direct from Ujung Pandang, cutting out many of the middlemen and so reducing prices. By the end of August, a building was under construction on a prime commercial site on the corner opposite the market. Soroako was buzzing with rumours that the owners were relatives of the District Chief. They were, in fact, close associates of his wife, from the same region and involved in the same church. The builder was her cousin. This apparent abuse of authority by the official, to further the interests of his associates, caused much anger and bitterness. I asked the family who owned the building how they had acquired the land, and they replied with apparent embarrassment, 'A gift from the government.' This was the business enterprise the District Chief had spoken of, but when the store opened, its goods were not cheaper than the other stores in Soroako.

This early scandal was a sign of things to come. The process of reorganising the village became, on the whole, a saga of disputed land ownership. There was growing bitterness among the indigenous Soroakans that they were losing ground to the newcomers. Many said, 'We have become stepchildren in our land.' The principal area of dispute was the land in New Village that had been vacated by the immigrants. The District Chief claimed that this land had formerly been unoccupied (*tanah liar*) and consequently the government could assume ownership. The Soroakans, on the contrary, claimed that much of this land was owned, the rights deriving from use for cultivation or pasturage by their forebears. In addition to disputing the ownership of some of the land, the Soroakans were angry at the manner in which the government was reallocating the 'unowned land.' The following examples illustrate the nature of the many multifaceted conflicts that occurred.

First Dispute. An immigrant woman received an order to demolish her shop-house in New Village. She had built on the land with the consent of a Soroakan woman who claimed to own the land because her father had used it as a horse paddock. The two women had been planning to build jointly on the site, which the Town Planner had listed in the name of Soroakan woman's younger brother. The women responded to the district government that there was no need to demolish until the new building was ready to go ahead. However, the district government insisted on demolition. None of the surrounding buildings were demolished.

In mid-November, the Soroakan woman heard that someone had applied to the village government to build on the site. The permission was refused but, as her informant commented, 'People are refused permission in the day and put up a house at night.' The woman went to the District Chief, asking for assurance that no one would build on the land. Meanwhile, someone began building on the site, so she then obtained a demolition order from the District Chief against the new construction. However, the opponent was a niece of the District Chief's wife (herself a district official), who was reported to have sympathetically intervened for her niece, saying the 'poor thing' had sold all her land in Toraja in order to go into business, and she should be allowed to proceed. She commented at a later stage of this dispute, 'What's does it matter which of them builds a house?', a view in direct opposition to the provincial government's ruling on the allocation of housing land in Soroako. She was later heard to threaten that if her husband proceeded with the demolition order, 'Just see what I'll do.' The Soroakan woman told me she'd commented to the District Chief, 'What we have now is a *sistem famili* ' (i.e., people obtaining land through their connections to people in power), to which he replied indignantly that what she was alleging could not be true, because if it were he would have to leave his wife.

The District Chief verbally supported the Soroakan woman's claim to the land, but he took no action to protect those rights. He promised to come to Soroako to invervene, but he failed to appear. By early December he still had not come. He was sighted at the company offices nearby, and people commented that he was not bold enough to come and face up to the problem of solving this and a number of other disputes. In this atmosphere of contradictory orders from the District Chief and his wife and the lack of decisive action, the immigrant decided to 'tough it out,' saying she would demolish her house only when the other illegal structures were demolished. Her attitude paid off, and her house remained. The compromise offered the Soroakan woman was a piece of land owned by another indigenous Soroakan (whose rights the government was refusing to recognise).

Second dispute.   A food stall owned by an immigrant stood in the way of a proposed road. It was moved onto a desirable corner block, next to the village government office, as a temporary measure. This land belonged to the son of the former missionary school teacher then living in the townsite, who had planned to build there. One of the indigenous Soroakans took up his case with the Town Planner, asking how long the stall would occupy the land. His plan had it divided into four house sites. All the indigenous Soroakans regarded the land as belonging to the estate of the former teacher. However, the Planner said, in the course of this discussion, 'But he can't take all of it.' He said the man could take only one of the four sites. This expression of opinion conflicted with the Planner's insistence at other times that he had no say in the allocation of land; he just measured. On hearing of this conversation, the owner began fencing the land, and the Planner commented: 'Let him finish the fence, and then I'll knock it down.'

The deceased teacher's son sought official permission to build on the land, but the District Chief refused to sign the building permit. The landowner and his wife had an association with the District Chief through the church, and were very upset that he failed to support them.

Third Dispute.   The Planner ran into problems when he tried to construct a vegetable market on land owned by a Soroakan. He chose the site of a former fish pond (*empang*) built by the landowner's father. The land had been surveyed, and the Planner was ready to commence construction, when the owner told him that he would knock any construction down. The owner sought the intercession of the brother in Jakarta, who spoke with the Planner. The Planner claimed that the acting Village Headman had told him there were no problems with the land. The Headman had never asked anyone in Soroako, this being in keeping with his style of government. The owners validated their claim on the land by saying they had collected rent from the immigrants who had built on the land before it was bulldozed. The market was never built.

Disputes over ownership arose not only over housing land. The Planner and local government officials failed to recognise claims on land needed for roads. For example, my household was disturbed one day by the young boy of the house shouting, 'Grandma, come quickly. The bulldozers are knocking down your banana trees.' Most unused land with the overcrowded village was squatted on by immigrants, or rented out by the indigenous owners to supplement household income. This household was fortunate in that they still had some land planted in fruit trees and vegetables—the land now being bulldozed. The old lady became very angry and distressed. She shouted at the driver in Bahasa Soroako, as she did not speak Indonesian. He did not understand her words but the meaning was clear. The driver said to others in the family: 'I'm only doing my job, obeying orders.' She replied, 'Why didn't you ask us before, so we could at least collect the leaves and fruit?' The land was being prepared for a road, and the acting Headman justified his peremptory action by saying that he only had the use of the bulldozers for one day and was anxious to complete as much as possible. The old woman raced about collecting her fruit, meanwhile watching that the driver took no more trees than necessary. Her daughter was anxious lest the old woman be hurt, but she cried out, 'What does it matter if I die? My husband is already dead.' The nervous driver exercised greater care than usual, limiting destruction to 26 trees out of about 200. Another old lady whose house-yard garden was being destroyed under the Planner's supervision was reputed to have run out carrying a knife shouting, 'I'd rather you kill me than destroy my livelihood.' Apparently this display caused him to go away.

Such peremptory destruction of property was not uncommon, and because of careless work it was often greater than necessitated by the plan. On one occasion, Inco employees digging drains knocked down a newly completed fence. The owner had offered to remove the fence before work commenced, but had been assured this was not necessary. A little more planning and more careful use of equipment could have minimised such destruction.

Whether or not consideration was given to people's rights seemed to depend on the person giving the orders. The acting Village Headman was very authoritarian in his commands. There was a second occasion when the old lady's banana garden was threatened. An employee of Inco Town Administration planned to dig a drain through the rest of the garden to prevent a recurrence of flooding. The acting Village Headman told him to go ahead, but he said, 'I could see that someone owned the land, so I thought I had better ask permission first.' The old lady refused permission for more of her land to be taken (she was planning to build there) and a compromise was reached. A new road was transformed into a stormwater drain. The man responsible, an Inco foreman, had displayed a greater sensitivity to people's rights and a more conciliatory approach than the majority of government officials and company personnel involved in the redevelopment.

Denial of Customary Land Rights

The District Chief and the acting Village Headman (appointed from the District Government office) constantly attempted to deny the local people's customary rights in land, whether these rights derived from former or current use. People were ordered to move their houses to make way for roads, and in some cases, homes for other people. The District Chief refused to recognise the claims by Soroakans to rights in certain land in New Village, claiming this had all been unoccupied land. He refused to sign the documents people needed to transform their customary rights in land into rights under the modern law. He justified this by arguing that he was the most knowledgeable person with respect to customary law (*ketua adat*) in the district. (His claim was based on his membership in the Padue group, a separate and distinct local group who had been subordinate to the Makole Matano in former times.) In one case when a man attempting to have his customary rights translated into rights under modern law said to the District Chief, 'I can prove it's my land by a mark on the boundary.' The official replied, 'That's a new boundary.' thereby implying that he had never owned the land, that he was making it up. There was no dispute among the Soroakans about his rights to that land; it had been cultivated by his grandfather. The man had spent a number of years in Jakarta and was not easily deterred from seeking his rights. When he threatened to take the case further with the help of relatives in Ujung Pandang, the official relented.

In an interview with the District Chief in 1979, I attempted to clarify the situation with respect to the Soroakan rights under Indonesian Land Laws, for he was still refusing to sign the relevant papers. He said, in a pained fashion; 'Yes, they do have rights to the land, but if I recognised those rights, how would we implement the plan?' Like the Planner, an official of the higher level Provincial Government, he ignored these customery rights.

Illegal Building

Compared with the immigrants, the indigenous Soroakans were slow to take unilateral action to occupy house lots. They waited for government permission.

Throughout 1978, new houses were constantly being constructed, especially in New Village, almost all by immigrants. By the end of that year, only 22 of the more than 200 houses in New Village belonged to indigenous Soroakans. They resented the government's failure to act in their interests or to protect their rights. The Soroakans often commented on the greater willingness of the immigrants to act in defiance of government orders. 'It's a *sistem berani*' (system of boldness), one of the commented. 'Whoever is bold enough to just take action and put up a house wins here.' However, not all the immigrants acted without permission. Many of the immigrants received approval from someone in local government, either because of personal connections, as in the case described above, or else through the payment of bribes. If it was not a *'sistem berani,'* it was a *'sistem famili'* (family system) or a *'sistem amplop'* (envelope system), a rather picturesque way of describing the way one discretely handed over a bribe.

The government was seen as favouring the immigrants, the well-connected, and the rich. As one woman said, 'The people have no right to decide where to move anymore. Only the government has the right.' As the pressure for land grew and the likelihood of Soroakans obtaining any land decreased, another woman commented: 'The Soroakan people will be thrown away into the lake. There is nowhere else for us to go.' People expressed anxiety about the future of their children. Where would they be able to build? Many joked about extending their houses upwards; there was nowhere else to go.

The Soroakans constantly referred to the stipulation in the plan that only indigenous Soroakans could build in the village. This reinforced the idea of autonomous Soroakan community with sharply defined boundaries, since the implementation of the plan as it was set out would have brought advantages to the indigenous community. It was in their interest to support such a notion of local group membership. However, the Soroakans also expressed concern about the unfairness of the plan with respect to those immigrants who had been in the village a long time and who had acted properly by getting local government permission to build. They were especially resentful that the people who benefited from corrupt practices (the *sistem famili* and the *sistem amplop*) were new immigrants.

The boldness of the immigrants in taking unilateral action to build derived in part from the failure of government officials to act in such cases. The legitimacy of the government was weakened by the obvious venality of district officials. One immigrant commented, 'If the District Chief's family can build, so can I.' Some immigrants would respect claims of an indigenous Soroakan to land, but ignore the orders of the government. As one put it, 'If the government comes and tells me I can't build, I don't listen, but if an indigenous Soroakan says someone owns the land, that is different.' Another immigrant said that he thought it was all right to build on government-owned land without permission, though he would not do so on land owned by a Soroakan. He justified his illegal construction of a house, saying that he was contributing to development (*pembangunan*), so how could the government object? The District Chief wanted Inco to deal with those who had illegally built houses, arguing that they had the responsibility, as most of the culprits were project employees. The company did not agree with him, arguing that they had taken the step of refusing to give housing loans for construction in Soroako, unless the employee had an official letter certifying his entitlement to a housing lot. Such letters were provided to immigrants by corrupt officials. The District Chief's attitude illustrated confusion about company and government roles. After all, the company had participated in bulldozing slum dwellings.

In only two cases did the District Government match the toughness it had displayed in getting the development under way by taking firm action against illegal constructions. It was not clear why they chose to act in these instances—whether the builders were particularly brazen in flouting government authority, or if they were concerned that the redevelopment plan was stymied by the lack of available land. In April 1978, the District Chief supervised the demolition of the framework of two illegal dwellings that had been erected on land set aside for homes of indigenous Soroakans, homes that were occupying land intended for some other purpose. In one case, the immigrant accepted his bad luck. In the other, the Soroakan house subsequently moved onto the site was vandalised. This was a tragedy for the owner, a relatively poor person with no regular source of income. The perpetrator of the crime was never apprehended. The house was only two doors from the house of a government official. It was odd that he did not hear the destruction taking place. Village gossip had it that in his capacity as a builder he had supplied the wood and the tradesmen for the illegal house, and it was assumed he had given tacit approval for its construction. Whether true or not, the fact that the villagers believed it shows their distrust of those in authority.

Changing Values Concerning Land Ownership

In the past, nonirrigated land in this remote and sparsely populated community had no monetary value (see chap.5). This changed after the development of the nickel project, especially when the redevelopment programme began. Land in the village became a scarce commodity, and in this monetised economy the cost to rent or buy land soared. Until 1977, most landowners had only rented land, but in that year people began responding to offers from out-siders to sell land at high prices. The first person to do so sold land to a Chinese trader. It was a large plot that did not correspond to a house site on the plan. The District Chief refused to legalise the sale. The trader wanted to buy an adjoining piece of land. The owner's wife said to me, 'If it was a Soroakan, we'd just give it away, but when we heard it was a Chinese, my husband said, "The Chinese never want to give anything to us; they just want to take from us." So we decided to sell.' Subsequently there were a number of land sales (none of them legalised), the price escalating with each one. This led to a rise in land rents, too. Many Soroakans, tiring of the wait for the government to allocate them a housing lot, had built homes on rented land, and the rise in rents was an extra frustration.

As a consequence of the sales of unoccupied land, people in the village began making demands for payment for use of occupied land. Many indigenous Soroakans had built homes on farmland. In accord-ance with customary law, they had received permission from the cultivators. The descendants of those former cultivators began demanding payment for the land at current prices, even though the land had been continuously occupied since long before the project. At first, this was a controversial matter, with some people refusing to take such action over land to which they could claim rights. For in-stance, one woman said she had discussed with her younger brother the possibility of asking for payment from someone who had built on their father's land. Her brother had replied, 'He's poor. What would we want to do that for?' However, by 1980, as the infusion of capitalist rationality proceeded apace, this kind of action was taken for granted. The couple cited above, who said they would sell to the Chinese but give to the Soroakans, were collecting money from the Soroakans who had long ago built on their land. This caused bit-terness for those who had to find money to pay for land that they had come to regard as their own.

All this was precipitated by the shortage of land, caused by the delimiting of the village boundaries by the land alienation, and ex-acerbated by the failure of local government to protect the interests of the indigenous Soroakans by ensuring enough house sites for them. The Soroakan Village Headman told me that the problem was that the government had given away any unowned land in New Village to immigrants, and the only land left already belonged to people. The landowners did not want their land given away to anyone, whether they were immigrants or Soroakans. The District Chief tried to prevent the sale of land by refusing to recognise the sales, by not signing the appropriate forms. This caused resentment. One landowner said, 'We live in a democracy. They can't tell me not to sell my land to an immigrant.' They did not object to immigrants buying land, but resented their being given land by the government.

Those most disadvantaged by this situation were the poor and powerless. The wealthy elite, who owned a lot of land, were struggling with the District Chief to have their rights formalised, but in the meantime the land sales were going ahead, with people just not bothering about the papers that would properly legitimate the sales. Meanwhile, the poor and powerless lost any chance to obtain land for housing.

CONFLICTS WITH LOCAL GOVERNMENT

Conflicts of Authority

The implementation of the redevelopment plan depended on the labour of village residents working in mutual cooperation (*gotong royong*) every Sunday (the workers' day off). They moved houses, dug drains, built roads and bridges, and collected rubbish. In 1977–78 the commonest activity was moving houses. Many were moved only a few feet, to make way for widened or new roads. Many houses were moved to new sites, to fit with the plan, or because someone claimed ownership of the land. The houses were moved by attaching a timber frame to the support posts; then a host of men would lift it on their shoulders and carry it to the new site.

When the acting Headman arrived in 1977, there had been *gotong royong* every Sunday for some time. Initially, the indigenous Soroakan men responded with enthusiasm to the regular Sunday calls. They felt it was the right thing to participate in *gotong royong* as an expression of the solidarity of the community. Also, they made such work enjoyable with much laughing and joking. When a house was being moved, the householders would provide refreshments.

However, enthusiasm for *gotong royong* waned as time went by. People became dissatisfied with the way the redevelopment was affecting them and also with the style of government of the acting Headman. He ruled in a peremptory manner, which was at odds with the expections of the Soroakans. In particular, he wanted to govern with minimal consultation with respected community leaders.

I witnessed the following interaction at a small ritual feast held by an old woman who had just recovered from an illness. All the male community leaders were present, including the functionaries of the village government. The men began a lively discussion about the practical details of the next day's *gotong royong*. They began speaking in Indonesian, in deference to the presence of outsiders (such as the acting Headman) but soon lapsed into Bahasa Soroako as they easily slipped into a familiar mode of making such plans. The acting Headman grew visibly annoyed and tried to stifle the discussion, saying he would solve the problem and make the decisions. The men ignored him and continued their discussion.

People objected to his behaviour in such incidents as the razing of the banana trees already mentioned, where he would destroy fruit trees or othe crops in the way of houses or roads without asking permission of the owners. One man commented:

> This plan is supposed to be implemented through working together (*kerja sama*) between the government and the Soroakan people, but it's not. The acting Headman just gives orders. According to the plan they should cooperate with local people, but they don't. No compensation is paid. It's difficult in Indonesia. In a foreign country they wouldn't get away with it.

His comment reflected the resentment growing among the indigenous Soroakans. The failure of the government to pay compensation for crops destroyed in the redevelopment was a source of great resentment. If trees were in the way of a road, or any other public facility, no compensation was paid. If a house was moved on the orders of the local government officials, the householder himself/herself had to pay compensation for any fruit trees cleared from the new site.

The resentments were expressed by people failing to turn up in response to the call for *gotong royong*. The exhortations necessary to obtain participants increased. It reached a crisis point in January 1978.

So few people responded to a call to move a house that the task was abandoned. The woman who owned the house was very distressed. She had been ordered to move some months before, but the new site allocated to her was occupied by immigrants. She had to wait until they moved. She had already prepared the new site, after their departure. She went in great distress to the acting Headman and implored him to try again to raise the necessary number of men. The second time was successful, and the house was moved. She told her new neighbour that if she had not wept, her house would not have been moved. The move was very much against her will; her husband had left her and she supported herself by selling from a small shop under her house. Her old house site was on the main road to the market, the new one in a less favourable position. Also, the new site was in New Village, where she did not know people, and she would have to build up a clientele.

This case probably focused opposition to the local government because many people knew she was being moved to make way for a wealthy immigrant trader, who had given the acting Headman a motorcycle. People were very angry about this, but also pleased at such public proof of the venality of this particular official. Because most bribes were discreet payments of money, suspicions were hard to prove. But no one could deny that the acting Headman was riding around on a motorcycle that, a week before, had belonged to the trader to whom he was allocating land.

The implementation of the redevelopment plan increased the confusion in Soroako concerning who was in authority; was it the government or the mining company? In particular, this came about because of the nature of Inco's involvement with the redevelopment plan. They paid the Planner (in addition to his government salary), provided machinery and personnel for slum clearance and road building, and provided the financing for much of the new building through interest-free housing loans. The confusion over authority was shared by the District Chief, for example, in his request to Inco to take action against employees who had constructed illegal dwellings.

The plan provided for a very limited kind of redevelopment. Road building was given priority and no consideration was given to the provision of clean water or proper sanitation. The plan did not even provide for a system of drains (built by the Town Administration as part of the aftermath of a flood).

For the Soroakans, the scramble for land increased the disunity among them by hardening the class division between landowners and nonowners. They also felt great bitterness as a group about the mode of the plan's implementation, especially under the authority of the immigrant acting Headman who did nothing to safeguard their interests. The loss of village land to immigrants increased their sense of dispossession, of becoming like stepchildren of the development occurring in their village.

In the early stages of the redevelopment plan, the company provided heavy equipment to bulldoze the slum dwellings and begin making roads. This involvement was intermittent: work would often be left unfinished (for example, the roads that were graded, but not gravelled). A sever flood, in late 1978, precipitated a renewed high level of activity by the Town Administration in the village. Village residents blamed the flood on the company, calling it a consequence of the excessive runoff from the denuded hills and interference with watercourses. They demanded compensation for property destroyed in the flood. This request was not met, but he company did accept responsibility for cleaning up the village and for constructing an adequate drainage system to cope with future flooding. The Town Administrator, shocked by the squalor of the village, undertook to do additional work, completing the roads, cleaning up garbage, and so on. However, his effort was opposed by other company managers, who did not approve of his spending money to refurbish the village.

This was the pattern in Soroako, with respect to solving the problems of the village grown into a small town. Local government lacked the resources to rectify problems of drainage, garbage collection, and so on. Many of the village's problems stemmed from Inco activities, and the local government lacked the power to confront the company. The company had the resources (and occasionally the will) to solve the problems, but its involvement was a kind of largesse, dispensed in an intermittent fashion. These problems are all well exemplified in dispute about water between village residents and the mining company.

CONFLICT WITH THE COMPANY

Disputes about Water

Clean water and sanitation were constant problems in the daily lives of residents of Soroako village. Disputes over water were one of the biggest sources of tension, especially between indigenous

Soroakans and immigrants. Water pollution was the most dramatic consequence of the mining company's despoiling of the environment.

When the village was still a small agricultural community, there were no problems with clean water, or sanitation. Houses were built in rows parallel to the lake's edge, those fronting on the lake jutting out over the water. Often the slatted bamboo floors of their kitchens overhung the lake, allowing for direct disposal of waste. Others had drains that fed wastes to the lake or a stream. A series of jetties were constructed out from the shore, from which people would wash themselves and their clothes, collect water for household use, and relieve themselves. People would defecate in the irrigation channels for the paddy fields (located just behind the village). Drinking water was obtained by paddling out from the edge of the lake in a small canoe and filling bamboo containers. Many people did not boil drinking water, the vastness and flow of the lake, as well as the sparse population, ensuring its cleanliness.

Inco's decision to house only the upper half of the work force in the townsite, coupled with the land alienation, which squeezed the burgeoning population into a small and delimited area, created overcrowding in the village. The arrangements that had served in the past for disposal of waste and faeces and for obtaining clean water were no longer adequate. The lake's edge, where people bathed, became fouled with human faeces. Because the village had no garbage disposal service, rubbish also ended up in the lake.

The town planning consultants engaged to choose the townsite had advised against the Soroako plain. They predicted the problems of water pollution, both industrial pollution and human waste. However, the problem of pollution from townsite sewerage has mainly affected village residents.

Inco installed a number of expensive sewage treatment plants in the townsite. The outlet from the *F* area came out in the middle of Old Village (map 2.3). It was intended that, after treatment, the outflow from this pipe would be clean water. However, the plant did not work effectively, and the pipe discharged raw sewage into the lake at certain times of the day. A company engineer claimed that the Indonesian population of the *F* area ran too much water into the system. Consequently, the relative volume of solids to liquids did not facilitate the natural decomposition process on which the plant depended.

Mining also led to water pollution. Strip mining in this area of heavy rainfall induced the clayey soil from the hills to wash into the lake when it rained. Streams that once ran clear had become yellow. These streams emptied on to the village shoreline and thus contributed to its pollution. The shore was thick with the silt whipped up by the afternoon winds. This made bathing unpleasant and the effective washing of clothes impossible.

In addition, the lake was fouled by liquid wastes from the plant, discharged through a drain at the boundary of the village. I was told that the wastes comprised mainly soot.

Between 1977 and 1979, regular tests carried out by the Inco hospital showed that, in areas near the village, *E. coli* counts reached acceptable levels only at distances of 25 metres from the shore. Company personnel were discouraged from swimming in certain sections along the lake shore (especially in front of the Old Camp, where a foreigner had contracted meningitis allegedly from swimming in the polluted water).

I could not obtain the precise results of those tests. However, in January 1981, I had samples of water tested at a laboratory in Ujung Pandang. I took them from these places were commonly used for washing clothes and bathing. Results from all three showed *E. coli* counts of more than 2,400 parts per million. The acceptable level for body contact in Australia is 200 parts per million. These high levels were obtained even after a reduction of the pollution from townsite sewage, following improvements in the method of treatment, described below. The levels must have been far higher in the 1970s, from the disposal of raw sewage from the townsite, as well as from the small number of toilets in the village itself.

The villagers believed they suffered seriously from problems of dirty water. They were as much concerned that the silt in the water made it unsuitable for washing and bathing as they were that faeces endangered their health. Although they did not understand the role of germs in causation of disease, they did connect the polluted water with an increase in the incidence of illness, especially stomach diseases and itching after bathing. The villagers unequivocally blamed Inco for the water problems, and they took action to persuade the company to accept responsibility and rectify the situation.

The problem of the village water supply came to the attention of an expatriate Inco employee, a Turkish-Australian Muslim who, by virtue of his religion was close to the villagers, especially the Imam. He arranged a meeting between representatives of Inco and village residents, early in 1977. The company representative accepted responsibility for the water pollution and agreed to truck in chlorinated drinking water in the short term, and in the long term to install forty-two standpipes in the village, which would provide the population with the same chlorinated water as townsite inhabitants. When I arrived in July 1977, five pipes had been installed and this number remained static during my field work. By 1980, the number had been increased to ten, and the village government was still trying to have installed the other thirty-two that had been promised.

Many of the villagers took the water into their homes by a complex arrangement of metal and plastic pipes. People queued often for several hours to affix their hose to the standpipe. They then waited while the pipe was affixed, to ensure that no one pulled out the hose. When water pressure was low, it could take as long as half an hour or more to fill the container in the house. Many people, especially women, would wake in the middle of the night for a turn when the queue was shorter and the pressure better, and then wake a friend or neighbour take her turn. There were frequent fights over access to water as people jumped the queue or pulled out a hose they felt had had a long enough time.

Because of problems in access to the standpipes, many people used the chlorinated water only for drinking and continued to wash clothes and bathe in the lake. The standpipes were so distributed that not all people could affix a hose; others had to carry water in containers. This occurred especially at either end of the village, where there were fewer standpipes and water pressure was lower.

There were changes in household organisation that exacerbated the problem of access to clean water. Fetching water was regarded as children's work, but with children staying longer at school and often attending high school away from the village, their labour was no longer available in the home. This loss was especially felt by women with very young children, who had to find time in the midst of child care to wait by the standpipe to obtain water. Since it was not considered appropriate for young children to be out alone at night, older children or parents had to wait by the standpipe. The problems of clean water were ameliorated a little in 1978 with the provision of the standpipes, as well as by the reduction in village population because of the winding down of the work force and the movement of immigrants to Wawandula and Wasuponda. However, difficulties with water were still a cause of constant complaint and an obvious health problem to the people of Soroako. They had hopes that the original promise would be fulfilled, giving them one standpipe to four dwelling units, the ratio Inco had supplied to Wasuponda and Wawandula. They believed that the company had a moral obligation to carry out its promise.

In July 1978, another meeting was held between the Village Government and company personnel to discuss the health problems of the village. The meeting was arranged by a doctor working for Inco (an Australian) who was constantly striving to extend the involvement of the Inco Medical Services to the health care of nonemployees in the district. Present at the meeting were the Soroakan Village Headman, eight other Village Government officials, and the nurses from the government clinic of First Aid Post (*Balai Pengobatan*) status. Three doctors came from the company hospital: the paediatrician, the community health doctor, and the Australian doctor. Also present was the Health Inspector from the company. I was presented by invitation of the Village Headman.

The village officials hoped that the meeting would give them the opportunity to make reasonable demands concerning matters that greatly troubled them. However, one of the company doctors chaired the meeting (even though it was in the government office), and it soon became obvious that he was intent on deflecting most of the villagers' demands by demonstrating that the problems were of their own making and that they were capable of resolving them by themselves. This was a strategy I saw used with great effectiveness by company officials on a number of occasions. An ideology of self-help was used to argue that it would be detrimental for Inco to assist in any way, even in solving problems Inco had created. The people who put forward such arguments had many aspects of their lives catered for by the company and would have been most indignant if these privileges and services had been withdrawn. It seems it was only the poor who needed to practise self-help.[7]

At the meeting the Village Headman began by identifying water supply and sanitation as the main health problems.

> We don't have enough water outlets, so people fight over them. There are no toilet facilities, so people have to use the lake and this fouls the water. We did not have this problem in the past. The population was small, the lake was clean, and

we had so much land behind the village and all the irrigation channels to use for relieving ourselves.

The company public health doctor turned responsibility for the state of the affairs back on the Village Government, countering their request for standpipes with a question about the number of wells in the village. He suggested that the basic pollution problem was that people used the lake as a toilet, so the problem was theirs to solve. One of the other doctors suggested that the fights over water were a consequence of misuse and poor management (by the officials present), and not a result of absolute shortage.

> Your main hope must be with the wells, and only secondarily with the standpipes. The pipes are for drinking water only, and yet I often see people bathing at them. Why is this so? Can't the village government better police their use?

Again, the problem was thrown back on the Village Government; one of the village officials replied in a voice that thinly concealed his anger.

> We can't bathe in the lake any more because the faeces from the townsite are dumped through this pipe which outlets to the lake in the middle of the village, and because of the mud in the lake after rain. Even the wells get dirty after floods.

The paediatrician was surprised at the man's comment and thanked him, saying he had not understood those problems.

Many of the new areas of the village were built on former rice fields where the ground was swampy and unsuitable for wells, the water being brackish. Other areas on the lake shore were sandy and not suitable for wells, so it was not realistic to insist that every household dig one. However, the small number of wells was seen by the doctors as an indication of laziness or intransigence. Many of those who could afford to, and who lived on suitable terrain, had dug wells, and many people had invested in hand pumps. The doctors also insisted people build toilets (pit latrines), which increasing numbers had been doing. However, the small size of the house lots (15 by 20 metres) and the fact that the land sloped toward the lake made it difficult to dig wells the necessary 15 metres from pit latrines. The insistence on village self-reliance also ignored the earlier promise to provide adequate numbers of standpipes.

People's expectations and habits had changed in this village community, which was incorporated into the most modern mining town in Indonesia. The Village Headman said, in response to the suggestion that they should build more wells, 'People are now used to the standpipes, and like to use them.' The water was known to be clean, and because of the elaborate system of pipes, many families no longer had to carry water up into the house. Also, habits with respect to use of water were changing. Many people followed the example set by the Village Headman, building a latrine and bathroom on the ground floor of their houses. The amount of water needed to flush the toilets, and to fill the drum to allow everyone to bathe indoors, was too great to be met by fetching and carrying. Even those without a proper bathroom would often erect a little shelter near the house in which to bathe.

Only people with no option—because of poverty or distance from a standpipe—bathed in the lake. The village residents were caught between rising expectations and worsening conditions.

At the meeting, the question of building pit latrines was also discussed. The villagers were told that the company would provide supervision (from the Health Inspector) to make the toilet bowls, but the people would have to provide sand, labour, and cement. The villagers were happy to do the work; they were willing to work together when they knew it was for their common benefit. However, the Village Headman commented later, when I asked what he'd thought of the meeting:

> Nothing was fixed. We weren't given a date when they would come and show us how to make toilet bowls. And about the sand: if we have to provide it, we have to go in small boats to the other side of the lake. Yet one truck load from the company would be enough.

He saw the ludicrous side of the argument about self-reliance. In a situation where the company is in control of so much complex machinery, they were insisting that the villagers do unnecessary time-consuming tasks with the most primitive technology—yet another example of unrealistic insistence on self-reliance.

There were no immediate consequences of this meeting. When I returned in 1980, a few toilet bowls had been made, but the more enterprising had obtained bowls through their contacts in the company, or bought them from a store. With respect to water supply, a few more standpipes were installed. However the new ones (and two of the original five) were of a different style. The original type allowed no permanent attachment of a pipe: users could only temporarily affix a plastic hose. The second type allowed for the permanent fixing of metal pipes, which led to a situation in the New Village where groups of individuals had permanently fixed pipes to some standpipes. This meant casual users could neither fill containers nor bathe in the flow of the pipe. Households that were not part of the group controlling the outflow had to ask for water from one of the group members.

Many households close to the F area had illicitly tapped the townsite water supply, running pipes directly into their homes. The security forces turned a blind eye to this practice, once these households had in turn provided them with their own piped water. People did not regard tapping the water supply as a form of theft. Because the houses in the townsite had piped water, they saw it as their right. However, this was not the only self-reliance being practised. As can be seen from table 7.1, many people had dug wells and latrines. This was regarded as a high priority when renovating one's home.

There have been improvements in the treatment of townsite sewage. By 1980 Inco had dug settling ponds behind the village, where the sewage lies for a while, and this facilitates treatment and presumably reduces the level of pollution. However, probably the settling ponds, which border on the village, have brought a new health hazard, the mosquitoes that breed in them.

The Village Administration comprised mainly indigneous Soroakans. Since none of them was paid a salary, tasks connected with their offices were additional to their income-earning activities. Nonetheless, many were in the office every day. Their experience in government derived from the days when Soroako was a small rural community, and they lacked the resources to administer a semi-urban community that needed, among other things, a water supply and garbage service. No higher level of government authorities intervened in these public health matters to protect the interests of the residents of Soroako village.

The Inco Town Administration intervened unpredictably in providing services to the village. The undertaking to clean up after the flood led to a greater involvement, most notably in cleaning up rubbish, and a promise of regular garbage services. But, like the prom-

TABLE 7.1.

THE DISTRIBUTION OF LATRINES AND WELLS IN SOROAKO VILLAGE, 1980

Location	No. of Houses	Houses With Latrines (%)	Houses With Wells (%)
Old Village			
Neighbourhood 1	58	63.8	19.0
2	61	32.8	18.0
3	76	15.8	11.8
4	53	5.7	17.0
N =	248		
New Village			
Neighbourhood 1	65	55.38	27.69
2	63	50.80	26.98
3	43	74.42	6.98
4	93	25.80	9.68
N =	264		

SOURCE: P. T. Inco Medical Services.

*The poorest of the Soroakans, those whose incomes were irregular, were concentrated in neighbourhoods 3 and 4 in Old Village. This is reflected in the smaller proportion having wells and latrines.

ised standpipes, or help with making toilet bowls, it never eventuated.

The village government and community leaders tried to develop a direct liaison with Inco so the company would help in alleviating some of the village's problems (as in the meeting already described). However, even though the townsite was formally under the jurisdiction of the Village Headman, it meant nothing in practice. The townsite, except for the F area, had not yet been organised into neighbourhood units, the smallest unit of local government.

In discussing this problem, the District Chief commented that he understood its source. It was the status hierarchy of the mining company. He said employees had contempt for the village people, an attitude exacerbated, he thought, by the fact that some village officials, including the Headman, were former workers. The high-ranking employees would not place themselves under the jurisdiction of someone who had been their subordinate in the company, he said. However, the District Chief did not back his wisdom with action, he failed to support village officials in their disputes with the company.

Conclusion

The Soroakans were relatively powerless in disputes with both the company and the government. Government action favoured the interests of the company, as did its inaction at the local level, which meant that there was no one to support the villagers in putting legitimate grievances to Inco. This did not stem from a malevolence towards the people. At the national level, the ruling elite no doubt believed that their development strategy would benefit the people, consequently, the main concern was to get investment and growth moving. At the local level, there was the additional complication of the venality of some officials, who could not resist using their positions to benefit personally from development in the region.

The Soroakan people's own leaders, the traditional elite, were not given a legitimate place in the structure of authority of the new nation state. Indeed, they were treated as miscreants when they did represent the interests of their people.

In conflicts with the company and the government, the Soroakans have tended to act as a unitary group, and this unity has its expression in their distinctive ethnic consciousness (see chap. 10). But in the contemporary situation, there were also forces dividing them. The same village leaders who represented the mass of the people in dealings with Inco and the government were the landowners profiting from their control of a scarce resource, to the detriment of the rest. The following chapter takes up the cultural expression of those unequal relations.

NOTES TO CHAPTER 7

1. Governor's decree (*Surat Gubernor Kepala Daerah Sulawesi Selatan*)
    No Agr 16/26/15, 5 October 1973.
    Regent's decree (*Surat Keputusan Bupati Kepala Daerah Luwu*)
    No 75/II/KDL/72, 11 December 1971
    No 65/II/KDL/73, 22 October 1973
    No 66/II/KDL/73, 25 October 1973.
2. Regent's decree No 29/II/KDL/74, 29 May 1974.
3. List issued by the Regency Compensation Committee (*Panitia Ganti Rugi Kabupaten Luwu*) 15 June 1975.
4. Governor's decree No 34/I/1977, 25 January 1977.

5. Letter of agreement (*Surat Persetujuan*) between Inco and the Provincial Government, 29 November 1977.
6. Letter from the lawyer to the Governor, 20 August 1980.
7. Schumacher's book, *Small is Beautiful* (1973), was very popular in Indonesia generally, and in Soroako. However, the ideas of self-help were deemed relevant only to the poorer segments of the population. The more advantaged people living in the townsite were not seen to derive advantages from digging their own wells or making their own toilet bowls.

Photo 7. Women returning from the fields through the appropriate rice land.

Chapter 8

The Wedding of Hijra: Changing Social Relations

Proletarianisation has brought changes in customary social relations in this community, even in the short period since the inception of the project. In particular, there are differences in relations between old and young, men and women, and also between households and household groupings, which were the fundamental producing units in the peasant economy. In the first part of this chapter, I describe the institution of marriage, in order to illuminate the nature of these changes.

Many of the new forms of social relations derive from the monetisation of the economy and from the related tendency of services previously conducted as part of the assembly of kin and community obligations to become commodities. Commentators on the development of advanced industrial societies have noted similar changes in marriage and the family. In particular, productive work, which in the peasant economy was carried out as an integral part of household activity, is now outside the home. This has led to a separation of work and home and corresponding 'domestication' of women (Rogers 1980) for whom there are few jobs in the capitalist enterprise.

In the latter part of the chapter, I investigate the ways in which new forms of status, the cultural expression of capitalist class relations (see chap. 2), are expressed by the Soroakans in the staging of weddings, the most important public ritual events in the community.

215

The familiar symbols employed for status affirmation in the precompany period are being assimilated to the new forms of class-derived status relations.

Wedding of Hijra

In order to discuss marriage and its ritual celebration, I have focussed on one particular wedding, the most elaborate of the dozen or more I witnessed during 1977–79. The wedding was that of a girl named Hijra, the daughter of Ruslan, who was at the time the only indigenous Soroakans to be employed by Inco at the level of 'skilled worker.' The status that his higher pay and position conferred was evident in his possession of a motorcycle and in the eligibility of his children to attend the company school in the townsite, a privilege denied unskilled workers. His rise was partly the result of the patronage of a 'boss' from West Java. This association allowed other privileges, for instance, the boss's wife obtaining goods for Ruslan's family from the company store.

The wedding of their daughter was an opportunity for this family to demonstrate their relative wealth and new status. The parents arranged a marriage between their daughter and a young worker from another upwardly mobile local family.

Marriage in Soroako

In the precompany economy, marriage played an important role in the reproduction of a social form in which households were the production units. Marriage cemented a relation between the husband and wife in which they were copartners in production, and it established the household within a network of kin and affines that formed an important basis for the cooperation so crucial in the agricultural economy. Parents arranged the marriages of their children with an eye to the constitution of successful units as well as the establishment of economic ties. In this village, where kinship is cognatic, a woman's female affines joined her female kin as her closest associates, and uxorilocal residence after marrriage cemented an association between a new husband and his male affines. These relations were important in economic cooperation.

Economic motivation is evident even in the new ideas about arranging marriages, where paid employment is the most important criterion of eligibility for a young man.

For the individual, marriage was the path to child bearing. The care of children was primarily the task of women, but for both women and men, the primary personal satisfaction marriage afforded was through having children, rather than through personal attachment to the spouse. One man commented, 'Why do we men marry if not in quest of children?' Sexual desire between partners was not regarded as the basis of marriage, though it was assumed passion would develop once they were married.

Hijra's marriage was 'traditional' in that it was arranged between the two sets of parents. Such negotiations were always shrouded in secrecy, as an unsuccessful approach could cause shame. The negotiations were between the parents of the prospective couple, but other kin and intermediaries could become involved. There were often whisperings about negotiations in progress, but many prospective unions came as a surprise when announced. Formerly, and even occasionally in contemporary Soroako, the girl was as much surprised as everyone else. One woman told me that she was deceived into thinking the elaborate preparations going on in her home were for her sister and was shocked to learn that it was she who was to be married. The provisions of the 1975 Marriage Law made it an offence to marry a girl against her will (Soewondo 1977). To guard against this, both parties to a marriage are required to sign consent forms ten days before the wedding.

This did not ensure that girls were no longer married against their will. Few girls dared disobey their parents. They were respectful, in awe (*takut*) of their parents. Women said, because parents love their daughters, they arrange matches in their children's interest only. Besides, as several women pointed out, if a girl acceded to her parents' wishes and the marriage was not a success because of the husband's shortcomings, the parents were obliged to take her back. To marry against a girl's parents' will meant that escape was closed. A recognition of women's economic dependence on their parents and husbands was clear. This dependence has been exacerbated by the changing nature of production in Soroako: there were few jobs for women in the nickel project. They were dependent on the husband's pay packet for themselves and their children. The improvement in their legal position with the new marriage law was offset by a decline in their autonomous role in production (Robinson 1983).

However, some women did resist their parents' choice of spouse. 'You can raise the roof,' women said to me. In such cases, they often refused to consummate the marriage. One young woman, who was in love with an immigrant worker, put up strong resistance to her parents' choice of a marriage partner. She refused to eat and thus was hospitalised. She then ran away, causing the marriage to be postponed for a week. At the reception, she was diffident, and she collapsed before proceedings had finished. Her behaviour was roundly criticised by many of her close female kin—even by some of her unmarried nieces who themselves entertained fantasies of romantic matches—because she was shaming the family by her actions. The groom's kin, the family of an engineer in the townsite, also felt shamed through being party to this course of events and claimed that the parents of the girl had told them she had consented to the match. Their explanation was that she had been bewitched by a young man in Soroako who desired the girl himself. The bride's next strategy was to refuse to consummate the marriage. She was treated by a sorcerer (*dukun*), on the assumption she had been bewitched. People waited anxiously for news that she was *baik* with her husband, i.e., that the marriage had been consummated. The theory that her behaviour had resulted from the malevolent actions of a young man was not accepted by people who were not members of the families involved; to others it was a clear case of a young girl's being married against her will. The *dukun*'s treatment did prove effective, however, and the marriage was consummated.

The people of Soroako, unlike rural people in some other parts of Indonesia,[1] were aware of the provisions of the new law and spoke as if forced marriage were a thing of the past. The modern view was that parents should arrange their daughter's marriage, rejecting suitors they felt to be unfit, but obtaining the daughter's consent before agreeing to a match. However, the distinction between forced marriage and coerced consensus is a difficult one, especially considering the vulnerable emotional and economic situation of young women.

Hijra offered no resistance to her parents' choice of a shy, homely youth, although it was clear from her constant weeping during the preparations for the reception that he did not meet her romantic fantasies.

Negotiations between the two sets of kin concerned the amount of money the groom would provide for the wedding feast, which the bride's parents host. In 1979, the usual cost of a large reception was Rp.100,000 (about US$243) and a buffalo. In Hijra's case, the groom agreed to provide Rp.175,000 and a buffalo. Her parents contributed a further Rp.100,000. (People often commented on the rising cost of weddings.) The money paid by the prospective groom was called *uang dikasih naik*, a rendering of the Bugis term *dui menre* B. meaning 'money which rises' (Lineton 1975, p.105), indicating the Bugis influence on the conduct of wedding rituals in Soroako. The Bugis negotiated both a bridewealth payment and the *dui menre*, but the Soroakans had not adopted the payment of bridewealth (although I heard one old man refer to the cost of the feast as the money 'to buy a girl'). However, it seems that commoner Bugis are more concerned with the *dui menre* than with bridewealth. Since the latter serves to affirm the status of the bride, it is more a concern of aristocratic families (Lineton 1981).

When the economy was based on subsistence cultivation, negotiations concerned not an amount of money but a quantity of provisions from the groom; principally rice and a buffalo, but also spices, tea, and sugar. Contributions from neighbours and kin were also significant. In the contemporary situation all the provisions had to be bought.

Formerly, resources were controlled by their older generation and this gave them some leverage in enforcing control of their children's choice of spouse. Young men earned the money in modern-day Soroako, and parents realised they were thus losing control of their children's choice of spouse, especially their sons. Contributions to a wedding feast, once an aspect of the dense web of interpersonal relations in the community, increasingly took the form of commodities. Economic relations, not personal relations, were the mediators. Those people who commanded the best wages from the company had the advantage of access to new commodified goods and services, which were distributed in accord with the distribution of rewards for wage labour. The only exception was the small group of villagers who had become wealthy through trade.

Changing Forms of Marriage

Marriages and their arrangement were important in reproducing crucial social relations, between men and women, old and young, households and groupings of kin, and the people of Soroako and those of nearby marriage-related villages. As social forms and the constitutive social relations have changed with the development of capitalist class relations, so have the mechanisms of their reproduction.

The separation of work and home, occurring as part of the process of proletarianisation, and the related constitution of the household as a unit of consumption rather than production, had profound effects on marriage and the family in Soroako. The family increasingly served as the locus for reproduction of labour power in a capitalist economy, rather than reproducing the relations of prior forms of economic organisation. This was reflected, for example, in the stress parents placed on formal education of children, a manifestation of an understanding that in the contemporary world they have nothing to sell but their labour power. With respect to marriage, ideas about the importance of romantic love were gaining currency, and there was a growing stress on marriage as the union of two romantically involved individuals, rather than the outcome of the alliance of two families. The idea of romance, of sexual desire and passion, was not new. The new element was the attitude that this was a necessary and appropriate basis for marriage.

A number of writers have commented on the way in which the family becomes a sphere of emotional life, under conditions of capitalist production.

> The organisation of production around alienated labour encouraged the creation of a separate sphere in which personal relations were pursued as an end in themselves (Zaretsky 1976, p.66).

For people labouring in the capitalist enterprise, the family becomes the realm of 'happiness, love and individual freedom' (Zaretsky 1976, p.80) or as Roberta Hamilton put it: 'Privacy has become the compensation for alienation from one's labour' (1978, p.27). This clearly contrasts with the situation in Soroako prior to the project, when marriage and the households it created were not principally a realm of private life.

Along with the family's becoming the sphere of emotional life during the development of capitalism, there are profound changes in the relation between husband and wife. They are no longer interdependant in production. Generally, the husband is the wage earner, engaged in alienated production, and the wife oversees the household, now a sphere of consumption separate from production. The decline in the importance of women's role in production, and its significance for the low status of women in developing capitalist societies, has often been noted (see, for example, Boserup 1970, Rogers 1980). The wife is trapped in the domestic realm by her economic dependence on her husband.

With the development of capitalism,

> (w)omen's economic dependence upon their husbands was matched then by an emotional dependence; their sense of self was to come from the reflection in their beloved's eye (Hamilton 1978, p.101).

Under conditions of alienated labour in the capitalist enterprise, the economic rationale of the household changes. The wife is no longer a productive worker; instead, she performs domestic labour that is critical for the reproduction of labour power for the capitalist enterprise. Conditions of alienated labour and the changes in customary relations with proletarianisation provide fertile ground for the ideology of romantic love. (Women's unpaid domestic work, for example, is performed 'for love.') The family becomes a realm of personal life, constituted out of personal relations rather than social relations.

Ideas of Romantic Love in Soroako

Ideas about romantic love were transmitted to the villagers as part of what Hildred Geertz has called the 'metropolitan superculture' (1963, p.35). Though these ideas may have originated in the West and been taken up in Indonesia as part of the ideological form of capitalism, they have been reworked and reinterpreted in the Indonesian context. In Soroako, it was the values and lifestyle of the Indonesian elite in the company townsite that had power for the village residents, rather than the values and lifestyle of the foreign 'bosses.'

The villagers were exposed to new ideas through their association with the more urbane immigrants. For example, many of the Indonesian townsite residents were happy for their adolescent children to 'date,' and village boys home for the school holidays joined in the dating activities. They observed the more relaxed behaviour of townsite residents in public places, like the movies or the beach.

Movies were important in transmitting urban values. During the construction phase (1973–77), there were outdoor screenings of foreign and Indonesian films once or twice a week. In 1978, a movie theatre opened on the outskirts of the village. Since 1980, Soroako has had television. In 1981, I observed that the most popular programmes for adolescents and adults were dramatic films (sandiwara) that were, as often as not, about love and romance. Such programmes were eagerly watched and then discussed for days.

Half of the indigenous Soroakan households owned radio cassette players, and these too were important vehicles for a popular culture conveying new values. The most popular 'pop' music in Soroako was Dang dut—rhythmic, Indian-influenced tunes with themes mostly of love, passion, and desire. The songs I remember hearing most were of love at first sight, unrequited love, and the pain of love that could not be realised because of parental opposition. The lyrics of many Dang dut sing openly of passion, sexual desire, temptation, and sin. Country style songs concerned with love, usually sung by women, were also popular. (The more 'cerebral' Indonesian pop music, popular in the cities, had no following in Soroako.) These songs provided the young with the argot of the Jakarta streets for matters relating to romantic love, which they used when flirting or fantasising about romance.

For many young Soroakans (as in Hijra's case) these ideas remained fantasy. But there, unlike many other parts of Indonesia, conditions existed for such fantasies to be realised. In that semiurban environment there were more opportunities for socialising between unmarried men and women than there had been in the past. Many families had unrelated male boarders. In January 1981, I attended two weddings, each between the daughter of the household and a male boarder. In the past, households would have contained only unmarried men who were too closely related to be considered marriage partners (muhrim). Some households included small shops, which were attended by the daughters of the house. These attracted groups of young workers on their motorcycles in the evenings, to chat and flirt. A few girls worked as servants in the townsite; others attended movies or football matches. The mining town was a bigger place and more potentially anonymous than the peasant village. It included strangers who were not concerned with safeguarding the honour of an unknown young woman. In the past, any gathering of young men and women (in the fields, or at a wedding, for instance) was certain to include at least one young man who was a girls' classificatory 'uncle,' a relationship that gave him responsibility for safeguarding her honour. I often noticed a flirtatious young woman having her ear tweaked by an equally young uncle.

Many of the older Soroakans saw it as their duty to safeguard the honour of young immigrant women, as part of a general concern to uphold the familiar moral order. (The girls regarded this interest in their affairs as prurient interference.) Especially in the early days of the project, many couples were forcibly wed by the village government when it was felt they had gone 'too far' in their association. This could mean that the young man had visited the girl's house too often, a sign of intention to marry, or that the couple had been found to have a sexual involvement. The village Headman assured me he still adopted this guardian's role. However, I feel that standards of acceptable social intercourse between men and women have shifted as time has passed.

A number of young Soroakan men were forced to wed immigrant women, who were without the protection of male relatives and were seen to be too free with the young men. Some of these girls were pregnant at the time of marriage. An old man, a functionary at the village mosque, told me he had forced his son to marry after the boy had failed to sleep at home for a few nights and the father discovered him with his girlfriend. This was despite the father's belief that they were too young to marry.

Such weddings were usually joyless occasions, celebrated in simple fashion. People referred to it as *kawin pisang goreng* (a 'fried banana wedding') because the full festivities, involving the slaughter of a beast, were not carried out. At one such wedding the groom's mother wept throughout the proceedings. The parents' anguish at not being able to arrange a match they approved of was often exacerbated by the fact that the girls concerned were Christian immigrants, the ideal spouse being a good Muslim.

Such weddings contrasted markedly with Hijra's. Her wedding was arranged by her parents and was considered a good match. It enabled the parents to plan a wedding feast that enhanced their reputation and standing in the community.

Because the young men by and large supplied the costs of the wedding feast, it was more difficult for parents to enforce their choice of spouse, a fact recognised by many of their older generation. It was possible under such circumstances for young men to choose their own bride, on the basis of romantic involvement. Young women could threaten to bring shame to the family by immodest behaviour with a boyfriend, if their own choice of husband was not accepted.

However, young couples who married according to their own will might not receive the same degree of parental support as those who contracted an arranged marriage. In particular, some immigrant women who married into Soroako had hostile relations with their mothers-in-law. This exacerbated the trend to privatisation of the individual family unit. Much amusement was caused by one such marriage, in which the immigrant daughter-in-law was tolerated in the mother's house only so long as she had a separate kitchen.

In another instance, a family who had successfully arranged the marriage of their first daughter agreed to allow a second daughter to wed a man from Ujung Pandang, with whom she was romantically in volved. He initially complied with Soroakan custom, living uxorilocally, sharing the front room with the other newly wed couple, but it was not a happy situation. He was an office worker and contemptuous of the village people. They, in turn, had little respect for him. 'He doesn't know how to work. He just sits in an office and writes all day,' his mother-in-law said. After only a few months of marriage, he took his wife to live in his cousin's house in the townsite. The father was very angry, saying that he would not have agreed to the match if he had known that the husband would take her away. The girl, caught between her parents and husband, was very upset. In marrying according to individual will, a young Soroakan lost much of the parental support that normally eased the transition to marriage.

In the contemporary situation, even in the case of some arranged marriages, the new husband had already built his own house (with money saved from his wages and perhaps with the aid of an interest-free housing loan from Inco), and so the new couple dispensed with the customary period of postmarital uxorilocal residence. This happened to Hijra. It made the adjustment to marriage harder for the girl, who in the past would not have left her parent's home till at least the birth of her first child. This also added to the tendency towards the privatisation of the nuclear family. Postmarital uxorilocal residence, in the peasant economy, was tied to bride service, which established economic ties between fathers-in-law and sons-in-law that continued when the couple moved to their own home (see chap. 5).

Stability of Marriage

In the customary situation, when the two spouses were not the only ones with an interest in the success of a union, and when high expectations were not held about the emotional content of marriage, marriages were very stable. A long-term monogamous union was the ideal. The few divorcees among older Soroakans were women who had been married (often forcibly) to the Darul Islam rebels, many of whom fled the district, leaving wives and children when the rebellion was crushed. However, marriages between Soroakans or with partners from the nearby marriage-related villages rarely ended in divorce.

The instability of marriage to outsiders was a feature of the contemporary situation. Soroakan families were reluctant to marry their daughters to immigrant men, because they knew of too many cases of what was locally termed 'contract marriage' (*kawin kontrak*). The contract referred to was not one between the bride and groom. On the contrary, it referred to a practice (especially common in the construction period) whereby immigrant workers married in Soroako, and when their work contract ended, left Soroako and their wife and children. These men were often married before coming to Soroako, unbeknown to the second wife. It was common for them to disappear without saying they were leaving, or to go on 'vacation' to their natal village, never to return. A sad indication of the bad faith with which many immigrant workers contracted marriages was given by the enormous number of unclaimed *Buku Nikah* (marriage certificates) sitting in a dusty cupboard in the local office of the Department of Religious Affairs, which was responsible for all Muslim marriages. The officials in the office said they had never before experienced such a phenomenon.

Suspicion of immigrant suitors had declined a little by 1980, when I witnessed a number of marriages between Soroakan girls and men who had been in the village a long time. Figures obtained from the Nuha District branch of the Department of Religious Affairs show an increase in proportion of marriages between indigenous Soroakans and immigrants, between 1970 and 1980. There was a corresponding decline in marriages with customary marriage partners (table 8.1).

A small number of indigenous Soroakan women had married immigrants in the early seventies, but these unions were unstable and many had already ended in divorce. The instability was a consequence of the marriage's being an agreement between two romantically involved individuals, rather than a pact between two families, both of whom had an interest in maintaining it. The commonest reason for marital trouble and divorce in these marriages was that the husband took a second wife. That is, he sought another romantic involvement, the passion of the first marriage having faded.

Some women found themselves inadvertently in polygamous unions, when husbands failed to inform them that they were already married, and this led to marital conflict. Previously, polygamy was almost unknown in Soroako. In one instance, a young Soroakan woman was courted by a boarder in her parents' house. He returned to his natal village to inform his parents of his intention to marry, and they immediately arranged a marriage with a kinswoman in his own village, in South Palopo. They were no happier than the Soroakans at the thought of their son marrying an outsider (*orang lain*). He returned

TABLE 8.1.
CHANGES IN PROPORTION OF MARRIAGES WITH
CUSTOMARY MARRIAGE PARTNERS, 1970–80

	Marriage Partners	1970	1975	1980
a	indigenous Soroakan + indigenous Soroakan	.36	.43	.29
b	indigenous Soroakan + same district	.28	.16	.07
a + b	between customary marriage partners	.64	.58	.36
c	indigenous Soroakan + immigrant	.36	.42	.64
	N =	11	31	14

SOURCE: Nuha District Office of Religious Affairs, January 1981.

to Soroako and went ahead with the wedding originally planned. Eventually the first wife arrived in Soroako and demanded to live with her husband. He joined her, leaving the second wife with her mother. Both wives gave birth to three children, but the first wife's children all died. He became more committed to the second wife, the mother of his living children. The trouble between the women grew worse, with the first wife demanding not only her husband but the children as well. (Indeed, she registered them at the hospital as her own children.) There were frequent public fights between the two women. Meanwhile the husband built a house, on land owned by the second wife's mother, where the second wife lived with her children. The first wife began demanding that she live there, and the second wife return to her mother. The second wife then said to me, with great anger:

> I would be ashamed to do that. Why do we women marry, except as our livelihood (*pencarian*)?

Her response to the situation was based more on insecurity bred of her economic dependence than on sexual jealousy. After a particularly violent fight with the first wife, she sarcastically proposed a solution: 'I'll cut his penis in half. She can have half and I'll have half.'

In another instance, an immigrant man had married a local widow. After some years of childless marriage, he pressured his wife to permit him to marry a younger woman from his own village, since her permission was necessary under the new marriage law. After weeks of pressure, she acquiesced, but his Australian boss refused to give him leave for the occasion. He went without permission and so lost his job. The Imam told me that he regarded the man as foolish. He had counselled him against taking a second wife, saying:

> You have a good wife, a happy home and a house. Now you are upsetting your wife and your home because you want to have childeren. You can't always have everything.

Then he added to me:

> And now he's lost his job, too. The Koran says you can have a second wife provided you treat her exactly the same as the first wife. But what human being can do that?

As no ordinary mortal could behave in accord with the prescription, the Iman felt it was better not even to try. His views reflected those of most Soroakans. However, the customary ideas about marriage were coming under pressure in the contemporary situation.

A number of the older married Soroakan men enjoyed their new freedom to frequent bars or visit immigrant households in the comparative anonymity of New Village. There were instances of entanglements with immigrant women, leading to the breakup of established marriages. One such man left his wife and six children to live with a snack vendor from Java. Soon after he left, his wife contracted a rare eye disease that blinded her. She assumed this was a consequence of black magic on the part of the other woman. The man's family was greatly shamed by his behaviour and took the wife's part, doing what they could to help her. The old father, who had arranged the match between his classificatory niece and his son, was so shamed that he left the village to live at his field hut. He told me he was reluctant to arrange the marriage of his youngest son lest he be shamed again. He saw that times had changed, that family honour and parental powers were not what they had been.

In an even sadder case, a Soroakan man took to drinking and frequenting prostitutes in New Village. He was not regularly employed, and spent all he earned (and a lot that he borrowed) on such pursuits. His family suffered, often going hungry. He tried to rape his daughter while drunk. The wife fled with the children to take refuge with a government official who was also her kinsman. She asked the village officials to help her obtain a divorce, but they urged her to return to her husband. He again tried to rape the daughter and the wife stabbed him. When the officials went to the house to investigate, they found not a scrap of food.

The changes in Soroako, such as the growing size of the community, the monetisation of the economy, the commodification of many customary services, and the cultural influence of the newcomers, were all putting pressure on customary Soroakan forms of marriage. The changes did not benefit women, who lost much of the protection afforded by traditional forms of marriage. The decline of their independent role in production made them extremely vulnerable.

Men talked a lot about the possibility of taking a second wife. It was a common male fantasy and a common female fear. The men often joked about it; but the women were never amused. In a typical instance, a man jokingly asserted that he would like a second (younger) wife, and his wife commented that such jokes made her very unhappy. 'It's all right for him,' she said, pointing to another man who was present, 'He only has one child. My husband has seven. Who will support them?' The fear of second wives was always expressed in economic terms. It was assumed that a man would favour the second, younger wife and the children of that union. In a similar vein, the blind woman, already mentioned, complained most about her economic problems in supporting six children. Her husband was pressured by the village government to marry his mistress to regularise the situation. The first wife commented:

> If he fixes up the house, I'll sign the papers [for him to take a second wife] ten times over.

The fear of husbands taking second wives, like unmarried people's fantasy of marrying for love, had more chance of being realised in the current situation becuase of the increased pool of women from which men could draw. Many married men became involved with women of dubious virtue by village standards. The villagers called such women 'second wives,' whether there had been a wedding or not. The economic insecurity threatened by a second wife was especially ominous because both the subsistence of the village economy and women's autonomous role in production had been eroded. The women whose husbands had second wives, and those who had been deserted (and it was often hard to differentiate these two categories), had hard lives as they tried to support themselves and the children, usually through petty trading. Some of the young immigrant women who had been deserted turned to prostitution.

The new marriage law and ideas of marriage based on romantic love might seem to herald new forms of personal freedom for women and men. However, just as the serf is not free, the social relations within which he labours tying him to the feudal lord, the individual in a peasant society is not free to choose a marriage partner. The marriage binds them in a web of relations that extend beyond the conjugal pair, and the very arrangement of the match is an expression of such ties. By contrast, the ideology of romantic love as the foundation for marriage denies the union as anything but a contract freely entered into between the partners. Like the wage labourer, the parties to such a marriage are nominally free, but they enter into social relations that offer them the isolation of the individual as opposed to the formal interdependence of the peasant community.

Weddings and the Affirmation of Status

Weddings were the biggest public ritual events in Soroako. Even the poorest families marked the marriage of their daughters with a feast at which they slaughered a few chickens. More affluent families provided a feast for hundreds of guests, for which they slaughtered a cow, or better still a buffalo. The importance of the wedding ceremony as a public occasion reflected the significance of marriage in this community—as a social event and as an event in the life of the individual.

The centrality of marriage and the associated wedding rituals in the highly status-conscious Bugis society is well documented (see, for example, Chabot 1967; Lineton 1975). The amount of bridewealth paid attests to the degree of hereditary status, and the wedding ritual provides an opportunity for the affirmation of status.

To perform an elaborate ritual, one needed to be able to call on the labour and contributions of a large following to prepare the feast, as well as to attract a sufficient number of guests, including a few people with standing in the community. Wealth in itself was not sufficient to achieve high status in South Sulawesi. It was also necessary to demonstrate that one was held in high regard, through the possession of a following. The pattern of attribution of status followed that of the mobilisation of political support in the precolonial polities. Indeed, the public rituals of the rulers in those polities were one of the most important ways in which they demonstrated political effectiveness (Errington 1981).

The status-conscious and politically competitive Bugis society provided the cultural form for the validation of social status in Soroako. In the performance of weddings, the protocols observed were mainly Bugis (not those of their ancestors), and when the Soroakan spoke of traditional attire for the bride and groom (*pakaian adat*), they meant the colourful Bugis silk sarong and the transparent blouse, rather than the costume worn by their forebears. The adoption of Bugis cultural forms was tied to the Islamisation of the community.

In contemporary Soroako, the claims to status asserted in the public feast accompanying a marriage were not only those arising from customary status relations. Within the village, households that had done well from the nickel project whether through long-term employment, or through successful trading, attempted to affirm or assert high status through the staging of elaborate weddings. The claims were not intended for their fellow villagers alone. The Soroakans were very aware of the status hierarchy of the townsite community, too, and they aimed to affirm status within that domain also.

The following analysis focuses on Hijra's wedding to illustrate these processes of change, though the analysis draws on the many weddings I attended. In many ways, although it was a very traditional occasion, there were important innovations related to the concern to realise status in the context of the hierarchy of the mining town.

Hijra's Wedding

Her parents wanted to make their daugher's wedding an occasion to be remembered, to impress everyone with their wealth and their standing in the community. They received a lot of help from the father's patron, the boss who had overseen his rise in the company.

They engaged the services of another village woman to organise the feast. She was chosen, not for her knowledge of customary ritual, but because she was the most urbane of the indigenous Soroakans. She had good contacts in the townsite, was innovative, and knew what would impress townsite residents.

It was quite an organisational feat to prepare a feast for the several hundred guests anticipated. The shopping for spices and other provisions went on for weeks prior to the event. Hosts aimed to feed as many guests as possible, but with the greatest economy.

The legalisation of the marriage (*nikah*) was normally not a public ritual in this community. It usually took place quietly in the days preceeding the wedding, attended by only the necessary witnesses and perhaps a few close kin. Occasionally, those attending might be served tea and a snack, such as fried bananas.

The important public event was the reception, when the bride and groom sat together on a 'throne' before the assembled guests (*duduk bersanding*). However, Hijra's wedding involved an elaborate feast for the legalisation as well. The parents sent out formal invitations to guests, mainly from the townsite, and killed five chickens. The guests sat in the parlour while the legislation took place in the bedroom. Hijra sat on the marriage bed, secluded behind drapes and dressed in a white bridal gown. The bride became very tearful as she was being dressed. Few brides seemed happy at their weddings. It is partly because custom dictated they affect a modest demeanour, with downcast eyes. A bride should not seem too eager to enjoy the delights of marriage, lest she be thought immodest. But it was also true that women were usually sad at the time of their wedding. Women said they cried in sorrow at the changes in their lives, but they were often sad that the timing of the wedding and the identity of the groom were not of their choosing. In Soroako, the girl was not an active participant in the legalisation, except to sign the final papers. The groom recited his vows in front of her male kin. This contrasted with some other parts of Indonesia, where the bride and groom sat together while he recited his vows.

The groom arrived with a retinue bearing elaborate cakes, which his brother-in-law told me were part of Bugis wedding custom (*adat*). He also carried the marriage payment (*mas kawin*), a bundle of white cloth. In accordance with Islamic practice, the payment given at the legalisation was nominal. It was regarded as a gift from the groom to the bride to express their solidarity, and it is appropriate that it has some religious significance. It is often a koran or a prayer mat. In this instance, it was white cloth for the garment women wear while praying.

The legalisation in this case was held two weeks before the reception (because the reception was to occur in the Muslim month of Muharram, an inauspicious month for weddings). For the next two weeks, Hijra remained secluded behind the drapes on the marriage bed, her face and body covered in a paste (*bedak*) made of rice flour and aromatic roots. This was believed to make the bride white, and therefore beautiful, for her wedding day.

Meanwhile, the women proceeded with the preparations, mainly cooking biscuits to serve to guests in the days before the reception. On Saturday, one week before the reception, the family called on other villagers to help them with the customary extension of the house (*sambung rumah*). This was done by extending a tarpaulin out from the house, to create a space to accommodate the anticipated several hundred guests, and also provide a temporary kitchen, to prepare the feast.

The men called to help were fed in recompense. On this occasions, the father borrowed his patron's gun and bagged a deer, which he stored in the patron's refrigerator until needed.

The provision of meat for the helpers added to the prestige of the wedding. The extension was electrically lit by an Inco generator borrowed with the aid of the patron. This, too, gave prestige to the event.

On the Thursday preceeding the wedding, two women were delegated to invite all of the indigenous Soroakan women to help cook. Usually, a smaller number of close kin and neighbours were invited. I counted eighty women in the kitchen on the night preceeding Hijra's wedding. All of these helpers had to be fed rice and meat, adding to the cost and the prestige of the wedding. The number who come to help is taken as a sign of the respect afforded the hosts, and thus an indication of their status in the community. The Village Headman's daughter spoke with pride of the number of people at her wedding. They had come without being asked, and at the time of the extension of the house there were so many they were 'like ants.'

The long night's work provided great opportunities for socialising, not the least of this being flirtation between the girls who were cooking and the young men attracted like bees to honey by the chance to chat with the girls and impress them with their wit and their skill in playing the guitar. For the villagers, this part of the ritual provided the most pleasure.

Also, on the evening before a wedding, it was customary at elaborate weddings like Hijra's for the bride to be 'graduated' in reading the Koran (*Tamatkan Koran)*), a ritual held in front of assembled guests in the presence of Imam. Next, the groom arrived with his relatives to sit in the company of the bride's family and friends, while she remained out of sight. This was referred to as *tudam penni*(B.), a Bugis term meaning 'to sit in the evening.'

According to custom, the bride and groom ought not to sleep on the night before their wedding. However, they usually did. The girls' unmarried female friends were required to spend the night with her in her bed, in order that they too should soon marry. Hijra's bed was suitably packed on the wedding night. The girls engaged in a lot of joking and teasing, fondling, and caressing. The teasing was usually about the anticipated delights of the marriage bed, to which the girl should respond with indifference.

On the following morning, the groom would return to the home of the bride for the reception. According to custom, he would be escorted to meet her in the inner bedroom of the house. He approached her with downcast eyes, showing no emotion. She would sit on the bridal bed, hidden behind drapes. On the occasion of Hijra's wedding, the groom was escorted by an old man, who stamped his foot as he stepped over the threshold and again as he entered the inner room, in order to make the girl respectful (*takut*) of her husband and willing to consummate the marriage. A mock struggle usually took place between the woman sitting with the bride and the groom's male escort. The man 'paid' by scattering sweets and coins, to open the drapes. The groom was then required to touch his bride. Hijra's shy young man nervously shook her hand, so his male companion took his hand and placed it on the girl's head. They then descended to the extension of the house, to sit on the elaborate throne. After a number of speeches, the assembled guests ate the meal the women had stayed up all night to prepare.

Formerly, when weddings were primarily village affairs, guests sat on woven mats and ate from banana leaves. In contemporary Soroako, it was mandatory to provide guests with plates, spoon, and forks (usually borrowed from neighbours) and, if possible, to provide chairs. For large weddings, this meant arranging the loan of folding chairs through a 'connection' in the company. The Women's Savings Association (*arisan*) in the village had bought a supply of plates and cups to be used at weddings.

Much of the preparation for a wedding was carried out by the voluntary labour of neighbours and kin, but increasingly aspects of the preparations were being commodified. For example, the most prestigious weddings engaged the services of young Balinese workers to prepare elaborate palm leaf decorations for the reception area. The wedding costume in contemporary Soroako was likely to be hired, from one of a number of women in the nearby town of Malili. These women also dressed the bride, taking over the role of the village wedding ritual specialist, which was to dress the bride and accompany her throughout the ceremony, advising her on protocol and providing moral support. This customary role was being made redundant by the growing preference for hiring elaborate wedding costumes, rather than borrowing them within the village. In 1981, the ritual specialist did not even return to the village from her field hut for some of the weddings I attended.

The costumes hired were usually elaborate Bugis silk sarongs, coloured blouses, and matching jewellery. Occasionally girls chose Western-style white dress and veil. The choice of Bugis costume mirrored the fact that the form of the ritual regarded as customary (*adat*) in Soroako today is actually Bugis. The ritual on the night preceeding the wedding, the style of the reception, and the custom of presentation of reverse dowry (see below) after the wedding all derived from Bugis custom. The Soroakans used Bugis terms to describe these phases of the ritual.

For Hijra's wedding, the parents agreed to a suggestion from the father's patron that the bride and groom should wear Sundanese costume. 'If the Soroakans don't have their own customary dress (*pakaian adat*), I would be really pleased if your daughter wore Sundanese costume.' The father was proud to comply. The drab brown and blue sarongs, and the bride's white blouse contrasted markedly with the vibrant colours of the customary Bugis dress. There was also an attempt at some emulation of Sundanese procedures, with the parents sitting uncomfortably with the bride and groom on the dais. These innovations were not well received by the other Soroakans. Criticism abounded on the drab nature of the dress, but it was as much a criticism of the attempt to ignore what was accepted in the community as the symbols expressing Soroakan identity, even if to the outsider the identity appeared to be a borrowed one (see chap. 10).

The sitting together on the 'throne' before the assembled guests (*duduk bersanding*) was regarded as the socially significant event in the wedding ritual, more so than the legalisation, when the marriage was validated, in the legal sense (*sah*). At a couple of weddings when the bride's mother was no longer alive, other women would weep at the thought that the deceased had not been able to witness the daughter sitting in state on the wedding day.

At the reception, an honoured guest would make a speech. At simple weddings it was usually the village Headman, but at more elaborate ones, a boss from Inco was often asked. It was always delivered in Indonesian, never Bahasa Soroako. (At one wedding, it was delivered in both English and Indonesian, for the benefit of foreigners present.)

At Hijra's wedding, a boss was invited to make the speech. He took the opportunity to deliver an exhortation to the assembled guests to support the government-sponsored family planning programme.

The reception concluded, the bride and groom returned to their respective homes. There is a further stage of the ritual, which was now often observed. Following Bugis custom, they enacted the *marola* B. The bride went to the home of the groom; some people described this as the presentation of the bride to her mother-in-law. She was given an indirect dowry (Goody and Tambiah 1973, p.2), that is, the parents-in-law presented her with goods that became her property and would remain hers if the marriage should end in divorce. Formerly it took the form of land, trees, or livestock. Some of the girls who married men from neighbouring villages still received such presentations, but in contemporary Soroako it was more likely to be gold, a sewing machine or, in one case, an elaborate kerosene stove. In very simple weddings, or when the groom was an immigrant from far away, this would not necessarily be carried out.

In keeping with the elaborate nature of Hijra's wedding, the *marola* B. was a big affair. The groom's family circulated printed invitations and extended their own house with a marquee to accommodate the guests. Other *marola* I attended were very much family affairs, with older female relatives and a few others accompanying the girl to her mother-in-law's house, where tea and cakes were served. If there were to be a presentation of reverse dowry to the bride, it took place then.

Because wedding rituals were concerned with a demonstration of status, the gossip by which a ritual was evaluated was as important as the event. Everyone would ask how many invitations were distributed, and to which parts of the mining town they had gone. Printed invitations were distributed for the most elaborate weddings. Formerly, as for simple weddings today, the guests were verbally summoned. The next question was whether it was lively enough (*cukup ramai*) and whether there were sufficient guests in attendance. It took me some time to understand why they did not send invitations R.S.V.P. Although hundreds of invitations would go out, there would be no knowledge of how many of the invited guests would turn up. But the number who attended, and their status, was a measure of the prestige of the hosts. I was always pressed to distribute invitations to foreigners. Apart from the company bosses, other prestigious guests included local officials and the *haji*. The other important question was the type of meat to be served. Chicken was a very poor showing. Beef was better, but buffalo was best. A number of buffalo was best of all. There was also comment on the bride's dress, how much it cost to hire, and the cost of any special effects, like decorations, entertainment, and the like. All these factors contributed to the prestige of the host family.

Hijra's family were keen to boast that the wedding was electrically lit, and about the number of people who had come, both as helpers and as guests. (The guests had numbered several hundred.) The gossip in the community did not accept their claims. Not only was there criticism of the dress, but also the proud assertions about the number of helpers were countered with the damning criticism that there had been too little meat to feed all of the helpers. Indeed, it was said there were 'too many people' involved in preparations.

The aim however was not to impress fellow Soroakans only, but the higher-status people from the townsite, too. These people were also scornful of the family's effort, belittling their emulation of Sundanese custom. The adoption of Sundanese dress was taken as further proof that the Soroakans lacked 'culture.'

However, the fact that so many high-ranking people (including a few expatriates) attended the wedding attested to the status of the parents in the eyes of the community. In spite of the criticism, the family were certainly not shamed by the wedding. The bride had been well behaved, and there had been a lot of guests, including a few bosses. These factors all conferred prestige.

The orientation of the biggest weddings towards the community of the mining town (rather than the village) was sorely felt by some of the poorer people in the village. They no longer felt comfortable as guests at such weddings. They would come to help with preparations, but they watched the proceedings from the sidelines, not participating as guests as they would at simpler weddings.

Although customary relations, based on ideas of mutual obligations to kin and affines, were still important in the staging of rituals, increasingly it was the consumption of goods and services that could be bought that were the important markers of status. The development of capitalist class relations meant that people increasingly confronted each other in terms of relations forged in the economic sphere, rather than the mutual dependence expressed in the idiom of kinship and community, which had pertained in the past. Soroakan people often expressed the view that the mutual aid given in the preparation of ritual feasts was the manifestation of the unity (*persatuan*) of the community. However, they also commented on the ways in which the monetisation of the economy had eroded some aspects of mutual help. In particular, there is the way in which new status is expressed through the purchase of commodified services.

The range of rituals I attended, from simple weddings where a few dozen neighbours and kin gathered together to eat a feast of chickens, to the elaborate ritual staged by Hijra's family, indicated the 'stretching' of differences in wealth, and therefore life chances occuring in this community. In the performance of weddings, we can see the expression of claims to status, as well as the extent of the differentiation between those doing well and those being left behind by the development of the nickel project. In particular, there is a marked difference between those who have had stable employment and those whose income was irregular. Proletarianisation in Soroako has had profound consequences, not only for forms of economic organisation, but also for social relations and their cultural expression.

We can also see the way in which some people were maintaining tradition, in arranging their children's marriages or accepting the arrangement of their own marriages, but also utilising customary cultural forms to express new kinds of status relations. Other people, feeling less constrained by traditional ideas and practicies, have been very open to new ideas and opportunities, such as the young people who insist on their right to marry for love.

NOTES TO CHAPTER 8

1. Peter McDonald (1980) has found that villagers in rural Java are largely unaware of the provisions of the law.

Chapter 9

Race Relations
and Class Domination

Racism was important as a legitimating ideology for European colonial expansion and domination. European superiority was used to justify intervention in native societies (see, for example, chap. 3) as well as to legitimate the class structure of European colonial rule. The internalisation of racist ideology by the oppressed facilitated European domination (Ross 1982).

The value of racism as an ideology of the dominating class in the world system does not end with the political independence of former colonies. It is an aspect of the new forms of domination that have arisen in the modern world, through the internationalisation of capital and the growing importance of the multinational corporation.

Chapter 2 discussed the differential rates of exploitation of labour in the mining town, which gave rise to a particular expression of class differences in a status hierarchy. When the company job ladder is mapped onto the place of origin of workers in each category, there is a degree of fit between the occupational hierarchy and a ranking of racial and ethnic groups (fig. 9.1). In particular, top managers were mostly white. 'Expat' was synonymous with 'white' in local parlance, in spite of the fact that some of the expatriate employees were Filipino and Korean.

An ideology that racial differences gave rise to inequalities in status, position, and power served to mask the class basis of the community and to justify the differential distribution of rewards to different segments of the labour force. Expatriate employees justified their privileged position in terms of their superiority to Indonesians.

The ideology of racial difference served the interests of capital in justifying the low pay of Indonesian workers. The white managers who propagated this ideology were representatives of capital in the mining enterprise (see chap. 2). In a similar fashion, high ranking Indonesian employees justified their privileges relative to the mass of workers in terms of their own superiority. (Chapter 10 examines the way in which an ideology of ethnicity provides an interpretation for the form of relations between Indonesian workers.)

This chapter deals with racist ideology and its role in the construction of everyday social experience in the mining town.

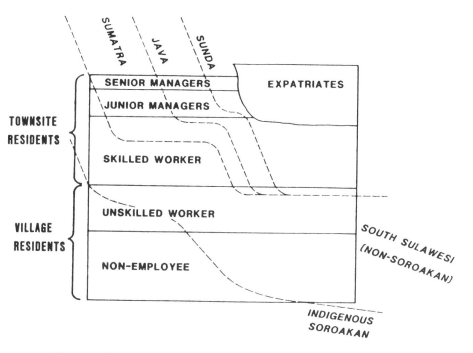

Fig. 9.1 Diagram of the superimposition of the hierarchy of racial and ethnic groups on the company job ladder.

The 'racial' and 'ethnic' groups tended to interpret each other's behaviour in terms of stereotypes that identified negatively evaluated behaviour as generated by inherent characteristics of each group. The different fortunes of people at the various status levels were seen to arise as a consequence of those negative characteristics, thus masking a perception of the ways in which inequality arose from the class struggle. The most negative stereotypes were held by people high on the status ladder, about those at the bottom. In particular, expatriates 'understood' the behaviour of Indonesians in terms of racist stereotypes.

The racist liturgy had a familiar ring to it; Indonesians were seen as stupid, unclean, and morally inferior to whites. In the context of the work place, Indonesians were regarded as less competent than expatriates. This was displayed, for example, in anxiety about the Indonesianisation programme set out in the Contract of Work (chap. 4). It was assumed that the plant would not function without the foreign experts. The Indonesian manager of the government-owned nickel project at Pomalaa, Southeast Sulawesi, had experienced these attitudes. A party of engineers from Inco, after visiting his project, had expressed disbelief that it functioned without a single foreigner. (They expressed their lack of regard for the Indonesian management by arriving for the meeting wearing shorts and without shirts.)

The expatriates' assumption of superiority to the Indonesians, and their feeling of separateness from them, was manifested in the use of the personal pronouns 'they' and 'them' to mean Indonesians, without any prior referent. Racist ideology validated the superior social and economic position of expatriates as 'natural,' deriving from inherent superiority. The poverty and degradation of some of the Indonesian people was taken as proof of their inferiority, and of white superiority.

There was on the part of the expatriates an indifference, even, in many cases, hostility, to Indonesian people and their way of life. For instance, it was a common assumption that when taking holidays one would leave the country as soon as possible. Very few expatriates took the opportunity to explore other parts of Indonesia, although they would visit other Asian countries. These assumptions were sustained by an unreflective cast of mind. In a typical encounter, an Australian engineer asked me if I had met any Indonesian academics, and how they compared with scholars back home. When I replied that I found them much the same he paused for a moment and then replied:

Well, I suppose they are a bit more sophisticated than the
ones we have to deal with, who have just come down from
the trees.

When I pressed him concerning the performance of his Indonesian labourers, he agreed it was quite remarkable given their lack of
formal education and work experience. He said that their work compared favourably with the performance of an Australian unskilled
worker. But he did not see his reply as contradicting his expressed attitudes.

Indonesian-Expatriate Relations in the Townsite

The C and D areas, and the Old Camp (map 2.2), housed both Indonesians and expatriates. Initially, it was intended that all expatriates would live in the C area, but the increase in the scale of the
project and the underestimation of the number of expatriate
employees had meant that the C area could not accommodate them
all, and many had to live in lower standard D accommodation. This
led to resentment among those expatriates who felt that they had
been allocated substandard housing—substandard because it was initially intended for Indonesian employees.
Residential integration did not ensure any social integration.
Many expatriates had no desire to mix with Indonesians outside of
the work place. Neighbours of different races usually did not know
one another's names. Few of the expatriates spoke Indonesian, and
few of the Indonesian women in the townsite spoke English fluently.
However, a few close, mixed-race friendships had developed between people at management level in the early days of the project.
One of the long-term Indonesian residents confided to me (in 1980)
that, since those particular expatriate families had left, 'there was no
one [from among the expatriates] that we can feel close to.' Her point
was starkly illustrated a moment after she made the comment. We
were at a gathering to bid farewell to an expatriate woman who had a
close friendship with her Indonesian neighbour. Some expatriate
guests arrived, women I remembered from my first field trip. They
did not know the Indonesian women present, although they had all
lived in the C area for several years. When introductions were made,
one of the expatriate women said (to an Indonesian woman), 'I know
the face.' I took it to be a joke, the kind one makes when a third party

introduces one to an old friend, but in fact it was a serious comment. It was an indication of the racial gulf, even in the C area.

It was rare for Indonesians and expatriates to be present together at informal social gatherings. At the lunch just mentioned, women of the two racial groups did not sit together. If I attended a dinner or a party in townsite, it was usually an all-Indonesian or all-expatriate affair.

I only once attended a party given by expatriates to which they invited many Indonesian guests. The Australian hosts invited their Indonesian neighbours (about forty adults and children) and about half a dozen expatriates. The evening began rather stiffly, until the Indonesian guests entertained us with traditional dance, and the Australians reciprocated by showing some Super-8 cartoons. The hosts served rice and curries, showing consideration for their guests' tastes. The evening ended on a merry note, with everyone dancing to rock-and-roll music, including women who had come in traditional dress. It was a rare gesture of good will from expatriates toward their Indonesian neighbours and fellow workers. The party took place in the Old Camp, where the expatriates were all on lower rungs of the job ladder and where, by 1979, the majority of the population were Indonesians.

The only other social occasions regularly attended by both Indonesians and expatriates were semiofficial functions, such as cocktail parties for distinguished visitors, or dinners to bid farewell to expatriate bosses. The only exceptions to the rule were the long-term residents mentioned above, who had mixed race friendships dating from the early days of the project camp, and who attended each other's social gatherings.

The Club (a feature of all mining towns) was the focus of organised social life, having film screenings and other organised entertainment. It was called the All Nations Club (*Taman Antar Bangsa*). Perhaps there had been a dream that it would serve as a meeting place for all townsite inhabitants, but it was predominantly an expatriate domain. Expatriate men gathered at the bar after work, and mainly expatriates ate in the restaurant. Some Indonesian families would attend the Sunday night Happy Hour, where cheap meals and half-price drinks were served. On these occasions they always sat in groups separate from the expatriates, sipping soft drinks while the expatriates imbibed alcohol. I found these occasions awkward, feeling caught between the two groups. If I was sitting with Indonesian friends, for instance, expatriates who came to chat with me would not interact with my companions.

The Club provided the venue for the activities of the Soroako Women's League, which included luncheons, card days, and craft lessons. Membership was open to all, though on the whole it attracted expatriate women. A few of the elite Indonesian wives from the C area were members, but as proceedings were always in English, this excluded most Indonesian women. There was no concession to Indonesian notions of propriety at the group's functions. The raucous behaviour at some of the luncheons embarrassed the Indonesian women. The organisers of a United Nations Day function served a meal that included pork, taking no account that all but two of the Indonesian women present were Muslims.

By and large, expatriates disliked having Indonesian neighbours. Those who lived in the D area resented that their accommodation was inferior to that of the C area and felt demeaned by the large number of Indonesians there. There were constant complaints to the Town Administration about the behaviour of Indonesian neighbours. A common protest concerned Indonesians' keeping of chickens in their yards. The man who dealt with the complaints (an Indonesian) said to me, bemusedly:

> They object to being woken by roosters. But it is our custom (*adat*) to keep chickens. We regard it as lucky, because they wake you for the dawn prayer.

Indonesian residents of the D area were amused by the fact that their neighbours found them too noisy. A friend who had moved from the village to the D area joked about the sensitive hearing of her expatriate neighbours:

> I often shout at the kids, or call out to them and then (she giggled) I remember that I'm not on the edge of the lake anymore, where my voice can be carried by the wind.

An American woman who had just moved out of the Old Camp told me she had been glad to leave, as the suburb was being ruined by the influx of Indonesian families, who were moving in as the American construction personnel left. I repeated her comment to another expatriate woman who replied 'People in the Old Camp do have to put up with their neighbours stealing from them.' When I asked how they knew their neighbours were responsible, she said 'When the Indonesians moved in, the number of thefts went up.' (The thefts were being committed by retrenched workers whose unemployment stemmed from the same cause as the exodus of American personnel: the end of the construction phase.)

In the townsite near the dam construction at Larona (map 2.1), the residents had even expressed a desire to enclose the settlement with a wire fence to keep Indonesians out. At a meeting to discuss the matter, it was pointed out that the only Indonesians entering the remote township were the household servants and the shop assistants in the company supermarket. The plan was dropped.

Residential integration in no way ensured social integration, nor did it promote racial harmony and understanding. Segregation in other company facilities reinforced the ideas of white superiority used to justify the whites' more privileged position in Soroako.

Segregation

The Inco hospital had separate Indonesian and expatriate clinics, where doctors consulted patients of their own race. The waiting rooms were segregated, the expatriate section being inside the hospital entrance. It was air-conditioned and less crowded, with more comfortable seating than the Indonesian waiting room, which was an annex with a concrete floor, outside the main entrance. There, patients waited for hours, sitting on hard benches, to see a doctor. High-ranking Indonesians could consult the expatriate doctors. However, there were complaints from expatriates when their doctors treated Indonesians, especially if the 'interlopers' were treated before a waiting white person.

The company store was also segregated. Apart from being accessible only to employees of 'skilled worker' status and above, the store had two sections: a duty-free section that sold imported items to expatriates and a section selling Indonesian products to Indonesian employees. Senior manager level employees had won the privilege of shopping in the duty-free section, but by and large the store was segregated. Few expatriates shopped in the 'local' section.

The schools were similarly segregated by occupational status and race. Only children of skilled workers and above could attend company schools. They were further divided between children of skilled workers, who attended the all-Indonesian school in the *F* area, and the children of junior and senior managers, as well as expatriate children, who attended school in the *C* area. The Junior High School (in the C area complex) was open to all children of Indonesian employees of skilled worker status and above.

The C area school had been intended as an experiment in multicultural education. Its founder, an imaginative expatriate teacher, felt that in addition to children studying a basic curriculum in their native language (English or Indonesian) the school should provide integrated activities in sport, music, and art. This would enrich the learning experience. In particular, expatriate children could realise an opportunity for an education that took advantage of the exotic physical and social environment in which they were living. Her ideas were given some thrust from a provision by the Indonesian government that Indonesian children study English at the school, and vice versa. Despite opposition by many of the expatriate parents and the Australian school teachers, she was able to implement some innovations in this direction. Indonesian and English classrooms were arranged alternately, while class times and recreation coincided in both streams. Hence the children could play together. (Parental opposition stemmed from an anxiety that their children might be disadvantaged by their absence from their home country. They did not wish their children to have a novel educational experience: indeed, the idea appalled many of them.)

Her innovations did not survive this teacher's departure. A fight between an expatriate and an Indonesian child on the overcrowded school bus from the Old Camp provided an excuse for the teachers to stagger class times, so the Indonesian children began school earlier and had breaks at different times from expatriate children. It was argued that this would prevent overcrowding on the buses. Further, classes were located in different sections of the building. The teachers began demanding that the library and sporting equipment be segregated, to prevent more of the damage they claimed was inflicted by Indonesian children. The expatriates thus sabotaged plans that the school provide a focus for interracial cooperation and mutual understanding. Indonesian parents, on the other hand, had not objected to the way the school was organised.

By and large, the motivation for the expatriates in coming to Soroako was not to seek adventure and exotic experience. The contract employees were attracted by the opportunity to earn large salaries. The Canadian permanent Inco employees were following a company directive that posted them overseas. In this the teachers were no different from the majority of expatriate employees; thus, they provided no counter to the narrow attitudes of the majority of parents.

Nor did the sporting facilities in the townsite help to integrate the community. Indonesian professional and managerial employees used the tennis courts and golf course, but usually they did not play with expatriates. Volleyball was popular, but attracted only Indonesians. However, a soccer competition established by a group of expatriates and elite Indonesians did attract support from all sections of the community. Teams represented sections of the company (mining, exploration, and so on) and the village also fielded a team. A few expatriates played on the teams. The games were enthusiastically watched by a largely Indonesian crowd.

Racial Conflict

The soccer matches also gave rise to one of the few incidents of overt conflict between Indonesians and expatriates. Enthusiastic supporters, like their counterparts elsewhere, would stop at nothing to ensure their team's victory, including harassing the opponent's goal keeper. In the competitive atmosphere, violence sometimes erupted. On one such occasion, an expatriate intervened in a fight between two Indonesian players. He probably felt secure that his status as a white man and a boss would give him the necessary authority. However, he was also punched. His assailant was immediately detained by Inco security guards. Later that evening the club house near the soccer field was burned down, and rumour related the incident to the fight. News of the fights and its aftermath swept Soroako and a number of different interpretations were made of the events. The expatriate response was very paranoid, interpreting the incident as antiwhite racism: the man was punched because he was a white. Indonesians interpreted the events in more particular terms: he was hit because he had intervened in a fight, and the fire was an act of revenge by the detained man's friends. I was interested in the expatriate response. It indicated that they saw themselves in an embattled position, where there was always the possibility of racial violence. The event indicated to them a degree of antiwhite feeling that they felt existed, despite a lack of tangible evidence. In fact, such violent incidents were extremely rare. The incident became a *cause celebre* among the expatriates, and its import was greatly exaggerated.

Regular conflict between Indonesians and expatriates occurred mainly in the bars in New Village. White men would become drunk and aggressive, causing offence to the Indonesians. A hostess in one of the bars told me her main job was keeping the expatriates and the Indonesians (by which she meant the village policemen) away from each other. In a typical incident, a drunken expatriate returned to his car to find his jacket missing. He angrily pounded on the door of what he thought was the bar where he had been drinking. He forced the door open, but it was the house of an Indonesian policeman whose wife and children were asleep inside. The angry policeman (who was absent at the time) let it be known that he had a bullet waiting for the expatriate. After this, and similar ugly incidents, Inco quickly flew the offender out of Indonesia.

Another incident that caused a stir in the expatriate community occurred at a bazaar held by the Women's League, at which second-hand goods were on sale. Such cast-offs from expatriate households were highly desired by Indonesian women. The foreign clothes and household goods were the concrete symbols of the higher status of the whites and were desired for the status they conferred on their new owners. The behaviour of the Indonesian customers at the bazaar shocked the expatriates; they crowded in, fighting and pushing for the goods on sale. The incident that created the biggest scandal during the bazaar was the disappearance of a carton of (imported) milk, from the self-service morning tea table. It was assumed that it had been taken by an Indonesian woman. The expatriate women discussed the behaviour of Indonesians at the bazaar for weeks. The actions of an English woman who tried to control the crowd of customers became legendary; she took on the character of a heroine.

The behaviour of the Indonesian women stemmed from fetishizing the material rewards for high status in Soroako. The avariciousness displayed mirrored that of the expatriate women, who filled their houses with goods obtained on trips away, and sold off unwanted household items when leaving, rather than give them to their neighbours. (Some even sold already opened jars of imported jam or bottles of alcohol.)

The infrequency of social interaction across racial lines meant that misunderstanding and conflicting expectations were bound to occur. Neither group was sufficiently aware of the norms of daily behaviour of the other.

Servants

All expatriate households had one or two maids and usually a gardener, providing the main interaction most expatriates had with Indonesians. These relations were fraught with tension and misunderstanding. Few of the mistresses spoke Indonesian, and few of the servants, English.

The 'servant problem' was a favoured topic of converstion when white women got together, and old hands were always giving newcomers the benefit of their experience. Women would remember their initial frustration and anxiety at having a stranger in the house, someone they were supposed to order about, and yet, with whom they could not properly communicate. One woman remembered hiding in the bathroom and trying not to cry when her new maid sulked about the wage. It seemed odd that the first thing new arrivals did was engage a maid. Almost universally, the expatriates were unaccustomed to having servants before arriving in Soroako, and the stress of handling the new relationship became an additional anxiety in the alien environment. However, an adequate complement of household staff was regarded as an important aspect of the expatriate lifestyle, and it was taken for granted that every newcomer would follow suit. Since the modern houses did not require a lot of daily upkeep, which was easily carried out by the maids, the women were left with little to do. They filled a life of boredom with luncheons, card games, and sporting activities.

It was at these gatherings of bored women that the servant probbem would be discussed, for example, the appropriate level of wages for them. The anxiety was always about paying too much, never too little. Expatriates paid servants between Rp.7,000 and Rp.8,000 (US$17 and $19) per month. This compared favourably with between Rp.5,000 and Rp.8,000 (US$12 and $17) per month paid by Indonesian employers in the townsite.

It was accepted that the more highly paid expatriates should pay a higher wage. However, many expatriates viewed the payment as an ordinary wage and accepted no further responsibility for their servants. Indonesian employers construed the relation in a different way: besides paying the monthly wage, the employer accepted responsibility to feed and clothe the servant, and often to provide lodgings. At the end of the Muslim fasting month it was customary for servants to receive an extra month's wage and a new set of clothes. This responsibility, when mentioned in a discussion at the Women's League, was generally rejected by the expatriate women. They felt they paid enough. In a paradoxical fashion, the fact that they could employ labour at such exploitative rates transformed itself into a fear of being cheated. It was assumed that the boss set the wage, and a maid who asked for more was regarded as 'cheeky.' The rationalisation was also often made that it would be doing the servants a disservice to pay them a higher wage, because this would engender rising expectations, which would not be met when the expatriates left. I have often heard the same argument from tourists, arguing that, if they paid a higher than local price for goods, it would set in motion an inflation of prices for the locals: therefore, their moral duty was to pay a low price. The locals, of course, are not stupid and cope easily with multitiered price or wage systems, charging what the consumer will bear.

A related anxiety of white mistresses focussed on what to give servants to eat. A common, and convenient, idea was that Indonesians ate only rice. I heard the opinion expressed that one should not give a maid eggs, because soon she would be asking for chicken or fish. The maids could not comprehend such meanness on the part of people who had so much. Women who were offered only rice for lunch would open refrigerators and find them stacked full of (forbidden) food.

A number of young women resigned as a result of such meanness. In discussing expatriate bosses, it was acknowledged that many were very generous, bringing their employees gifts when they returned from home leave, and so on. As one put it, 'But if they are mean, their stinginess is beyond belief' (*Kalau mereka kikir, bukan main kikirnya*). Another common manifestation of meanness was the refusal of some employers to pay a servant's bus fare to work after Inco cut out the free bus service. It cost the women Rp.300 per week, a sizable chunk of their monthly wage—but less than the price of a packet of cigarettes for an expatriate.

The pervasiveness of hierarchy and status differences in Soroako infused all relations with an exaggerated concern with inequality. For many of the expatriates, who came from societies where daily inter-actions were based on more egalitarian principles, this gave rise to discomfort and confusion. These problems are well exemplified in the following incident.

An American woman was in tears because she had just fired her maid, for whom she and her son had developed some affection, but who had suddenly become careless and unreliable a few weeks previously. She related the events while sitting sobbing on a neighbour's verandah as we watched the maid leave on the bus. In spite of her anguish at having to treat someone 'so unequal,' it did not occur to her that something may have upset the servant to lead to so dramatic a change in her behaviour. The American woman was simultaneously distressed at having to sack the maid, thus acting as a superior, and at not getting her money's worth.

Another woman told me of her irritation and indignation on discovering that her gardener, whom she had paid Rp.4,000 (US$10) per month, owned extensive rice lands and livestock. The man said he had sought employment out of curiosity about expatriates. She was most indignant at this disturbance of the proper hierarchical order, saying to her husband, 'Do you realise he's worth more than you?' (This was a dubious assertion.)

Simone de Beauvoir made a telling comment about the expatriate obsession to stay on top in any economic transaction with the poor of the Third World. Describing negotiations between tourists and a boat man in Algeria, she wrote:

> Three young, beared Frenchmen, anxious not to be 'had', were chaffering over the price of their passage in an arrogant way that ill-concealed their avarice, when in a poor country. They would have felt exploited themselves if they didn't ex-ploit the populace (1965, p.307).

Stealing

Theft was one of the main motifs in interracial relations in Soroako. Company management were concerned at the amount of stealing from the work place, which ranged from petty pilfering of light bulbs, seat belts, paint, and writing paper to the theft of expen-sive equipment. One incident involving the theft of a scientific instrument worth $20,000 had apparently been the work of a well-organised gang, operating on a previously placed order for the apparatus. The theft of food from the mess in the camp (men taking more than they needed and giving it to others) was also a major concern. Indeed, one manager argued that the loss of food from the camp balanced out any obligation Inco had for the welfare of the unskilled workers living in the village.

There was also a lot of stealing in the townsite—both pilfering by household servants and break-ins, especially while the householders were absent on leave. In the village, by contrast, theft was rare. Expatriates were always amazed that I did not keep my possessions and money under lock and key.

Inco had a private police force, whose major responsibility was the security of company installations. All people leaving the project area, by road or plane, were subject to search by these guards. They were arbitrary in their style of enforcement, and remarkably inefficient in preventing crime. It was widely believed, even by company managers, that they were involved in much of the theft, or at least turned a blind eye in return for a share of the profits of crime.

Stealing was an obsession with the expatriate community. They talked about the subject constantly. It was another focus for their anxiety and guilt. The high level of theft was a constant reminder than they were a privileged, affluent elite in a community where some of the people were extremely poor.

Much of the theft from the work place was of items people desired in order to improve their homes; timber, paint, and pipes and hoses to bring water from the standpipes. The pilfering by servants derived from the temptation presented by the abundance of consumer goods they saw in their employers' homes. They stole Coca-Cola, radios, jeans, and other such potent symbols of modern life, indeed the very consumer goods whose desirability kept them striving for a foothold in the modern market place. Household servants were the lowest paid workers in Soroako, yet they faced at closest quarters the abundance of consumer goods that they were the least able to afford. The high level of theft was related to the rising expectations of Indonesians living in the mining town.

The attitude of the thieves, that people with so much should share it around, was constantly validated by the fact that petty theft would often not be noticed for some time. The conspicuous consumption of wealth by the expatriates was constantly remarked on by Indonesians, even the relatively well-off, living in the townsite. Market traders always countered expatriates' efforts to bargain over a price with the statement that they had lots of money (the implication being they should spread it around). This always met with an indignant or angry response. It hit a responsive nerve and could not be laughed off. Many expatriates seemed to believe their own protestations that they were really hard up.

There was a marked increase in the amount of theft at the time when workers were being retrenched. In the case of house breaking, this was a consequence of the number of recently unemployed people waiting around in the hope of obtaining another job. There was also an upsurge in pilfering in the work place. Doubtless much of this was by people taking a chance, when they knew they were leaving, that they could not be sacked if caught. But such behaviour also derived from feelings of bitterness against the company. As one man put it:

> I have been a faithful employee for eight years. The company has used me up, and now I'm being thrown away. Lots of people are in the same situation. We feel upset and resentful (*sakit hati*) towards the company. That is why we steal.

They were confused at the impersonal nature of the wage relation, and felt loyalty on their part ought to be reciprocated. They understood their relation to the company in terms of the inappropriate model of patron-client ties that were totally inconsistent with the impersonal nature of the wage relation.

In a dramatic occurrence in 1979, a group of indigenous Soroakan men stole a quantity of aircraft fuel, which was used by the project manager for the light aircraft he flew for recreation. The thieves were rounded up by Inco security and handed over to the police. It eventuated that the fuel had initially been stolen by an Inco employee. He pitied some friends who, having been retrenched, were trying to make a living from farming. They travelled to their fields by motorised boat and, without a regular source of cash income, fuel was hard to come by. He told the men that the fuel he gave them was being dumped by the company. (The story was not implausible, as Inco often threw away items like timber and oil drums that village people could use; indeed, some men had been in trouble with the security guards for taking such refuse home.) Believing the Inco employee, the Soroakan men themselves stole more of the fuel.

The incident caused great shame to the indigenous Soroakans; it was the first time any of them had been caught stealing. The police chief in Wasuponda believed their story, and sent them home after a night in gaol. They were very ashamed and concerned to explain themselves. For example, two of the men who were friends of mine felt it necessary to visit me to give an embarrassed explanation of their involvement in the matter.

Besides censuring their behaviour, many of their kinsmen were keen to point out that the events were inevitable, given the increase in unemployment. 'If men can't get work, what other option is there?' people asked. Stealing was unequivocally related to the troubled times, and village residents constantly predicted that the incidence would increase further, with more retrenchments.

To the expatriates, all that the stealing proved was the fundamentally flawed nature of the Indonesian character. Theft figured in racist jibes and jokes among the expatriates. In a typical instance, a group of white women were complaining at the small size of the bunches of celery on sale in the company supermarket. 'The Indonesians must have been at it' (i.e., stolen some of the sticks), one commented. I was surprised to hear the racist joke from that particular woman: she had been sensitive to, and critical of, the uncharitable stereotypes of Indonesians when she first arrived, but was coming to accept those views herself.

Expatriate attitudes towards stealing entailed a fundamental hypocrisy. Many goods were hard to come by in the remote area, the company having to import them for its own use. This contributed to the high level of theft, in which the expatriates were also involved. Expatriates extended their company houses and made household items from materials plundered from the company. An expatriate friend (who was scrupulously honest, never deriving any advantage from his position in the company) told me the following story. A dinner guest arrived at my friend's home in an angry mood. He had just visited the work place on a Sunday afternoon and discovered an Indonesian employee taking some wood. He expostulated angrily on the thieving nature of Indonesians. My friend asked why the man had gone to work himself on a day off. He replied that he had just been picking up some of the matierals he needed to build a raft. My friend asked what difference there was between his behaviour and that of the Indonesian. The man replied (getting angrier) that if he came to work in such a remote place and suffered such difficult work conditions, it was his right to have access to things that made his life pleasant, like a raft for outings on the lake. So, in Soroako, even theft was a privilege that accrued to those of high status. There were many pleasure craft, all manufactured from materials stolen from Inco or the contractors, as well as barbeques and other household items illegally manufactured in company workshops. The project manager had decided to turn a blind eye to such behaviour by expatriates, but Indonesian workers had been punished for theft that arose from similar motivations (for example, the desire to improve one's house in the village, thus enhancing one's quality of life). The hypocrisy of this stand was not lot on the Indonesians, who saw the evidence of their bosses' pilfering as they went boating on the lake on weekends.

Expatriates and the Village

The expatriates' ignorance of the customary behaviour and conditions of daily life of Indonesian people was most profound with respect to the inhabitants of the village. Many foreigners never entered the village, and for those who did it was usually to shop in the market and adjacent stores, or to patronise rattan factories and tailors.

They were ignorant of the ways in which the village had changed as a result of the project, and they regarded the poverty and dirt as the outcome of its inhabitants' laziness or ignorance. For example, one woman criticised the villagers for 'letting things go.' Her view was that they had lost pride in their village and neglected things, once the company came. She supported her argument by making invidious comparisons with the other villages on the shores of Lake Matano, which had not felt so directly the impact of Inco's presence, and so still retained their rustic charm.

In a similar vein, an Australian teacher advised the Town Administrator not to be too hasty in his plan to provide water, sanitation, and garbage services to the village. 'You musn't move too fast and have these pople coping with a level of facilities that they are not used to.' I asked him if he thought their villages of origin were as filthy as

Soroako. Had he not noticed that other villages in the region coped with these problems, that they were within their capacity to solve? He took the point, but time and time again I found that unreflective attitudes fed racist prejudice.

When expatriates did enter village houses as guests, they were often so concerned about unhygienic conditions that they would refuse all food and drink offered. The village residents commented on this, and interpreted such behaviour as indicating that the expatriates thought the Indonesians would poison them. It was my experience in Sulawesi to be always warned against accepting food from people in villages where my protectors had no kin. People felt vulnerable in the role of stranger. The expatriate anxiety about accepting food stemmed from the same anxieties about the strangeness of unknown others. Although expatriates claimed that their refusal derived from a rational precaution against disease, the anxiety was held to an irrational degree. The Indonesians' explanation of their behaviour held a lot of truth. The most bizarre instance of this kind of behaviour was the practice of some women of roasting any food they had bought in the F market before eating it.

Expatriates were totally ignorant of the economic conditions of the village residents' lives. They were unaware that village residents farmed the mountains, even though all phases of the agricultural cycle were visible from the townsite. Some told me of the strange primitive folk they saw coming down from the hills—the villagers in work clothes returning from the fields. I heard an account of comments made by some expatriate women, as they noticed smoke in the distance, while they were playing golf (on the site of the Soroakans' former paddy fields). One said, 'Look at those stupid people, burning off the jungle and destroying the environment.' My informant told me she replied: 'Not so much as Inco has already.' (The strip-mined hills were in the foreground of the view from the golf course.) This women clearly felt she was presenting an enlightened attitude to me. She was, however, surprised when I told her there was a rational reason for the burning, in that farmers were preparing their fields for the sowing of rice.

The tendency to see poverty and hardship for the people at the bottom of the hierarchy as arising 'naturally,' as a consequence of their own shortcomings, was evident in the expatriates' responses to the increasing unemployment in Soroako. They were totally ignorant of the possibilities retrenched workers had for making a living. For example, an expatriate woman commented that she had seen some Indonesians hawking pots and woven mats in the townsite:

> Thank God they are getting off their backsides and doing something now they've been laid off, and not just waiting for the company to provide everything.

(They were in fact itinerant peddlars from Ujung Pandang.) This was a common belief, that the Indonesian residents of the mining town (who received least from the company in wages and other benefits, even when they were employed) expected the company to provide everything. The expatriates who held this belief *did* have everything provided by the company, and complained bitterly about shortcomings in the service, for example, of shortages of particular foods in their store or slow service from Town Maintenance for routine repairs to their houses. The woman who made the above comment lived a life of complete idleness; in the course of our conversation in the hospital waiting room, she complained that she would miss her card game because of the long wait. The common expatriate philosophy could be characterised as 'The more you have, the more you deserve.'

Such tough-minded attitudes seemed to derive from the uneasiness the expatriates felt as members of a wealthy elite, facing every day the realities of the inequalities of contemporary capitalism. Many of them were ordinary working people back home in Australia, Canada or America, unaccustomed to seeing themselves as part of management, their interests so closely allied with those of capital. Many felt guilt in the unaccustomed position, but the guilt manifested itself as anger. They thus denied their complicity in the generation of the poverty and misfortune they saw around them.

Nowhere was this more evident than in the village market, one of the few exotic experiences available to the expatriate women. Though it was difficult to buy goods costing more than a few dollars there, the women were extremely anxious about the prices they were charged. In the market place, economic inequalities were out in the open. The stall owners, mostly Bugis, were tough-minded in their dealings with expatriates, and their frequent reminders to the expatriate shoppers that they had lots of money made the latter angry. Expatriate shoppers always seemed tense, and bargaining made them anxious, since they always felt they were being 'ripped off.'

Few expatriates had social encounters with Indonesians resident in the village, and such encounters were usually tension filled. Just as they felt awkward in interactions with townsite Indonesian residents, for example, in the Club, they were gauche in dealing with people in the village. An expatriate woman made a rare visit to my house, bringing some old bottles (to be used for kerosene) for my hostess. I asked a young man to entertain her while I finished lunch. He spoke some English, and the visitor spoke little Indonesian. When I joined them she was speaking to him in her poor Indonesian, and address-ing him in the second person (*kamu*), a form of address that is very impolite in an interaction between strangers. She had not ascertained that he spoke English, and he was so appalled by the situation that he did not press the point. When I arrived, the situation worsened; she no longer addressed him directly, but asked me questions about him. She was so discomfited that she did not even exercise normal politeness.

Relations between expatriates and village residents did not grow closer with time. During the construction phase of the project, there were always some expatriate guests at all but the smallest weddings, including some whom I had been pressed to invite, and others in-vited by the families of the bride and groom. In the early days of the project, I was told that potatoes had been served to foreign guests at weddings because it was assumed they did not know how to eat rice. By 1980, there was a marked change, a number of weddings having no expatriate guests.

It seemed that insularity of the racial groups was increasing with time. On my way back to Soroako in 1980, I heard from a former ex-patriate resident that there was a plan to fence the village, to keep its residents out of the townsite. I heard nothing of such a plan in Soroako, but it is significant that an exresident could believe it to be true.

During my field work, a number of long-term expatriate employees, who had shepherded the project through its initial phases, left. Farewell parties were frequent. On only two such occa-sions did low-ranking Indonesian employees attend these functions. Both of these expatriate families had lived in the area since early ex-ploration days, and they had made an effort to establish friendships with Indonesian families of all levels. Many of the others remained impersonal and unknown 'bosses.'

My presence in the village provided a link with its population that was used by some of the expatriates. Some tried to exploit an assumed identity of interest, opposed to the village residents, in using me as an intermediary to negotiate boat hire, prices in the market, and so on, assuming I would press for a cheap price. However, there were a number of links established through me that derived from nobler motives. For example, the Women's League and another association, the Hospital Volunteers, became involved in welfare activities in the village, supplying equipment for the village clinic, even financing the completion of a new clinic, when Inco pulled out of the construction with the building only half-completed. These women later established a programme to weigh infants and distribute supplementary food to underweight children.

Indonesian Attitudes towards Expatriates

Just as expatriates saw the inferior status of Indonesians in the occupational and status hierarchies as natural, a product of their lesser intelligence, Indonesian residents in the vilage tended to assume that all white people were very clever, evidenced by their ability to make cars, aeroplanes, and other machines, as well as their superior status in the mining town. One old man came with me to visit a house in the townsite. He told his wife of the technological marvels of the house: running water, electrical appliances, and so on. The house had everything 'except human breath.' He was very impressed also that his grandchildren, who had accompanied us, had learned how to operate those marvels of modern technology.

The low-ranking Indonesian employees evaluated expatriate bosses positively. They were said to be free of the unfair and particularistic attitudes towards their underlings that Indonesian bosses were seen to have (see chap. 10). Their relations with expatriates were mediated by Indonesian middle-level personnel, the latter being viewed as the real cause of their failure to advance on the job ladder.

The higher-ranking Indonesians were less appreciative of expatriate bosses. These men, many of whom were highly qualified, resented the assumptions of inferiority based on race that were pervasive in the company. They resented the higher pay of expatriates who were performing the same tasks as themselves. Also, expatriates

were believed to be unnecessarily slow in passing on skills to Indonesians, thus 'hindering "Indonesianisation"'' (Kamm 1978).

A young Indonesian engineer expresed his resentment in the
following way:

> Sometimes I can barely stand working with expats. They treat
> us so much as inferiors. If we make a suggestion, it's not ac-
> cepted, because we're Indonesians. They shout at us and use
> rude words over the smallest matter and to us that is really
> rude (*kasar*). We Indonesians have more sensitive feelings
> than foreigners. (*Kita orang Indonesia lebih halus perasaan
> daripada orang asing*).

In many incidents expatriate foremen and supervisors acted in
ways that would have led to strikes in their home countries. For instance, a number of trade teachers protested at being driven to the
plantsite in the same bus as their Indonesian apprentices.

The townsite Indonesians in particular were aware of the expatriates' feelings of superiority. They were very resentful of such
racist behaviour as expatriates insisting on being served first in the
supermarket, or complaining about white doctors treating Indonesians as well as themselves. One Indonesian advanced the theory that
the Australians were racist because many of them had been in
Bougainville, where there was segregation of blacks and whites.
Manifesting his own racist attitudes, he said it was understandable
that whites would feel superior to black Bougainvilleans, but it was
incomprehensible that they should extend such attitudes to people
like himself.

In spite of their generally high regard for expatriates, villagers too
had their reservations. Most of the foreigners invited to weddings
would treat the occasion with the respect due an invitation anywhere.
They would dress in suitable clothes and behave politely. Unfortunately, this was not always so. In one of the worst displays of arrogant behaviour, a group of expatriates arrived late for a wedding in
Nuha. They were wearing shorts (which the hosts equated with
underwear) and no shirts, though they did throw on shirts as they
approached the pavilion. Nevertheless, they were treated as
honoured guests, and seats were provided for them in the front row.
They refused the food offered at the reception and persisted in their
refusal even when I told them such behaviour was impolite. In spite
of their gross behaviour, they continued to be treated with respect. I

was very angry, especially since the invitation had been made through me, but could not display my anger (which would have further evinced the grossness of foreigners). I later apologised to the organiser of their wedding. She replied that indeed expatriates clung too strongly to their own customs, that she thought the guests had 'come on too strong' (*terlalu terang*).

Heavy drinking by whites and the fighting that occasionally accompanied it was also commented on and criticised by all Indonesians. They noticed this behaviour in the village bars and also on the home-made rafts that sailed past the village on weekends.

The large size of expatriate men, and their propensity to violence when drunk, made some Indonesians frightened of them and fearful of chance encounters. Many people recounted meetings with expatriate men in the jungle that they found alarming. For example, one woman was alone in her rice field with her young son, when about fifty large white men came running past. The woman and child were terrified and ran to hide. It was the weekly run of the local chapter of the 'Hash House Harriers,' an institution found in most expatriate communities in Southeast Asia. The men run through the jungle, following a paper trail, and drink large quantities of beer at the finish. I was not surprised that such a celebration of the most 'macho' values was terrifying to the Indonesian woman and her son.

Some of the questions I was asked about the behaviour of white people made me wonder if the Indonesians, especially the village people, regarded us as truly human in the sense of being of the same mould as themselves. For example, I was often asked if white women breast fed. It was common conviction that we could not. It was also a widely held belief that we were unable to give birth to twins.

For Indonesians resident in the townsite, living at close quarters with expatriates gave them cause for reflection, as they could see that urban Indonesian culture was changing in the direction of Western culture. Some had reservations about aspects of the impending change. Some expressed the opinion that they would not want to manage human relations in the way their expatriate neighbours did. For example, they saw it as the expatriates' fault that they often did not know their Indonesian neighbours. One man commented that if you visited expatriates while they were eating they would ask you to wait until they were finished, whereas Indonesians would ask you to join them. Such behaviour was described as being 'too much' (*terlalu*). By contrast, townsite Indonesians would describe the Indonesians in a neighbourhood as a 'big family,' always eating in each other's homes, and so on. However, the ambiguous nature of their own position, in transition between the values of a peasant and a class-based society, was indicated by their attitudes towards the village residents, whom they viewed as 'too much' in the other direction. Villagers, for example, were regarded as having too many relatives living with them to support on a small wage. For the townsite Indonesians, the ideal was 'a middle path,' with a limited degree of cooperation and mutual help between kin and neighbours. For the Indonesian residents of the mining town, racist denigration by whites was often countered by negative stereotypes of whites. However these did not lead to a perceived unity of interest in opposition to whites (see chap. 10).

Conclusion

Contrasts in lifestyle were a daily reminder of differences in wealth and privilege between different strata of the mining town. These differences arose from the structure of economic domination, but at the ideological level they were represented as 'natural,' a consequence of inherent racial characteristics. Racist ideology provided a justification for the superior position of the whites who, in Soroako, represented the interests of capital: it had the same significance in the neocolonial situation as it had under colonialism.

However, race was not the only ideology of class domination. The significance of ethnicity in 'naturalising' class relations is examined in the following chapter, which also discusses the importance of ethnicity as an ideology that can mobilise resistance to class-based forms of oppression.

Chapter 10

Stepchildren of Progress: Ethnicity and Class Consciousness in the Mining Town

How have the indigenous Soroakans responded to, and interpreted, the changes brought about by the project, which has meant proletarianisation for some, semi-employment as part of the industrial reserve army for others, and for all a more complex social and economic environment? An important part of their response has been the assertion of a particular sociocultural identity, that of indigenous Soroakans (*orang asli Soroako*). This chapter examines the assertion of that identity in the context of the manifest form of social organisation that has arisen on the basis of capitalist class relations (as described in chap. 2).

The preceding chapter discussed white racism as an aspect of class domination. The whites related to Indonesians as a unitary group possessing racially distinct characteristics that justified their lowly position on the company job ladder, and hence their low status.

However, the Indonesian residents of the mining town in no way saw themselves as a single group. The hierarchical divisions of the company job ladder also correlated with sociocultural divisions among the Indonesians. They discussed these divisions in terms of ethnicity, using the Indonesian term *suku* (ethnic group), which is usually used in official discussion of sociocultural differences, or the more popular term *sekampung*. The latter term means 'of the same village,' but was used in the sense of a common place of origin. What was regarded as common was contextual: it could be a village, a district, a regency, a linguistic group, an island or (for foreigners) a nation state (see Suparlan 1979, p.58).

Just as an ideology of racial superiority validated for the whites their elevated position in both the company and the mining town, Indonesians explained the relative locations of different sociocultural groups by reference to an ideology of ethnicity: that the differences arose from fundamental cultural differences which justified the unequal distribution of status, privilege, and power.

There is a large literature on ethnicity in postcolonial societies.[1] Many writers follow Geertz, (1963b) in viewing such identities as part of the cultural baggage which peasants bring into the modern world, preventing them from developing the more rational forms of identity appropriate to the modern nation state, such as citizen. For example, in his study of a Sumatran city, Liddle concluded that ethnic or ethnoreligious loyalties based on the

> ineluctable primordial givens of social life produce deeply rooted hostilities which make compromise on local political issues difficult to achieve (1970, p.208).

Ethnic identity is taken as a given, as a fundamental aspect of social structure from which we can derive explanations of other social events, rather than as part of the cultural form we wish to explain by reference to aspects of social structure (See Kahn's critique of this approach [1981a].) The 'primordialist' view is still current in studies of ethnicity (Keyes 1982, p.viii). However, such identities cannot be regarded as structural principles of the same order as class, rather, they are products of consciousness, which can be related to class processes. Such identities arise not only from cultural distinctiveness, but on the basis of social and economic interest (Kahn 1981a, p.49).

Soroakan identity in the contemporary world, though deriving much of its form of symbolic expression from the historically specific experience of the Soroakan people, cannot be understood as simply a hangover from that past, but as a response to forms of class oppression. In certain contexts, their shared identity has served as a basis for political mobilisation and struggle against forms of oppression. However, it was counterproductive in relation to other struggles in that it masked the class processes generating inequality.

In investigating the importance of sociocultural identity[2] in the mining town, I first describe forms of social interaction between the different groups of Indonesian nationals. The categories into which they segregate derive from an intersection of the occupational hierarchy with a set of sociocultural identities based on linguistic and/or local group membership. The stress on such group differences derives from the ideology of regional differences propounded by the contemporary Indonesian Government. The country's motto, 'Unity in Diversity,' reflects the recognition of those cultural differences and the importance of forging higher level identities. However, the latter are defined in terms of the interests of the elite. The higher-level identities that are encouraged are national identities, or identities of common function (functional groups) organised under the umbrella of the ruling elite. There is no room for the forging of class-based identity of interest, as was happening under the influence of the Indonesian Communist Party in the Sukarnoist era (see Leclerc 1972).

Sociocultural differences are recognised by the Indonesian Government and their expression sanctioned, so long as they remain at the level of cultural practice: a distinctive style of dress, dance, house construction, and regional languages. This approach is similar to the concept of 'multiculturalism' being officially sanctioned in Australia. Just as, in Australia, the 'identity' of Yugoslavs may incorporate their customary dances, but not their experience of worker self-management in factories, Indonesians may express their sociocultural identity through the costumes they wear at their weddings, but not through asserting ties to particular tracts of land, if that land is required by the government for a development project.[3]

Divisions in the Mining Town

The differential distribution of rewards and privileges that arrived with the mining project gave rise to a status hierarchy that divided the population. There was envy of those deemed to be one's superiors and gloating over those who were worse off.

Even as expatriate employees were concentrated at the top of the company's pyramidal structure, there was a degree of fit also between levels of the hierarchy and a hierarchy of sociocultural groups. Top managers tended to originate from Java, especially West Java, and junior management and skilled workers, from Java or Sumatra with, however, an increased proportion of Sulawesi-born workers in the 'skilled worker' category. 'Unskilled workers' were principally natives of Sulawesi (see fig. 9.1, also fig. 2.1).

The division between the company townsite and the village was fundamental in the mining town. Residents of the two places differed in lifestyle, life chances, and status honour. Village residents were, on the whole, unskilled labourers for the project, or increasingly, in the ranks of the semiemployed.

Village and townsite were also divided in daily life. Employed village men mixed with townsite residents in the work place, but there were few informal social interactions. Village residents rarely visited people in the townsite. Relations between village and townsite residents were usually of patron to client. Townsite women would visit clients in the village, for example, to solicit help in cooking special rice dishes or to procure young coconuts for festive occasions. Such services were usually paid for: they were not organised as labour exchanges, as were such transactions within Soroako. However, the fee was usually established by the patron. Remuneration was often generous—though it could partly comprise cast-off clothes and household items—even so, it was outside the village women's control.

I was discussing the form of these relations with an old man who was a client to a number of families in the F area. He would bring them vegetables from his farm and water their gardens while they were on vacation. In return, they gave him cigarettes or souvenirs from their vacation. I asked him if it would not be better if he were paid at a regular rate for his goods and services. He replied, looking shocked:

> If you receive money, the feeling isn't good. It's better to have good feelings.

There was an assimilation of new social relations to a familiar model deriving from peasant society.

The gulf between villagers and F residents, in terms of wages and lifestyle, was not as great as that between villagers and management. This was reflected in more-regular contacts of a more intimate kind between the villagers and F residents. Indeed, many village residents (although few indigenous Soroakans) had kin and affines in the F area. Even between nonrelated people, in the *F* area as well as the village, ties of sentiment were sometimes strong. For example, in the case of the old man mentioned above, two of his many client families had great affection for him, regarding him as a surrogate grandfather to their children. He in turn valued the friendship of new and different people, and the chance to satisfy an immense curiosity about the way of life of others.

It was extremely rare for village residents to have kin or affines in the *C* or *D* areas, or for relations to take on the intimacy of fictive kinship. For the mass of village residents, there was little interaction with people in the townsite. Many had never even visited the company housing or the townsite shops, and the women in particular felt awkward and out of place in the presence of the more sophisticated people of the townsite.

The elite women's ties to village residents were construed as between patron and client and were more clearly based on the provision of services than were relations with *F* area residents. Ibu Mahmud, the woman with whom I lived, was the principal contact for most of the elite women. They usually requested help, for example, in provisioning feasts, from her. Her association with some of the elite families went back to exploration days, when the geologists and engineers had boarded in her house. Ibu Mahmud was proud of her connection to the elite (unequal though it was) and boasted:

> If the ladies from the townsite want anything, who do they come looking for? Only me.

She valued both their gifts and cast-off clothes and shoes and her visits to their homes, which enabled her to familiarise herself with the elite lifestyle to which she aspired. These connections enhanced her position as a leader in matters of style as well as a broker in the village. There was no doubt of the inequality pervading village-townsite relations, even for Ibu Mahmud, whose relations with elite women were the closest. I once accompanied her to a townsite house to collect an unpaid debt for rice. We were not offered a drink by our hostess before embarking on our walk back to the village. On another occasion, two of the elite women with whom she was most intimate visited our house, and conversation turned to their complaints about the degree of hierarchy in the mining town. They felt there were too many levels—of wages, housing, and such-like, and some people were contemptuous of those living in less prestigious areas. One said:

> We are not like that, but other people are. It wasn't like that
> when we first arrived [in the early 70's]. We set up Savings
> Associations [arisan]; we gave lessons in deportment, eti-
> quette, and so on. I even persuaded the women to stop bind-
> ing their stomachs in pregnancy.

Her well-intentioned statement attested to the force of status differences in Soroako. Good relations between the elite women and the
villagers were asssumed to be relations between superiors and in-
feriors. Respect and learning all went one way.

The assumptions of hierarchical ordering of sociocultural groups
in the mining town mirrored that current in contemporary Indonesia
wherby the people of rural areas, especially in the Outer Islands,
were regarded as backward (*masih bodoh*) and in need of uplifting and
illumination, by means of development (*pembangunan*). This ideology
infused the attitude of the elite Indonesians towards the Soroakans
(and to village residents in general). The Soroakans were frequently
described as backward (*masih bodoh* or *terbelakang*), and it was commonly asserted that they had been even more so at the commencement of the project.

This assumed superiority was always unself-consciously expressed. For example, at Hijra's wedding (described in chap. 8), the high-
status patron and his wife invited a townsite resident, a beautician, to
dress and make up the bride. Throughout the preparations, the
beautician and her companion made disparaging comments about the
state of the bride's skin and her unsophisticated undergarments.
They also chased away the crowds of young children who, at all
Soroakan weddings, sat wide-eyed watching the village girl's transformation into a Bugis princess. The elite women showed little concern for the villager's feelings, or any awareness that there might be
an alternative way of seeing things.

Organisations in the Mining Town

In Soroako there were none of the government-sponsored village
organisations found in other parts of Indonesia.[4] Outside of the work
place, the organisation that integrated people from different sectors
of the mining town were all established under Inco's auspices. In the

previous chapter, I discussed the activities of the Club, which very marginally involved village residents, and the sports activities, of which only soccer really attracted villagers. Here, I will discuss the Indonesian women's association, which did organise residents of all sections of the town, and the cultural associations.

The principal organisation for women was the Association of Inco Families (*Ikatan Keluarga Inco*) or IKI. This was established in 1972 by a group of managers' wives, with the aim of involving wives of employees from all levels. They sought leave from Inco management before proceeding. IKI had branches in all sections of the mining town, but the leadership were all members of the elite, hence it reinforced the status hierarchy deriving from the job ladder. The organisation's mode of operation also reinforced a view that the status hierarchy was indeed generated from a differential ranking of sociocultural groups. Principal officers were all from Sunda (West Java) or Java, and all were wives of managers. Indeed, I attended the 1978 annual meeting of the executive, and the majority were Sundanese. They conversed in their native tongue when official business (conducted in Indonesian) was completed.

The elite women had a patronising view of those lower in the hierarchy, and saw it as their duty to uplift and lead the less sophisticated. They enforced a conformity to modern, urban values at IKI functions: members wore Western dress on such occasions and were known by their husband's names, not the teknonymous terms common in the villages of Indonesia. Activities involved teaching the values and skills of the urban housewife (in cooking, child care, and entertaining) to the lower-status women.

The elite always assumed their way was best, and often their expressed superiority caused distress to village women. For example, in 1980 the IKI leadership organised a cooking competition, in which they judged the efforts of village members. The elite woman who delivered the judges' decision commented on the cleanliness, efficiency, and skills of each contestant. The village women were shamed by such public criticism. Later, one commented:

> We want to join in development (*pembangunan*) but how can we if we are treated like that? We only feel broken-spirited (*patah semangat*).

The irony was, much of the criticism was directed at the manner in which they had added the spices, which they had done according to the instructions of another elite woman, who had given the demonstration preceding the competition. The townsite women assumed village women did not know how to cook with spices, whereas, of course, they were skilled, but in a different culinary style. Few of the village members of IKI would attend functions held in the townsite, because they felt shy and out of place, although, by 1980–81, I noticed more of them attending a fete held in the F area.

The other organisation with exclusively Indonesian membership was a cultural association, an umbrella group for a number of smaller organisations representing the principal cultural groups among the elite. The most active groups represented townsite residents from West Sumatra and Sunda. Their major role was to organise cultural performances on such national days as Independence Day (17 August).

These groups reinforced the corporate identity of sociocultural groups (as well as providing entertainment and leisure activities for residents of the mining town). The notion of sociocultural identity, or 'ethnic identity,' reinforced by these groups followed that expressed in the dominant ideology; such identities were defined in terms of a shared 'traditional' culture comprising dance performances, dress and so on. Unity of interest was defined by shared culture, not shared socioeconomic position.

The indigenous Soroakans were never invited to perform at such events. Immigrants at all levels of the hierarchy regarded them as people with 'no culture,' because they no longer had a distinctive set of such 'flags' as dress or cultural performances or rituals (see chap. 8). Their claim to a common identity defined by shared descent and ties to place did not fit the prevailing view of what consituted 'ethnic identity.' As people with 'no culture,' they could be regarded as of no consequence. This served to eliminate any consideration of them as a distinct group of people who could be shown to have suffered disadvantages from the project's development. They were obliterated, and hence their anomalous position as the erstwhile owners of the soil, but at the lowest rung of the hierarchy, could be ignored.

The mixture of hostility and contempt the elite felt for the Soroakans was graphically illustrated when I addressed the Parents and Friends Association of the D School, prior to my departure, in March 1979. I showed slides illustrating the series of rituals involved in a Soroakan wedding. The event for which I had the most complete record in slides was Hijra's wedding. The all-Indonesian audience seized on the fact that the bride and groom had been wearing Sundanese costume, and in the ensuing discussion many of them expressed their contempt for the Soroakans as people with 'no culture.'

Relations between Soroakans and Village-Resident Immigrants

Within the village, there was a fundamental division between immigrants (*pendatang*) and indigenous Soroakans. The immigrants, like the Soroakans, identified with a group from a common place of origin (*sekampung*). The groups that had salience for individuals were contextually determined. For example, for the few village residents who originated outside Sulawesi, *sekampung* tended to be speakers of the same language. For the Sulawesi-born, the group of *sekampung* included people from a common district, or, if from nearby, a common village. For immigrants, their *sekampung* served as surrogate kin, providing them with support (even if only by speaking the same language) in the alien environment.

The immigrants were residentially intermingled with the indigenous population of Soroako. Many rented rooms or apartments in indigenous Soroakan houses or boarded with Soroakan families. There was contact between immigrants and the indigenous inhabitants in daily life: for men, in the work place; for women, while washing, shopping, or obtaining water.

However, there was a tendency for the village to be residentially segregated, with the majority of indigenous Soroakans in Old Village and an immigrant majority in New Village. This gave the two sections different character in the eyes of village residents.

In early 1977, the two sections looked very different, New Village having mainly small, impermanent dwellings, and Old Village, more permanent housing. However, the redevelopment (described in chap. 7) led to the construction of permanent dwellings in New Village. The redevelopment plan was also intended to change the social composition of New Village, but in this it failed. New Village continued to be principally an immigrant area, and as such it was perceived by many Soroakans as an alien and hostile environment. For them, it was inhabited by people considered as 'other' (*orang lain*).

The twenty-two Soroakan families who, by the end of 1979, lived in New Village regarded themselves as in exile from home. They would use the expression *pergi kampung* (literally to go to the village, but with the sense of going home) to describe a visit to Old Village. Indigenous Soroakans were reluctant to move there and resented government orders to do so, even though the move was only a few hundred metres. They agreed with the initial plan to move indigenous Soroakans to New Village, but because immigrants had remained the majority, they felt it to be a hostile environment. The social distance was too great; they were isolated from kin. A young Soroakan man (a retrenched Bechtel employee) who had been helping me with a survey of New Village refused to finish the work. He said the people were suspicious of him, and the situation was worse because he was down there alone, without a companion.

Some immigrants, especially those living in Old Village, grew close to their indigenous Soroakan neighbours, but generally there was little integration into each other's social lives. In times of trouble, such as illness or bereavement, the Soroakans would draw together for mutal support. It was rare to see immigrants in Soroakan homes on such occasions. Female immigrants were only rarely invited to help cook ritual feats. There were a few notable exceptions, usually among immigrants with affinal ties to Soroakans.

In a similar fashion, immigrants relied on their *sekampung* in times of need. In the socially complex situation of the mining town, such common identity served as a substitute for kin relations. I attended a children's birthday party in New Village, given by a wealthy trader. All the guests (except myself and Ibu Mahmud) were from New Village, and almost all were from the same area (South Palopo) as the hostess. I asked Ibu Mahmad to identify the guests. She wrinkled her nose in distaste and said, 'They're all from around here [New Village], all immigjrants.' Her behaviour was very arrogant, as she told the hostess how to organise the party, yet it was accepted, because of her high standing in the community.

Religious Differences

Religious affiliation was an important defining attribute of the self-identified groups in Soroako. In particular, the Bugis and the Soroakans strongly identified with Islam, and the Torajans and Mori, with Christianity. In spite of the similarity of the Mori language to Bahasa Soroako, the Soroakans felt a greater difference between themselves and Christians, than their difference from Bugis immigrants, who were Muslims.

Christians differed from Muslims on a number of issues relating to personal demeanour. Christian women almost universally wore Western-style clothes, in particular, short, sleeveless frocks regarded as immodest by Muslims. They were more likely to cut their hair, too. Christian women had greater freedom of movement than Muslim women. They mixed more freely with men, and girls working as household servants in the townsite were predominantly Christian. Many came to Soroako on their own which Muslim girls would never had done. These differences were often commented upon by the Soroakans, who made ribald jokes about the presumed 'looseness' of Christian women.

The eating of, or abstinence from, pork was a potent symbol of Christian-Muslim differences, indeed seeming more salient than any doctrinal differences between them. Christians ate pork with the same fervor with which Muslims rejected it. It was a 'badge' of Christian identity.

The mosques and churches (map 2.2) served as institutional foci, integrating people from different sections of the mining town. Indeed, the largest of the three churches was an Ecumenical Protestant Church,. which combined more than ten different Protestant sects, many of them regionally based. The expressed aim of establishing a unitary church had been to avoid the divisiveness of a number of small groups. The congregations of the three mosques also united for joint prayers on the occasion of major Islamic holy days. However, since the leaders of both Christian and Muslim congregations were managers in the company, these organisations, too, reinforced the status hierarchy of the mining town.

Christians and Muslims generally coexisted without overt hostility and conflict, but the jokes members of one group would make about the other were evidence of a degree of prejudice.

Marriage

One of the areas of value conflict between indigenous Soroakans and immigrants concerned sexual mores. Soroakans were concerned about sexual exploitation of their women, as well as seduction of their men by immigrant women. I have already noted the trend towards a higher proportion of Soroakan marriages with immigrants (chap. 8). One woman expressed the common fear: 'Who will be left for our girls to marry?'

A number of immigrant men (some of whom had married local girls) told me that when they first arrived in the district and were domiciled at a camp near the current plant site, they would come to Soroako seeking girls. The Soroakans did not know about courting (*tidak pintar main pacar*), and there were reportedly several incidents where angry fathers chased immigrant men with drawn swords. A number of couples were forced to marry. Such moral surveillance was still occurring the the late 1970s. One young immigrant woman complained to me that her Soroakan landlords spied on her when her boyfriend came to visit and were threatening to take her before the citizens' militia (*Hansip*) to force her to marry. The Soroakan Village Headman told me that the visited homes all over the village to uncover immoral behaviour. If a couple were too involved, he would force them to marry. And if they didn't comply? 'Then *out* of Soroako.' He had arranged about ten marriages in this fashion, mostly between immigrants, but occasionally between young Soroakan men and immigrant women (see chap. 8).

Soroakan attitudes about the limits of proper behaviour when courting, as well as intermarriage with immigrants, mellowed over time. The increasing number of intermarriages (not all of them forced) served to integrate at least some of the newcomers into the community. For example, the most respected midwife and masseuse in Soroako was a woman who had migrated to Soroako when her daughter married a local boy. She was often called to cook the rice at Soroakan weddings. (The degree of acceptance she was afforded was, however, exceptional.)

Organisations within the Village

There were no government-sponsored organisations within Soroako village that facilitated the integration of indigenous Soroakans and immigrants. The village administration had not coped with the sudden growth of the early 1970s, and officials were getting on top of their tasks only as the pace of change slowed down in the late 1970s. A few attempts were made to establish organisations like those found in other parts of Indonesia (see note 4), but with little success. The groups organised around the churches served to integrate the Christian community and to sharpen the differentiation from Muslims.

The village branch of the Association of Inco Families (IKI) was viable in Soroako village. There were two chapters: one in New Village, and another in Old Village. The only activity that was self-sustaining in the village chapters was the Savings Association (*arisan*). Members paid a fixed amount each month and then drew lots to determine who would take the pot. Each member had only one chance of winning, until each participant had a turn.

All the members of the IKI Savings Association in New Village were immigrants, whereas the Old Village chapter was almost exclusively Soroakan. In addition, the immigrant members were mostly Bugis. None of the Torajan women in the village were active (although Torajans resident in the F area were enthusiastic members of IKI). The principal organisers in the village were an influential Soroakan woman, an aristocratic Bugis woman (*Opu* B.) from Malili, and a Javanese woman, both of them Muslim. The Soroakan chapters were distinctly Muslim organisations.

The uncertainty pervading Soroako, because of the massive retrenchments, led to the demise of the Savings Association, in 1978. The women were reluctant to commit themselves to a new series, lest some members' husbands be retrenched. (The money came from their pay packets.) Indeed, during that year, an immigrant woman in the Old Village chapter did not pay her contribution for two months, contributing to the distrust of strangers that made continued commitment to the Savings Association difficult.

In August 1978, the two chapters met jointly to decide if the Savings Association was to be reconstituted. At that meeting, the Opu, mentioned above, regarded as a leader among Bugis immigrants, insisted on behalf of the other immigrant women that *all* IKI members in the village should meet in a single group. She said:

> The saving of money is not our only goal. It is also important that we all get together.

Indeed, the elite women in the townsite stressed that the Savings Associations were as much to forge bonds between people in the heterogeneous community as to help in saving money.

The Opu later explained to me her own thinking on the matter:

> If we meet separately, then we don't know each other, and there is a chance that one [group] might feel more elevated than the other. This way, we meet each other, and there can be no such misunderstanding.

She saw the Savings Association as a way of bettering relations between immigrants and indigenous Soroakans, rather than providing another avenue for hardening the lines of division. The joint meetings were indeed successful in bringing some village residents together.

However, the project's development had precipitated a situation in which indigenous Soroakans found themselves in intense competition with immigrants—for jobs, housing land, even safe water. The kinds of rapprochement achieved in groups like the Savings Association were important, but somewhat inconsequential with respect to the fundamental basis of conflict. Using the metaphor employed in the title of this book, one man commented:

> We indigenous Soroakans are treated like stepchildren. It's the immigrants who come out on top (*Kita orang disini dianaktirikan, orang lain yang menang*).

Sources of Conflict between Immigrants and Soroakans

In the atmosphere of mass retrenchments, the Soroakans felt themselves to be in intense competition with the immigrants. Their feelings were of dispossession: as the indigenous inhabitants of the area, they felt they had prior rights to the jobs the company created. Company assurances that they would be given such preferences had fostered that view of the world. Unfortunately, it did not mean that, in practice, Soroakan households were assured of income from wages (see chap. 6).

Failure to gain promised employment was interpreted by the Soroakans as the outcome of bosses 'favouring their own' (*main suku*) within the company, and it was a consequence of people's favouring their own that the Soroakans did not find work. Immigrants did not see the problem in the same light. For example, one man said to me:

> Immigrants come here with nothing, so they should be given preference in employment.

There was also intense competition between indigenous Soroakans and immigrants for housing land. The government plan allocated all housing land to indigenous Soroakans, yet they saw immigrants taking over New Village. This was often interpreted as the outcome of the government officials' 'favouring their own.' Throughout the implementation of the redevelopment, the acting Village Headman was an immigrant from South Palopo. Both he and the district officials (Christians from the local area and from Tana Toraja) were seen to 'favour their own' at the expense of indigenous Soroakans. One woman commented:

> We Soroakans will be thrown into the lake. There is nowhere else for us to go.

On the other hand, some of the immigrants resented the provisions for special treatment for Soroakans in the redevelopment plan. One man told me that he had no sympathy with the directive that only Soroakan natives could build in the village. He had built a good house, and so was aiding development (*pembangunan*). Since the government was 'for development,' it should support his effort, too. Another man commented angrily that as immigrants paid tax, they, too, should be regarded as indigenous Soroakans (*orang asli Soroako*).

Conflicts over other resources also took on 'ethnic' dimensions. Fights frequently erupted in the queues for water, and in such situations, lines were often drawn in terms of place of origin. In Old Village, the indigenous Soroakans could monopolise the standpipes, as they had more well-developed social networks. Older, influential women would bully other Soroakans to allow them to jump the queue. Immigrants, naturally, resented such behaviour.

Soroakans felt disadvantaged when the post of Village Headman was filled by an immigrant. On the other hand, the Soroakan Headman (returned to office in mid-1978) was more concerned with *his* 'own.' For instance, when discussing the problems of the village water supply, I commented that the residents of the outlying areas of New Village were the worst off. The Headman contemplated my statement for a moment and then replied in a dismissive voice, 'Oh, those Torajans.' Such people's needs were not his concern.

These conflicts arose out of competition for scarce resources, which were crucial for survival. The Soroakans were conscious of their position at the bottom of the hierarchy, with least access to rewards and privileges. They resented their objective situation and the lack of status honour that accompanied it.

To the immigrants, the Soroakans' inferior position was proof of their backwardness, their lack of worth. I was showing a young Soroakan girl a book with pictures of other parts of Indonesia. She looked up in surprise and said:

> They're all peasants (*tani*). Why do they (the immigrants) laugh at us, if they are all peasants, too?

The Soroakan Explanation

The indigenous Soroakans did not concur with the view that their lowly status derived from inherent lack of worth. They saw it as the outcome of a politicisation of sociocultural differences, described as *main suku* (favouring your own), which they believed operated both in the company and in the government.

In the context of the fierce competition for jobs with Inco, they felt themselves to be disadvantaged with respect to immigrants who had more contacts within Inco. A common experience and interpretation was related to me by a young Soroakan man. Following retrenchment from one of the construction companies, he attempted to apply to Inco. The personnel office would not accept an application because, they said, there were no jobs. In the meantime, he claimed, new people were being taken by Inco, but they were all immigrants. His father commented:

> If you have a *sekampung* in Personnel, it is easy. For instance, people from Tator (Tana Toraja) never wait. They are taken on straight away. We indigenous Soroakans are thrown the bones, after the newcomers have eaten the meat.

The objections were not to favouring your own (*main suku*) in itself, but to the fact that they were not well placed to benefit from it. It was widely assumed one *ought* to favour one's own, and most people agreed with criticism of people in company management who refused to give special treatment to people from their own region.

The Soroakans felt bitter about both the failure of many of their number to be employed and the fact that most of those in employment had not achieved promotion. It was a common belief that promotion, too, depended on the help of a patron who was usually a *sekampung*.

This did happen. Many employees did use their influence to gain employment or promotion for people with whom they were connected. Indeed, there were efforts by some high-ranking personnel to get rid of a fellow manager who refused to be party to such practices.

The Soroakans' bitterness was exacerbated by their belief that they deserved privileged treatment, because they were the original inhabitants of the area and because the company had taken their land. Inco gave some recognition to these special claims, in the promise of preference in employment, and in the promise to give interest-free housing loans only to indigenous Soroakan employees, if they were building in Soroako. In addition, by 1980, impoverished nonemployees could obtain free treatment at the company hospital only if they were indigenous Soroakans.

Consequently, Soroakan identity came to have, at least in theory, special entitlements. That this did not work in practice was largely the result of the prevalence of 'favouring your own' in the company.

Local government was also characterised by such 'favouring of one's own.' I have already discussed the manner in which such ties led to the fiasco of the redevelopment plan, whereby almost all the land in New Village went to immigrants. Many of these people built houses with loans from the company, using contacts in the government to complete the documentation necessary to prove eligibility for their loans (see chap. 7).

In spite of the ineffectiveness of promises of special treatment in protecting the interests of the indigenous Soroakans, such guarantees fuelled the tendency of Soroakans to see themselves as a special group.

The prevalence of 'favouring your own' in both the company and government masked the real bases of the objective position of the Soroakans. It masked the fact that their fundamental dispossession derived from the operation of capitalist class relations, and that their failure to obtain work also related to the bureaucratic rationality of the company, which sought particular skills (which the Soroakans did not have) for particular jobs.

Soroakan Identity

The Soroakan response to the new economic conditions and the new social milieu was the assertion of a particular kind of sociocultural identity and a political mobilisation around it. The cultural form in which it was expressed derived from their unique historical experience, but it has taken on new meaning in the context of higher rates of exploitation within the new forms of class oppression in Soroako since the project.

> Man makes his own history, but . . . he does not make it out of conditions chosen by himself, but out of such conditions as he finds close at hand. The tradition of past generations weighs like an alp upon the brain of the living. At the very time when mean appear engaged in revolutionizing things and themselves . . . do they anxiously conjure up into their service the spirits of the past, assume their names, their battle cries, their costumes, to enact a new historic scene in such time-honored disguise and with such borrowed language (Marx 1914, p. 9).

The indigenous Soroakans had a strong sense of themselves as a cohesive group, defined in terms of an ideology of common descent, shared language, and a common tie to the village as their place of origin (chap. 2). A commitment to Islam was a crucial aspect of that identity, stronger than any attachment to cultural symbols of dress or ritual practice dating back to their distant ancestors. Indeed, when they spoke of their custom (*adat*) they meant Bugis custom, for example, the dress and ritual forms used in weddings (chap. 7). Many customary practices were still performed, for example, in house moving or in cultivating rice, which were referred to as practices of the ancestors (*orang tua dulu*). (This Indonesian phrase has the same meaning as the phrase used by Torajans to describe their pre-Christian religion: *Aluk To Dolo*.) Such practices, however, are not the most public of Soroakan rituals.

Immigrants were quick to point out the derivative and eclectic nature of Soroakan public rituals. These are the cornerstone of the notion of custom (*adat*) promoted in contemporary Indonesia, and the apparent lack of a timeless traditional culture was used to denigrate the Soroakans.

However, the assertion of identity through borrowed symbols in no way indicated a lack of commitment to that identity; witness the rejection of the attempted assertion of status through borrowed Sundanese costume, described in chapter 8. Also, there were often contexts in the contemporary situation in which common identity was powerfully asserted, but not in a form having official sanction. These contexts derived from the political economy of the contemporary Indonesian state, rather than centuries of shared tradition.

The Soroakans saw themselves as 'stepchildren' of the progress associated with the project. This definition arose from their notion of themselves as the owners of the land, as people united by a common tie to place, validated by their descent from the founding ancestors. They asserted this identity in the context of the competition for survival in the contemporary situation.

The feeling of common descent was a fundamental aspect of their identity. *Tidak ada orang lain* (there are no outsiders) was the most commonly heard expression of this ideology. Soroakans felt themselves to be part of an extending web of kinship, united in their common tie to the village.

They made a fundamental distinction between themselves, as *orang asli Soroako* (people originating in Soroako) stressing the common place of origin, and *orang pendatang* (immigrants). Sometimes, they would use the terms *orang disini* (people of this place) or *orang kita* (we people) as opposed to *orang lain* (others, or outsiders).

In the changing social milieu, that distinction was not easy to sustain. Sociocultural group membership is not immutable. As a product of consciousness, it was necessarily flexible, and responsive to changes in the face of new circumstances. Many of the newcomers shared their religion and other important cultural traits. Many have lived there for some years, and some have become affines.

A small number of immigrants were regarded, then, as *penduduk Soroako* (literally, population of Soroako): an intermediate category of people who were not indigenous Soroakans but who, because of their involvement in the community, could not be regarded as 'other,' which the term immigrant implied. The Soroakans championed the rights of such people to obtain housing land in Soroako (chap. 7).

In modern Indonesia, language is an important defining attribute of sociocultural identity, as it was in the past in Central Sulawesi (see chap. 2). However, language was losing its importance in defining who was or was not an indigenous Soroakan.

In the linguistically complex environment of the mining town, Indonesian was the language of daily discourse. It was used in the work place, the school, and the market. Indonesian was regarded as the appropriate language in those areas of life relating to the modern world, such as govenment meetings, celebrations of national days, and IKI meetings. Proceedings at most weddings were conducted in Indonesian. It was also the language of flirtation. Almost all of the indigenous Soroakans spoke Indonesian (with varying degrees of skill). The older people had been taught Malay at the village school, and those early beginnings facilitated their language learning.

By 1979, all Soroakan parents were teaching their children Indonesian as their first language. Although Bahasa Soroako was the language of daily communication in Soroakan households, babies and infants were always addressed in Indonesian. Parents explained this practice by saying that Indonesian was necessary for education, and—because of the demise of the agricultural economy—they saw that their children's future lay with education. The common assumption, borne out in practice, was that children would learn Bahasa Soroako, 'from their friends in the street,' whereas they had to be taught Indonesian. The children were bilingual before beginning school, at 7 years of age.

This pragmatic response to changed circumstances contrasted markedly with the attitudes of Bugis mothers living in Soroako, who taught their children Bugis as their first language 'lest their tongues become stiff.'

Clearly, the Soroakans did not have an irrational conservatism, clinging to tradition for its own sake. Their form of expression of common idenity was pliable and was transformed in response to new circumstances. Just as the kind of identity asserted at the turn of the century related to the political construction of their relations with the world beyond the Lake, in the 1970s their identity was a response to new forms of domination.

False Consciousness or Class Consciousness

Soroakan identity incorporated a political dimension. It was an assertion of solidarity in relation to people seen as 'other,' with whom they were in conflict. They acted as a solidary group, united by their perceived common set of rights in response to forms of class oppression.

For example, they protested as a group the low price paid for their land, a political response to the state's championing of the interests of capital, to their detriment. They also protested the failure of the company to provide them with jobs and its disregard for their health in despoiling the environment.

However, the assertion of the commonality of Soroakan interests militated against their joint mobilisation with other village residents against forms of class oppression. The resented the failure of the government to protect their interests in the allocation of housing land, but they did not protest against the bulldozing of immigrant houses. They fought for the poor to gain free treatment at the company hospital, but they concurred in a plan to limit such free treatment to indigenous Soroakans.[5]

In fact, the company's response to promise special treatment for Soroakans (in jobs, housing loans in Soroako, and free medical care to nonemployees) reinforced their consciousness as a distinctive group, further eroding the bases for common mobilisation of people in the same objective circumstances. Few of the promised special benefits were obtained, however, thus adding to their feelings of frustration and dispossession.

Their negative feelings were directed more towards the immigrants in the village, with whom they saw themselves in direct conflict, than towards the managers, the representatives of capital. To the extent that they did feel bitterness towards managers, it was expresed as a feeling of personal betrayal, through the failure of the managers to observe an unspoken contract arising from a patron-client relation.

Land was the means of production in the peasant economy. The stress on tie to place as a fundamental aspect of their shared identity reflected their common class position in the peasant economy. In the contemporary situation they had all suffered dispossession of the means of production; in this regard, then, their consciousness was a correct understanding of their class position. However, their objective class position in the new order was the same as that of the immigrants, yet they saw themselves as having interests divergent from the newcomers.

In identifying low-status immigrants as the enemy, Soroakan identity mitigated against the formation of class-based alliances. But, on the other hand, it united different segments of the less privileged (the employed, semiemployed, and self-employed) as a group against forms of class oppression. The limited success of the mobilisation around the identity (most notably over the land compensation) was dependent on the role of the customary village leaders in mobilising the others. The patron-client ties between village leaders leaders and their followers were an important basis of the cohesiveness of the Soroakans.

Conclusion

In contemporary situation, the Soroakans felt themselves to be, and indeed were, in intense competition with newcomers over scarce resources. The scarcity of jobs, housing, land, and clean water were an outcome of the capitalist development associated with the establishment of the nickel project.

The status hierarchy, based on differential distribution of rewards, was the phenomenal form of daily social relations, but it arose on the basis of capitalist class relations (see chap. 2). However, in the consciousness of most residents of the mining town, the job ladder and the status order of the mining town were seen to arise on the basis of racial and cultural differences: the 'given' differences that capital uses to justify differential wages, and hence differential rates of exploitation.

The empirical reality of social differentiation in Soroako gave credence to the folk ideology. Top managers were mostly white, the high-level Indonesians all originating from Sunda or elsewhere on the Island of Java. The Soroakans, and Sulawesi natives in general, clustered at the bottom of the company job ladder, and a large mass of village residents were part of the semiemployed industrial reserve army, whose productive activities (and therefore life chances) had been crucially affected by the development of the project.

The degree of fit between the ordering of racial and sociocultural groups, the company job ladder, and the derived status hierarchy led to a conviction that the social order was generated through racial and ethnic differences. For those at the top, their position derived from naturally superior worth. Those below them to an extent internalised their devaluation as being naturally inferior, but they also saw their place as arising from the process of people in authority using their position to 'favour their own' (*main suku*).

What led the degree of fit between an ordering of ethnic groups and the status hierarchy? In part, it has arisen because of the different historical experiences of regions of the Indonesian archipelago.

Indonesia has a long history of an association between racial and ethnic differences, and relations defined in the economic sphere. Furnivall talks about 'racial castes' in the colonial period; groups defined in terms of racial differences (Europeans, Chinese, and natives) had different roles in production, as well as divergent economic interests (1944, pp.450–51).

Bruner argues that Furnivall did not go far enough in describing the manner in which colonial intervention altered relations between different groups of Indonesians (1974, p.255). In Africa

> (c)olonial regimes have played an important part in fostering tribalism by their policy of trying to channel all political and economic dealings between individuals and the State through the medium of 'tribal authorities' and by discriminating in favour of some tribes and against others, especially in their own recruitment policies (Leys 1975, p.199, cited by Kahn 1981a, pp.45–46).

Indeed, I have heard Indonesian intellectuals argue that sociocultural differences were exploited and thereby hardened into ethnic cleavages by Dutch colonial policy. For example, in Sulawesi, Christian Ambonese and Minahassans were used as administrators over the native peoples of the island.

Whether or not this argument holds in Indonesia, it is clear that the differing histories of the incorporation of regions of the archipelago into the colonial system, and into the modern world system generally, have been important in creating the differences in levels of education and skill that differentiate Indonesia's population, and, hence, the population of the mining town.

Most important, differences between the status of different sociocultural groups were not seen as the outcome of differences in life chances, whatever the reason for the differences might be; they were seen as proof of differential worth, consequent on inherent differences.

In contemporary Soroako, cleavages based on sociocultural identity and those based on class overlapped markedly, so that to organise on the basis of the former was in fact a form of fighting class oppression. If there had been no overlap, if the material conditions of existence did not reinforce an already existing idea of community and self, would the Soroakans have represented themselves and their interests in terms of an ethnic identity?

NOTES TO CHAPTER 10

1. For a review of writings on ethnicity see R. Cohen (1978) and Kahn (1981a).
2. I use the term 'sociocultural identity' rather than 'ethnic identity' because the latter term has become synonomous with a notion of a primordial attachment, and I wish to argue for a more contingent relation between past and current cultural forms than this seems to allow.
3. This interpretation of ethnic identity was parodied by Rendra in his play, *The Struggle of the Naga Tribe* (1979).
4. Such government sponsored organisations included the Village Welfare Institute (*L.S.D.*) and the official women's organisation.
5. Under Indonesian law, people are entitled to free medical treatment at government hospitals and clinics if they have a letter certifying inability to pay (*surat miskin*) from the village government. There was constant negotiation in Soroako to have the same system apply to the company clinic.

Chapter 11

Conclusion

This book has been principally concerned with the incorporation of a community of independent peasant cultivators into a world system in which the capitalist mode of production provides the overriding economic rationality. The immediate agent of the process of change described is a multinational mining company. However, neither the course of events nor the process of change engendered can be understood by an exclusive focus on the local area, nor by a study of the local population and the multinational corporation as institutional actors. To explain developments in Soroako, we need to attend to the structures that underlie the historically specific events; the mining project set in motion a process of proletarianisation, whereby the indigenous people of Soroako (the *orang asli Soroako*) became incorporated into a system of social relations organised around the appropriation of the means of production by a single class that exploits the labour of a nonpropertied class. Inco's impact in Soroako must be interpreted in terms of a model that explains the process of capitalist expansion everywhere. I have suggested that an anthropological study of a local community in the capitalist periphery should be informed by the perspective of world systems theory and dependency theory, and should employ the tools of class analysis to understand the ramifications of that historical process at the local level.

However, there is a tendency in structural Marxism to reify the abstract categories of class analysis, so that the formal properties of the capital-wage labour relation are seen as immediately and totally encompassing the social form of the local community. Such an approach directs our attention away from the historical and cultural specificity of particular transformations to capitalism, treating superstructural elements as functional impulses arising reflexively from the economic base. Because of their commitment to intensive field work, anthropologists should have more to say than students from other disciplines about cultural and ideological aspects of the development of capitalism.

I have considered here not only changes in the forms and relations of production (general structures of the capitalist mode of production), but also the particular social and cultural forms associated with capitalist relations of production in contemporary Soroako. The focus is 'micro,' but the tools used to explain the 'microprocess' have a generality beyond the specific instance.

Drawing on the perspective offered by world systems theory, Inco's intervention in Soroako can be seen as the latest chapter in a history of transition to capitalism, beginning with the expansion of mercantile trade networks in the nineteenth century. This process has been characterised by increasing loss of community autonomy and increasing dependence on economic relations with the world outside the village. The new forms of economic relations have allowed for an ever greater degree of exploitation, culminating in the loss of control of the principal means of production (irrigated agricultural land) in the contemporary period. (The change in economic organisation that had led to the increased dependence on settled agriculture had itself been an aspect of an earlier phase of capitalist penetration in the colonial period.)

The nickel project brought many of the material benefits of industrial capitalism to the countryside, including improvements in communication and transport, modern medical care, and labour-saving consumer commodities. However, these benefits were unequally distributed. The inequalities in Soroako mirrored those in the world system at large: the lowest paid, most highly exploited segments in the world proletariat are located in the capitalist periphery, and the most highly paid, in the metropolis. In Soroako, this was concretely manifested in the presence of highly paid workers from the advanced industrial nations. Within the community, capitalist class relations gave rise to a structure of inequality, culturally expressed in the unequal distribution of the goods and services that have been part of capitalist development, evaluated as differences in status.

The Soroakans anticipated that the project would bring a new level of affluence. Some had long-term, stable wage labour, which allowed them to pursue a lifestyle deriving from the consumer society of industrial capitalism, rather than the peasant society they were leaving behind. However, a large segment of the village was still dependent on a diminished agricultural sector for their livelihood. The mining company responded to the continuing world recession with cutbacks in production and retrenchment of staff, thus throwing an increasing proportion of village residents back into the agricultural sector. Changes in the organisation of production in agriculture meant that few families could meet all their needs from rice farming; thus, of necessity, they became part of the industrial reserve army of the semiemployed, seeking additional income from the cash economy.

The effect of absolute poverty, deriving from capitalist domination of production, was exacerbated by the increased incursion of the monetised market and the consumer values of capitalism, which tied people to that market. New felt needs meant that cultivators measured their needs and satisfaction, not against the lifestyle of the peasant community, but against that of the employed in the mining town.

The fortunes of the entire community were tied to those of the company. Even the nonemployed farmers and traders were dependent on the economic activity it generated. Like the wage labourers, they feared that the company would pull out, thereby threatening their livelihood. Traders (and landlords) hoped that the level of activity would increase, making Soroako again as lively as it had been in the days of project construction.

The indigenous Soroakans are survivors. They have shown adaptability in the face of a century of transformation. They adapted to the cultural and political forms of the Bugis realm of Luwu, the economic and political changes of the colonial period, the Islamic orthodoxy and isolation of the Darul Islam rebellion. They have responded with optimism and hope to the nickel project. In no way do they resemble the conservative peasantry presented in the modernisation literature as being dragged into the modern world. They positively evaluated the new social milieu. Soroako had become *ramai* (bustling, lively) whereas in the past it was *sunyi* (quiet, isolated). Work for the project was evaluated as providing new experience, in addition to being a source of livelihood.

The Soroakans, as well as the immigrant workers, recognised and appreciated benefits from modern technology: pressure lamps, sewing machines, motorcycles, and modern health care were all sought after. The electrification of the village provided the way for even more complex labour-saving commodities, and for television.

Protests by the Soroakans have not been against the project per se. When discussing the conflict over land, for example, many were keen to stress they had no desire to hold up (*menghalangi*) the project: they just wanted a better deal. As the metaphor, stepchildren of progress, suggests, there was profound disappointment that the benefits of the project did not fall more to themselves. Indeed, their positive evaluation of the modern goods and services that accompanied the establishment of the mining project made their exclusion from these even harder to accept.

> If only the company would give all Soroakan men jobs, everything would be good.
>
> If only the company would provide clean running water to village houses, everything would be fine.
>
> If only I could send my children to the company school and we could all be treated at the hospital, things would be good.

However, this view was based on a fundamental misapprehension of the nature of capitalism: they accepted the equation of growth with capitalist development. Their expressed hopes failed to take account of the fact that capitalist class relations are based on exploitation. The division of labour in detail, within the production process, allows the labour for each segment to be purchased at the lowest possible price. Skilled workers and professional and managerial employees were offered the salaries and privileges necessary to attract them to Soroako and keep them there. Racist assumptions about the relative capacities of Indonesians and expatriates led to a situation in which the company required significant numbers of expatriates at the upper levels of the organisation—and lured them to Soroako with generous pay and conditions. Unskilled workers, by contrast, could be had at a cheap price and were replaceable.

The Indonesian government hoped that the company would take the lead in developing the region: indeed, the company's public statements hinted at such an undertaking. Despite the activities of individual managers to enforce a commitment to the well-being of unskilled workers and nonemployees, community interventions, such as garbage collection in the village, or extension of medical treatment to the poor, were the first to be cut back in hard economic times.

Capitalist development in the advanced industrial nations did bring prosperity to the proletariat in general. However, as the history of early capitalist development shows, these benefits were won by workers, by means of industrial and political struggle. Different conditions obtain in the contemporary world system. The dispossession of peasants in proceeding faster than their incorporation into the industrial proletariat. The large size of the industrial reserve army in the periphery makes it difficult for workers to struggle for better pay and conditions. There is always the army of the poor waiting in the wings. Capitalist development in the Third World has led to increasing differentiation between a mass of struggling poor and what some have called a 'labour aristocracy': those segments of the proletariat who have relatively secure waged employment. Such a tendency was evident in Soroako, where the differences in lifestyle and life chances between the employed and nonemployed were becoming more marked with the passage of time. Apart from the effect of wage labour per se, relations between community members increasingly followed a capitalist model. Relations of labour exchange and mutual assistance, which existed in the less monetised peasant economy, were declining, and increasingly villagers performed services for each other in return for a cash payment.

To an extent, the emergence of new forms of inequality determined by the capitalist mode of production have arisen on the basis of a reworking of preexisting relations. These had, in turn, been a consequence of the reworking of even older patterns under the influence of mercantile expansion and colonialism. The relatively wealthy Soroakans—a few large traders and a small number of long-term employees who had additional sources of income—were, on the whole, from the old elite families who had owned the largest estates in the preproject economy. In the past, this wealth had been translated into political power, and in the contemporary situation they used their greater wealth to advantage, for example, in renting out land, or in trading. Wealth in contemporary Soroako was translated into status by such customary cultural means as the staging of elaborate rituals.

Even the relatively well-off in the village were differentiated from the Inco employees living in the company townsite, in particular, from the professional and managerial employees. The differences in income and access to certain privileges were culturally manifest as differences in status honour.

Within the village, the different fractions of the proletariat had contrasting evaluations of the changes in their lives since the establishment of the project. Long-term employees regarded themselves as better off. In the preproject economy, they had had to work physically harder in the fields, and the range of consumer goods was more limited. Many had been able to take advantage of recent improvements in transport to travel to Palopo or Ujung Pandang.

The nonemployed tended to evaluate their life as more difficult since the loss of irrigated land to the project:

> Now you have to buy everything. If you have no money—nothing.

> It's really difficult now, ever since we lost our paddy fields.

> Life is hard now. We only eat a little. The yield from the swidden is really small.

> Things are more difficult now, because of the problems in getting food. Clothes are less of a problem as we can get money for rattan and dammar, and cloth is cheaper. But whereas before we'd eat rice three times a day, now we often only drink, or eat bananas, in the morning.

Another man summed up his situation: 'I'm tired with the effort of living' (*sudah payah hidup*).

There was a recognition that the customs and values of daily life were changing, that life was more complex now than in the peasant society. A common view was that contemporary life demanded too much thinking. Most accepted the changes, with even old people accepting new styles of courting, new ways of arranging marriages, and the greater freedom of women to venture outside the home. Grandparents accepted having to speak Indonesian to grandchildren. However, some were disturbed by the changing nature of social relations: one of the village elite commented that the sentiment between people (*perasaan*, i.e., moral sensibility) had changed for the worse:

> There is a lot of affluence in Soroako, but if the sentiment is no good. . . .

He felt something was lost in the quality of relations among village members.

Others commented negatively on the loss of autonomy in work, consequent on their loss of land, and the change this meant in the nature of work:

> Before, we were free. Now you have to sell your labour power (*jual tenaga*). If you don't, you don't eat.

A worker's wife commented:

> If my husband missed a day (at the mine) he'd get the sack. But once we'd finished planting paddy, if you took a day off, it didn't matter.

The changes in the conduct of everyday life in contemporary Soroako have been profound, and they have been accompanied by ideological changes, such as new attitudes about gender roles and family relations, along with changing ideas about work relations. Many of these ideological shifts manifest the hegemonising tendency of ideology under capitalism. Consumer desires, for example, ensured their positive orientation to capitalist development.

However, this hegemony is by no means complete. Stealing from the company and industrial action were forms of struggle against class domination. In chapter 10, I argued that the expression of Soroakan ethnic identity represented a way of struggling against forms of class oppression, as in the protest over the land alienation, or in the claims of the Soroakan's right to work.

The role of the national elite has been important in dampening these struggles. Representatives of the Indonesian state have intervened in industrial disputes, as well as in the conflict over the price for the land. In relation to the latter, one man commented: 'If we protest too much they say we are Communists.'

The national Indonesian Government views an alliance with foreign capital as a means to attain development. The limited bargaining power of the proletariat in the capitalist periphery is further circumscribed by the actions of the national bourgeoisie, who establish a rule of law favouring the operation of capital, in particular, international capital.

There are many conflicting views concerning appropriate development strategies. There is general agreement that the aim is the eradication of poverty and hardship; the argument is about how to achieve that end. The proponents of growth argue that the benefits will eventually 'trickle down,' the experience of the advanced industrial nations being replicated in the periphery. This approach takes no account of either the historically different conditions of capitalist development in the periphery or the manner in which the achievement of generalised benefits relates to the class basis of capitalism, that is, that benefits were won through workers' struggle, which is not possible under the political conditions created by the alliance of national ruling elites and international capital in the Third World.

The proponents of growth assume that the interest of the mass of people will be met by modernisation or development. Studies of local conditions, such as this book, enable us to evaluate the human costs of this kind of development—its cost to the ordinary people in whose name such strategies are being pursued.

The story of Soroako is an unfinished one. The Indonesian Government hopes the project will bring development. The company is in quest of profits. Inco has already pulled out of its Guatamala operations. The company has considered the closure of the Soroako venture, but so far its response to the continued slump in the world nickel market has been to cut back expenditures. It remains to be seen whether this becomes yet another anthropological study of a short-term intervention by a multinational that then moved on. (See, for example, Eipper [1980], Partridge [1979].) Even in the mining company departs, the changes in the form of society left in its wake will remain.

Bibliography

Abendanon, F. C. 1915–18. *Midden Celebes expeditie. Geologische en geographische doorkruisingen van Midden Celebes (1909–10)*, Vols. 1–3. Leiden: Koninklijk Nederlandsch Aardrijkskundig Genootschap. Met medewerking van het Ministere van Kolonien uitgeveven.

Aditjondro, G. Y. 1982. Dapatkah Soroako dan Tembagapura menjadi pusat perkembangan daerah? *Prisma* 8; 47–65.

Adriani, N. 1901. De invloed van Loewoe op Midden-Celebes, *Mededeelingen van wege het Nederlandsche Zendelinggenootschap* 45; 153–64.

Adriani, N., and Kruyt, A. C. 1969. The Bare'e Speaking Toradja of Central Celebes, H.R.A.F., trans. (1951). *De Bare'e Sprekende Toradjas van Midden-Celebes (de Oost-Toradjas).* Amsterdam: Verhandelingen der Koninklijke Nederlandse Akademie van Wetenschappen, Afdeling Letterkunde.

Alavi, H. 1979. The State in post-colonial societies: Pakistan and Bangladesh. In *Politics and State in the Third World*, ed. H. Goulbourne. London and Basingstoke: Macmillan.

Alavi, H., and Khusro. 1970. Pakistan: the burden of U.S. aid. In *Imperialism and Underdevelopment*, ed. R.I. Rhodes. New York and London: Monthly Review Press.

Allen, G. C. and Donithorne, A. G. 1954. *Western Enterprise in Indonesia and Malaya : A Study in Economic Development.* London: George Allen and Unwin.

Amin, S. 1974. *Accumulation on a World Scale.* New York and London: Monthly Review Press.

Aminullah, Lewa. 1978. Pemakaman dan pemilihan Datu di Luwu. *Pedoman Rakyat* 18 December.

Andaya, L. 1975. The nature of kingship in Bone. In *Pre-colonial State Systems in Southeast Asia*, ed. A. Reid, L. Castles et al. Kuala Lumpur: Malaysian Branch of the Royal Asiatic Society.

———. 1981. A preliminary investigation of the economic foundations of Bugis-Makassar states in the 17th and 18th centuries. Paper presented at S.S.R.C. Conference on South Sulawesi, 9–11 December, at Monash University.

Andelman, D. A. 1977. Indonesia looks to Inco when the oil runs out. *Australian Financial Review* 23 February.

Anderson, B. R. O'G. 1972. The idea of power in Javanese culture. In *Culture and Politics in Indonesia*, ed. C. Holt. Ithaca, N.Y.: Cornell University Press.

Anderson, P. 1974a. *Lineages of the Absolutist State*. London: New Left Books.

———. 1974b. *Passages From Antiquity to Feudalism*. London: New Left Books.

Arndt, H. W. 1967. Survey of recent developments, *Bulletin of Indonesian Economic Studies* no. 7: 1–37.

———. 1968. 'Survey of recent develoments', *Bulletin of Indonesian Economic Studies* no.11:1–28.

Bailey, A. M. 1981. The renewed discussions on the concept of the Asiatic Mode of Production. In *The Anthropology of Pre-Capitalist Societies*, ed. J. S. Kahn and J. R. Llobera. London: Macmillan.

Bailey, A. M., and Llobera, J. R. 1981. The AMP : Sources and formation of the concept. In *The Asiatic Mode of Production : Science and Politics*, ed. A. M. Bailey and J. R. Llobera. London: Routledge and Kegan Paul.

Banaji, J. 1970. The crisis of British Anthropology. *New Left Review* 64: 71–78.

———. 1972. For a theory of colonial modes of production. *Economic and Political Weekly* 7(52): 2498–2502.

Barbalet, J. M. 1976. Underdevelopment and the colonial economy. *Journal of Contemporary Asia* 6: 186–192.

———. 1980. Principles of stratification in Max Weber : an interpretation and critique. *British Journal of Sociology* 31(3): 401–416.

Bedford, R., and Mamak, A. 1977. *Compensating for Development : The Bougainville Case*. Christchurch, N.Z.: Bougainville Special Publication No. 2.

Berita Soroako. 1977. Pidato Mr P. Savoy dalam peringatan 17 Agustus 1977 di Soroako. August vol. 1(8).

———. 1978a. Farewell Speech by B. N. Wahju. May, vol. 1(36).

———. 1978b. Speech by P. Savoy. August, vol. 2(36).

Beukers, G. A. J. 1916. Persoonlijke herinneringen betreffende het werk in Midden-Celebes, speciaal Mori. *Mededeelingen van wege het Nederlandsch Zendeling-genootschap* 60: 154–65.

Boon, J. A. 1977. *The Anthropological Romance of Bali 1597–1972*. Cambridge: Cambridge University Press.

Booth, D. 1975. Andre Gunder Frank: an introduction and appreciation. In *Beyond the Sociology of Development*, ed. I. Oxaal, T. Barnet and D. Booth. London, Boston and Henley: Routledge and Kegan Paul.

Borkent, H., et al. 1981. *Indonesian Workers and Their Right to Organise*. Leiden: Indonesian Documentation and Information Centre (INDOC).

Boserup, E. 1970. *Women's Role in Economic Development*. London: Allen and Unwin.

Bradby B. 1975. The destruction of natural economy. *Economy and Society* 4: 127–61.

Brandt, W. F. 1980. *North-South: A Programme for Survival*. London and Sydney: Pan Books.

Braverman, H. 1974. *Labour and Monopoly Capital*. New York: Monthly Review Press.

Bromley, R., and Gerry, C. 1979. *Casual Work and Poverty in Third World Cities*. Chichester: John Wiley and Sons.

Bruner, E. M. 1974. The expression of ethnicity in Indonesia. In *Urban Ethnicity*, ed. A. Cohen. London: Tavistock.

Byrne, J. 1979. Nickel bounces Back. *Australian Financial Review* 4 July.

Caldwell, M., and Utrecht, E. 1979. *Indonesia: An Alternative History*. Sydney: Alternative Publishing Co-operative.

Canadian International Development Agency. 1977. *Sulawesi Regional Development Study*, vols. 1 and 3. Report prepared by the University of British Columbia.

Chabot, H. T. 1967. Bontoramba: a village of Goa, South Sulawesi. In *Villages in Indonesia*, ed. Koentjaraningrat. Ithaca N.Y.: Cornell University Press.

Coedes, George. 1968. The Indianized States of Southeast Asia. ed. Walter E. Vella, tr. Susan Brown Cowling. Canberra: Australian National University Press.

Cohen, G. A. 1978. *Karl Marx's Theory of History: A Defence*. Princeton N.J.: Princeton University Press.

Cohen, R. 1978. Ethnicity: problem and focus in Anthropology. *Annual Review of Anthropology* 4: 379–403.

Collins, J. 1975. The political economy of post-war immigration. In *Readings in the Political Economy of Australian Capitalism*, ed. E. L. Wheelwright and K. Buckley. Vol. 1. Brookvale: Australian and New Zealand Book Co.

———. 1978. Fragmentation of the working class. In *Readings in the Political Economy of Australian Capitalism*, ed. E. L. Wheelwright and K. Buckley. vol. 3. Brookvale: Australian and New Zealand Book Co.

Dagg, C. J. 1978. *P.T. International Nickel Indonesia Community Development Programme*, Soroako: P.T. International Nickel Indonesia.

Dalton, G. 1971a. Theoretical issues in Economic Anthropology. In *Economic Development and Social Change*, ed. G. Dalton. New York: The Natural History Press.

————. 1971b. Reply to Frank. *Current Anthropology* 12: 237–41.

Davies, R. 1979. Informal sector or subordinate mode of production? A model. In *Casual Work and Poverty in Third World Cities*, ed. R. Bromley and C. Gerry. Chichester: John Wiley and Sons.

de Beauvoir, S. 1965. *The Prime of Life*. Hammondsworth: Penguin.

Deere, C. D. 1979. Rural women's subsistence production in the capitalist periphery. In *Peasants and Proletarians: The Struggles of Third World Workers*, ed. R. Cohen, P. W. Gutkind, and P. Brazier. London: Hutchinson.

Dobbin, C. 1980. Islam and economic change in Indonesia circa 1750–1930. In *Indonesia: The Making of a Culture*, ed. J.J. Fox. Canberra: R.S. Pac.S., Australian National University.

Eipper, C. M. 1980. The Bantry Bay Example: The Advance of Capitalism in County Cork, Ireland. Ph.D. thesis, Department of Anthropology, University of Sydney, Australia.

Errington, S. 1981. Personal communication.

Esser, S. J. 1927. Klank-en vormleer van het Morisch. *Verhandelingen van het Bataviaasch Genootschap van Kunsten and Wetenschappen* 67: parts 3,4.

Foster-Carter, A. 1978. Can we articulate 'articulation'. In *The New Economic Anthropology*, ed. J. Clammer. London and Basingstoke: Macmillan.

Frank, A. G. 1969. Sociology of development and underdevelopment of sociology. In *Latin America: Underdevelopment or Revolution*, ed. A. G. Frank. New York and London: Monthly Review Press.

Friedl, E. 1967. The position of women: appearance and reality. *Anthropological Quarterly* 40: 86–95.

Furnivall, J. S. 1944. *Netherlands India: A Study of a Plural Economy*. Cambridge and New York: Cambridge University Press and Macmillan.

Furukawa, H. 1982. Rice culture in South Sulawesi. In *Villages and the Agricultural Landscape in South Sulawesi*, ed. Mattulada and N. Maeda. Kyoto, Japan: Centre for Southeast Asian Studies, Kyoto University.

Geertz, C. 1960. *The Religion of Java*. New York: Free Press of Glencoe.

————. 1963a. *Agricultural Involution*. Berkeley and Los Angeles: University of California Press.

————. 1963b. The integrative revolution. In *Old Societies and New States*, ed. C. Geertz. New York: Free Press of Glencoe.

————. 1981. *Negara: The Theatre State in Nineteenth-Century Bali*. Princeton: Princeton University Press.

Geertz, H. 1963. Indonesian cultures and communities. In *Indonesia*, ed. R. McVey. Ithaca N.Y.: Cornell University Press.

Glassburner, B. 1978. Political economy and the Soeharto regime. *Bulletin of Indonesian Economic Studies* 14(3): 24–51.

Goody, J., and Tambiah, S. J. 1973. *Bridewealth and Dowry*. Cambridge: Cambridge University Press.

Griffin, K. 1981. Economic development in a changing world. *World Development* 9(3): 221–6.

Grubauer, Albert. 1913. Unter Kopfjägern in Central-Celebes: Ethnologische Streiszüge in Sudost-Und Central-Celebes Leipzig: R. Voigtländer.

Gusfield, J. 1967. Tradition and modernity: misplaced polarities in the study of social change. *American Journal of Sociology* 72: 351–62.

Hafid, A.; Sallatang, M. A.; and Makaliwe, W. H. 1981. Some socioeconomic aspects in developing a coastal village, the case of South Sulawesi. Paper presented at the S.S.R.C. Conference on South Sulawesi, 9–11 December, at Monash University.

Hall, S.; Lumley, B.; and McLennan, G. 1978. Politics and ideology: Gramsci. In *On Ideology*, Centre for Contemporary Cultural Studies. London: Hutchinson.

Hamilton, A. 1981. A complex strategical situation: gender and power in Aboriginal Australia. In *Australian Women: Feminist Perspectives*, ed. N. Grieve and P. Grimshaw. Melbourne: Oxford University Press.

Hamilton, R. 1978. *The Liberation of Women*. London: Allen and Unwin.

Harvey, B. S. 1974. Tradition, Islam and Rebellion, Ph.D. thesis, Cornell University, Ithaca, N.Y.

Healey, D. T. 1981. Survey of recent developments. *Bulletin of Indonesian Economic Studies* 17 (1): 1–35.

Hindess, B., and Hirst, P. Q. 1975. *Pre-Capitalist Modes of Production*. London, Henley and Boston: Routledge and Kegan Paul.

Hofstede, Geert. 1982. Cultural pitfalls for Dutch expatriates in Indonesia: lessons for Europeans in Asia. *Euro-Asia Business Review* 1(1): 37–41.

Hopkins, T. K., et al. 1982. *World Systems Analysis: Theory and Methodology*. Beverly Hills, London and New Delhi: Sage Publications.

Hunter, A. 1968. Minerals in Indonesia. *Bulletin of Indonesian Economic Studies* no. 11: 73–89.

Idris-Soven, A. and E., and Vaughan, M. K., eds. 1978. *The World as a Company Town: Multinational Corporations and Social Change*, The Hague and Paris: Mouton.

International Nickel Company of Canada Limited. 1974. *Annual Report*.

———. 1975. *Annual Report*.

———. 1976. *Annual Report*.

Jessup, P. C. 1977. Development aspects of the Soroako Nickel Project. Paper presented at Symposium '77, The Indonesian Mining Industry: Its Present and Future, 14 June, at Jakarta.

Johnson, R. 1979a. Histories of culture/theories of ideology: notes on an impasse. In *Ideology and Cultural Production*, ed. M. Barrett et al. London: Croom Helm.

———. 1979b. Three problematics: elements of a theory of working-class culture. In *Working Class Culture: Studies in History and Theory*, ed. J. Clarke, C. Critcher, and R. Johnson. London: Hutchinson.

Kahn, J. S .1978. Ideology and social structure in Indonesia. *Comparative Studies in Society and History* 20: 103–122.

———. 1980. *Minangkabau Social Formations: Indonesian Peasants in the World-Economy.* Cambridge: Cambridge University Press.

———. 1981a. Explaining ethnicity: a review article. *Critique of Anthropology* 16(4): 43–52.

———. 1981 b. Mercantilism and the emergence of servile labour in colonial Indonesia. In *The Anthropology of Pre-Capitalist Societies*, ed. J. S. Kahn and J. R. Llobera. London and Basingstoke: Macmillan.

Kahn, J. S., and Llobera, J. R. 1981. Towards a new Marxism or a new Anthropology? In *The Anthropology of Pre-Capitalist Societies*, ed. J. S. Kahn and J. R. Llobera. London and Basingstoke: Macmillan.

Kamm, H. 1978. Indonesia Nickel Project reflects 2 worlds. *New York Times* 14 April.

Keyes, C. F., ed. 1982. *Ethnic Change.* Washington, D.C.: University of Washington Press.

Kompas. 1982a. P. T. Inco terpaksa berhentikan 427 karyawan. 19 October.

———. 1982b. Permintaan Nikel merosot 426 buruh terkena PHK. 21 October.

———. 1982c. Kasus buruh P. T. Inco dianggap selesai. 12 November.

Kow, A. A. 1949. *Thirty Years in Indonesia.* London: Salvationist Publishing and Supplies Ltd.

Kristanto, K. 1982. The smallholder cattle economy in South Sulawesi. *Bulletin of Indonesian Economic Studies* 18(1): 61–86.

Kruyt, A. C. 1900. Het rijk Mori. *Tijdschrift van het Koninklijk Nederlandsch Aardrijkskundig Genootschap* 17: 436–66.

———. 1929. The effect of Western civilisation on the inhabitants of Poso (Central Celebes). In *The Effect of Western Influence on the Native Civilizations in the Malay Archipelago*, ed. B. Schrieke. Batavia: Kolff.

Kruyt, J. 1919. The numerals in East Mori. *Mededeelingen van Wege het Nederlands Zendelingen Genootschap* 63: 328–46.

———. 1924. De Moriers van Tinompo, (oostelijk Midden-Celebes). *Bijdragen Tot de Taal-, Land - en Volkenkunde van Nederlandsch - Indie* 80:33–217.

———. 1977. *Kabar Keselamatan de Poso, (Het Zendingsveld Poso.* tr. P.S. Naipospos). Jakarta: BPK Gunung Mulia.

Kunstadter, P., and Chapman, E. C. 1978. Problems of shifting cultivation and econmic development in Northern Thailand. In *Farmers in the Forest: Economic Development and Marginal Agriculture in Northern Thailand*, ed. P. Kunstadter, E.C. Chapman and S. Sabhasri. Honolulu: East-West Center.

Laclau, E. 1977. Feudalism and capitalism in Latin America. In *Politics and Ideology in Marxist Theory*. London: New Left Books.

Lebar, F. M., ed. and comp. 1972. *Ethnic Groups of Insular Southeast Asia*, vol. 1, New Haven: H.R.A.F.

Leclerc, J. 1972. An ideological problem in Indonesian Trade Unionism in the sixties: 'karyawan' versus 'buruh'. *R.I.M.A.* 6(1): 76–91.

Leys, C. 1975. *Underdevelopment in Kenya.* cited Kahn 1981a. London: Heinemann.

Liddle, R. W. 1970. *Ethnicity, Party and National Integration: An Indonesian Case Study*. New Haven: Yale University Press.

Lineton, J. A. 1975. An Indonesian Society and its Universe: A Study of the Bugis of South Sulawesi (Celebes) and Their Role Within a Wider Social and Economic System. Ph.D. thesis, School of Oriental and African Studies, University of London.

———. 1981. Personal communication.

Long, N., and Richardson, P. 1978. Informal sector, petty commodity production, and the relations of small-scale production. In *The New Economic Anthropology*, ed. J. Clammer. London and Basingstoke: Macmillan.

Lubis, T. M., and Abdullah, F., eds. 1981. *Human Rights Report, Indonesia 1980*. Jakarta: Penerbit Sinar Harapan.

McDonald, H. 1976. Indonesian makes new rules for mineral investors. *Australian Financial Review* 6 October.

———. 1980. *Suharto's Indonesia*. Australia: Fontana.

McDonald, P. 1980. Address to the Indonesia Study Group. A.N.U.

Macdonald, Wagner and Priddle, Consulting Engineers. 1970. *Soroako Engineering Investigations*. Report commissioned by P. T. International Nickel Indonesia.

McGee, T. G. 1979. The poverty syndrome: making out in the Southeast Asian city. In *Casual Work and Poverty in Third World Cities*, ed. R. Bromley and C. Gerry. Chichester: John Wiley and Sons.

———. 1982. From 'urban involution' to 'proletarian transformation': Asian perspectives. Paper presented to a Workshop on Proletarianisation in Asia and the Pacific, Dept. of Geography/Centre for Southeast Asian Studies, Monash Universtiy.

Macknight, C. C. 1981. The rise of agriculture in South Sulawesi before 1600. Paper presented to the S.S.R.C. Conference on South Sulawesi, 9–11 December, at Monash University.

Magubane, B. 1971. A critical look at indices used in the study of social change in colonial Africa. *Current Anthropology* 12: 419–30.

Makaliwe, W. H. 1969. An economic survey of South Sulawesi. *Bulletin of Indonesian Economic Studies* 5(2): 7–36.

Mangkusuwondo, S. 1973. Dilemmas in Indonesian economic development. *Bulletin of Indonesian Economic Studies* 9(2): 28–35.

Marx, K. 1914. *The Eighteenth Brumaire of Louis Bonaparte.* Chicago: Charles H. Kerr.

———. 1930. *Capital,* Vol. 12, (cited by Tracy 1981). London: J.M. Dent (Everyman).

———. 1973. *Grundrisse.* Hammondsworth: Penguin.

———. 1976. *Capital,* Vol. 1, Hammondsworth: Penguin.

Matheson, V. 1975. Concepts of State in the *Tuhfat al Nafis.* In *Pre-Colonial State Systems in Southeast Asia,* ed. A. Reid, L. Castles, et al. Kuala Lumpur: Malarpian Branch of the Royal Asiatic Society.

Mattata, H. M. Sanusi Daeng. 1962. *Luwu Dalam Revolusi.* Ujung Pandang: Yayasun Usaha Keluarga 'Kaitupa.'

Mattulada. 1977. Kahar Muzakkar—profil patriot pemberontak. *Prisma* 8: 77–86.

———. 1982. South Sulawesi, its ethnicity and way of life. In *Villages and the Agricultural Landscape in South Sulawesi,* ed. Mattulada and N. Maeda. Kyoto, Japan: Centre for Southeast Asian Studies, Kyoto University.

Meillasoux, C. 1981. *Maidens, Meal and Money.* Cambridge: Cambridge University Press.

Merdeka. 1982. Di PHK, 170 buruh P.T. Inco di Sulsel unjuk perasaan. 13 November.

Miles, D. 1967. A note on shifting cultivation and settlement. *Journal of the Siam Society.* 55(1): 93–99.

Mills, R. F. 1975. Proto South Sulawesi and Proto Austronesian Phonology. Ph.D. thesis, University of Michigan.

Mining Journal. 1979. Indonesian overview. 292(7502):1.

Mortimer, R., ed. 1973. *Showcase State: The Illusion of Indonesia's 'Accelerated Modernisation'.* Sydney: Angus and Robertson.

Nash J. 1979. *We Eat the Mines and the Mines Eat Us: Dependency and Exploitation in Bolivian Tin Mines.* New York: Columbia University Press.

Nash, J. 1981. Ethnographic aspects of the world capitalist system. *Annual Review of Anthropology* 10: 393–423.

Noorduyn, J. 1965. Origins of South Celebes historical writing. In *An Introduction to Indonesian Historiography,* ed. Soedjatmoko et al. Ithaca, N.Y.: Cornell University Press.

O'Laughlin, B. 1975a. Marxist approaches in Anthropology. *Annual Review of Anthropology* 4; 341-70.

———. 1975b. Production and reproduction: Meillassoux's *Femmes, Greniers et Capitaux. Critique of Anthropology* 8:3-27.

Palmer, I. 1978. *The Indonesian Economy Since 1965: A Case Study of Political Economy*. London: Frank Cass & Co.

Panglaykim, J. 1968. Survey of recent developments. *Bulletin of Indonesian Economic Studies* (9): 1-34.

Partridge, W. L. 1979. Banana County in the wake of United Fruit: social and economic linkages. *American Ethnologist* 4: 491-509.

Peacock, J. 1968. *Rites of Modernization*. Chicago: University of Chicago Press.

Pedoman Rakyat. 1982. Kasus PHK buruh P.T. Inco dianggap selesai. 9 November.

Pelita. 1982. 26 karyawan P. T. Inco Soroako diberhentikan. 26 October.

Penders, C. L. M. 1968. Java's population during the colonial period. *World Review* 8(1).

Peoples, J. G. 1978. Dependence in a Micronesian economy. *American Ethnologist* 5: 535-52.

Pleyte, C. M. 1981. De geographische verbreiding van het koppensnellen in de Oost Indische Archipel. *Tijdschrift Aardrijkskundig Genootschap* 2e serie 8: 908-946.

Polomka, P. 1971. *Indonesia Since Sukarno*. Hammondsworth: Penguin.

P.T. International Nickel Indonesia. n.d. *P.T. International Nickel Indonesia*. Publicity pamphlet.

P. T. International Nickel Indonesia. 1977. *Welcome to Soroako*. Publicity pamphlet.

Regan, R. J. 1978. Competition is killing nickel. *Iron Age* 15 May.

Reid, A. 1981. The rise of Makassar. Paper presented to the S.S.R.C. Conference on South Sulawesi, 9-11 December, Monash University.

Reid, A., and Castles, L. 1975. Introduction. In *Pre-Colonial State Systems in Southeast Asia*, Kuala Lampur: Malaysian Branch of the Royal Asiatic Society.

Reiter, R. 1975. Men and women in the South of France: public and private domains. In *Towards an Anthropology of Women*, ed. R. Reiter. New York and London: Monthly Review Press.

Rendra, W. S. 1979. *The Struggle of the Naga Tribe*, trans. Max Lane. St. Lucia: University of Queensland Press.

Republic of Indonesia and P. T. International Nickel. 1968. *Contract of Work*.

Robinson, K. 1983. Women's work in an Indonesian mining town. In *Women's Work and Women's Roles in Southeast Asia*, ed. L. Manderson. Canberra: Development Studies Centre, Australian National University.

Robison, R. 1978. Toward a class analysis of the Indonesian military bureaucratic state. *Indonesia* 25: 17-39.

Rogers, B. 1980. *The Domestication of Women : Discrimination in Developing Societies.* London: Tavistock.

Rogers, S. C. 1975. Female forms of power and the myth of male dominance: a model of female/male interaction in peasant society. *American Ethnologist* 2: 727–56.

Ross, R. 1982. Reflections on a theme. In *Racism and Colonialism: Essays on Ideology and Social Structure,* ed. R. Ross. Leiden: Martinus Nijhoff.

Rostow, W. W. 1960. *The Stages of Economic Growth.* Cambridge: Cambridge University Press.

Roxborough, I. 1979. *Theories of Underdevelopment.* London and Basingstoke: Macmillan.

Sacerdoti, Guy 1980. Clouds on the mining front. *Far Eastern Economic Review.* Feb. 1: 52–52.

Sarasin, P., and F. 1905. *Reisen in Celebes.* Wiesbaden: C. W. Kreidel's Verlag.

Schneider, H. K. 1975. Economic development and anthropolgoy. *Ann. Review of Anthropology* 4: 271–92.

Schumacher, E. G. 1973. *Small Is Beautiful.* London: Blond and Briggs.

Seddon, D., ed. 1978. *Relations of Production : Marxist Approaches to Economic Anthropology.* London: Frank Cass.

Short, K. 1979. Foreign capital and the state in Indonesia : some aspects of contemporary imperialism. *Journal of Contemporary Asia* 9(2): 153–74.

Silverman, M. 1979. Dependency, mediation and class formation in rural Guyana. *American Ethnologist* 6: 466–90.

Smith, C. A. 1978. Beyond dependency theory: national and regional patterns of underdevelopment in Guatamala. *American Ethnologist* 5: 574–617.

Smith, S. 1980. The ideas of Samir Amin: theory or tautology. *Journal of Development Studies* 17(1): 5–21.

Soewondo, N. 1977. The Indonesian Marriage Law and its implementation legislation. *Archipel* 13: 283–94.

Sundrum, R. M., and Booth, A. E. 1980. Income distribution in Indonesia : trends and determinants. In *Indonesia : Dualism, Growth and Poverty,* ed. R. G. Garnaut and P. T. McCawley. Canberra: R.S. Pac.S. Australian National University.

Suparlan, P. 1979. Ethnic groups in Indonesia. *The Indonesian Quarterly* 7(2): 53–67.

Sutherland, H. 1979. *The Making of a Bureaucratic Elite.* Singapore: Heinemann.

Swift, J. 1979. *The Big Nickel.* Ontario: The Development Education Center.

Tanaka, K. 1981. Agricultural adaptation by spontaneous migrants to northern Kabupaten Luwu. In *Villages and the Agricultural Landscape in South Sulawesi.* ed. Mattulada and Maeda. Kyoto, Japan: Centre for Southeast Asian Studies, Kyoto University.

Taussig, M. T. 1980. *The Devil and Commodity Fetishism*. Chapel Hill: University of North Carolina Press.

Taylor, J. G. 1979. *From Modernization to Modes of Production*. London: MacMillan.

Tempo. 1979. Wajah-wajah di Danau Matano. 2 April: 53–54.

Terbit. 1982. Buruh Inco yang diberhentikan akan ditampung pemda. 4 November.

ter Braake, A. L. 1977a. Letter to Mrs Pula, Soroako.

———. 1977b. *Celebes*, unpublished ms.

———. 1978. Letter to K. Robinson.

Thompson, E. P. 1965. Time, work-discipline and industrial capitalism. *Past and Present* 38: 56–97.

———. 1978. *The Poverty of Theory and Other Essays*. London: Merlin Press.

Tipps, D. C. 1973. Modernization theory and the comparative study of societies: a critical perspective'. *Comparative Studies in Society and History* 15(2): 199–226.

Tjondronegoro, H. D. 1976. The Canadian nickel mining project. *Indonesian Observer* 29 November.

Tracy, C. Lever. 1981. 'Post war immigrants in Australia and Western Europe, in reserve or centre forward?', Paper presented at the Ethnicity and Class Conference, 27–29 August, at the University of Wollongong.

Turner, Bryan S. 1978. *Marx and the End of Orientalism*. Boston: Allen and Unwin.

Van Dijk, 1981. *Rebellion Under the Banner of Islam*. The Hague: Martinus Nijhoff.

Vickers, A. 1983. Personal communication.

Vlekke, B. H. M. 1965. *Nusantara : A History of the East Indian Archipelago*. Cambridge: Harvard University Press.

Volkman, T. A. 1980. The pig has eaten the vegetables : ritual and change in Tana Toraja. Ph.D. thesis, Cornell University.

Wahju, B. N. 1977a. Nickel production in Sulawesi. Lecture to the Soroakan Women's League, 31 March.

———. 1977b. Sulawesi : an introduction to its geology, anthropology and history. Lecture presented to the Soroako Parents and Friends Association, April 6.

Wallace, P. 1978. King no more. *Wall Street Journal* April 20.

Wallerstein, I. 1974. *The Modern World System*. New York: Academic Press.

Warren, J. 1979. The Sulu zone : commerce and evolution of a multiethnic polity, 1967–1898. *Archipel* 18: 223–9.

———. 1982. Slavery and the impact of external trade : the Sulu sultanate in the 19th century. In *Phillipine Social History : Global Trade and Local Transformations*, ed. A. W. McCoy and C. de Jesus. Manila: George Allen and Unwin/Ateneode Manila University Press.

Weber, M. 1970. *From Max Weber,* ed. H. Gerth and C. Wright Mills. London: Routledge and Kegan Paul. (cited by Barbalet 1980.)

Williams, C. 1981. *Open Cut : The Working Class in an Australian Mining Town.* Sydney: George Allen and Unwin.

Williams, R. 1980. Base and superstructure in Marxist culture theory. In *Problems in Materialism and Culture.* London: Verso Editions and New Left Books.

Wright, E. O. 1978. The class structure of advanced capitalist societies. In *Class, Crisis and the State.* London: New Left Books.

Wolters, O. W. 1970. *The Face of Srivijaya in Malay History.* London: Lund Humphries.

Young, K. 1978. Modes of appropriation and the sexual division of labour : a case study from Oaxaca, Mexico. In *Feminism and Materialism : Women and Modes of Production,* ed. A. Kuhn and A. Wolpe. London: Routledge and Kegan Paul.

Young, K., et al. 1981. *Of Marriage and the Market.* London: C.S.E. Books.

Zaretsky, E. 1976. *Capitalism, the Family and Personal Life.* London: Pluto Press.

UNPUBLISHED HISTORICAL DOCUMENTS

Document 1. 1904. Draft: Memorandum from the Resident of Posso to the Governor of Celebes en Onderhoorigheden (17 February, 1904), Ag. No. 2421/04 (no archive number), held in Indonesian National Archives, Jakarta.

Document 2. 1904. Letter from the Governor of Celebes en Onderhoorighden to the Governor General of the N.E.I. (19 January, 1904), Ag. No. 242/04, No. 117/2, held in Indonesian National Archives, Jakarta.

Document 3. 1910. Memorie van Overgave van den Aftredenden Gouverneur van Celebes en Onderhoorigheden, A. J. Baron Quarles de Quarles, Macassar (4 August, 1910), Ag. No. 10915/1911 (no archive number), held in Indonesian National Archives, Jakarta.

Document 4. 1918. Zelfbestuur Luwu Reglement, No. 5, No. LI/7, Ujung Pandang Branch, Indonesian National Archives.

Document 5. 1921. Zelfbestuur Luwu Reglement, No. 8, No. LI/7, Ujung Pandang Branch, Indonesian National Archives.

Document 6. 1922. Zelfbestuur Luwu Reglement, No. 9, No. LI/7, Ujung Pandang Branch, Indonesian National Archives.

Document 7. 1932. Zelfbestuur Luwu Reglement, No. 39, No. LI/7, Ujung Pandang Branch, Indonesian National Archives.

Document 8. 1933. Salinan Keterangan dari Gamara tentang nama Makole wawa inia Rahampoeoe Matano yang diketahoeinya jang mana bisa didengar dari orang toeanja. Matano, 27–7–1933. Ms. in possession of Haji Ranggo, Soroako.

Index

309